MARKETING AND ECONOMIC DEVELOPMENT

MARKETING AND ECONOMIC DEVELOPMENT

by Erdener Kaynak

PRAEGER

New York
Westport, Connecticut
London

Library of Congress Cataloging-in-Publication Data

Kaynak, Erdener.
  Marketing and economic development.

  Bibliography: p.
  Includes index.
  1. Marketing—Developing countries.   I. Title.
HF5415.12.D44K39   1986   338.9′009172′4   86-91548
ISBN 0-275-90003-7 (alk. paper)

Library of Congress Catalog Card Number: 86-91548
ISBN: 0-275-90003-7

First published in 1986

Praeger Publishers, 521 Fifth Avenue, New York, NY 10175
A division of Greenwood Press, Inc.

Printed in the United States of America

∞

The paper used in this book complies with the Permanent
Paper Standard issued by the National Information Standards
Organization (Z39.48-1984).

10 9 8 7 6 5 4 3 2 1

Dedicated to the teaching staff of the Faculty of Economics of Istanbul University, who created in the author an unceasing interest in economic theory and thought, instilled in him an urgent curiosity, and assisted in the development and broadening of the author's intellectual capacity and horizons during the second part of the 1960s. For this, the author feels a special gratitude.

Contents

List of Tables

List of Figures

Foreword
by A. Coskun Samli

Marketing is a very powerful social force. As such, intentionally or unintentionally it has a critical economic impact. This impact could be positive or negative, and most of the time is not neutral. The relationship between marketing and the economy is not one that is simple or easy to understand. Rather, this relationship is extremely complex and delicate. Misunderstood or not at all understood, marketing's role in the economy can easily be an immense force. As such, if it could be unleashed and unchecked it could have a devastating impact on society. By the same token this powerful force and its profound impact can be, and indeed must be, unleashed under controlled conditions if it is to enhance the society's economic well-being to a substantial extent. Marketing thus far, in regards to societal issues, has taken three types of positions: pro-active, reactive, and inactive. While an inactive marketing stage can be less than satisfactory and wasteful in terms of not using such a forceful activity to the society's advantage, being pro-active without proper directions can be devastatingly dangerous. Reactivity, at best, produces very mediocre results. Thus it is extremely important to determine marketing's impact on the society. Perhaps the single most important impact is its economic constraints.

Since much of the scholarly research and writings on marketing in the United States and even around the world focus on the micro level, there has been a critical void in the area of marketing and economic development. Without proper understanding of the powerful impact that marketing has on the economy, it is not possible to provide proper direction to marketing for the benefit of society at large. Thus, pro-active marketing depends on proper understanding of the relationship between marketing and economic development.

This book plays a critical role in this all-important area. Professor Kaynak makes a major attempt first to explore the economic development process, then to examine marketing activity within the society and finally to relate the two in a constructive manner. He provides critical information and analytical tools for both public policymakers as well as marketing practitioners. He particularly emphasizes how unfavorable market conditions hinder economic development and what can be done to alleviate them. He reiterates the fact that it is the joint responsibility of public policymakers and marketing practitioners to provide sound marketing opportunities and practices in order to facilitate economic growth.

In an age when the gap between the world's poor and rich nations is growing, there is, more than ever before, a need for a book such as this one. Professor Kaynak's effort to fill the void is monumental and his intentions are noble. It is my sincere hope that many marketing and economist colleagues, public policy officials at all levels, and managers of international firms will read this important and thought-provoking book and think about its far-reaching message. It is definitely time to use marketing as a critical force in economic development. Too many other approaches have failed. And some of us feel that this is the fail-safe approach.

A. Coskun Samli
Virginia Polytechnic Institute
and State University
Blacksburg, Virginia

Preface

> It was illusory to think that a country could be industrialized by building factories: the reality was that industrialization meant building markets. Marketing, however, as part of the process of industrialization in the developing countries, has not yet received the recognition and attention that it merits.
>
> The late Paul Hoffman
> Former Administrator
> United Nations Development Program

This book explores the relationship between marketing and economic development. To this end, the book first of all examines the development process. Second, it describes the general features of marketing activity and processes in different economic settings in the world. Third, the relationship between marketing and economic development is operationalized. To achieve this objective, prevailing market conditions and marketing systems are related to stages of economic development of countries at varying levels of growth. Marketing systems and practices vary from one area of a country to another. In this book, these pronounced differences are related in a systematic way to the differences in the economic environment within which marketing systems operate.

One of the acute problems faced by public policymakers as well as global marketing managers in most parts of the world is the complete lack of reliable marketing data. The reason for this is the heavy emphasis placed on production and technological improvements; marketing is considered unnecessary under the given market conditions. In this book, the effect of unfavorable market conditions on the economic development process is examined.

There is a vital link between domestic and foreign markets that one often overlooks. It is necessary to produce products suitable for the market segment at home, but a country must also fit export requirements. Without trade there can be no true development of the economy or of industries in specific countries. As a result of this, the role of trade for economic development is looked at. Furthermore, the organization of marketing efforts of firms and the problems encountered in different economic settings are studied. To improve the marketing practices of firms and improve the workings of the economic machine of less-developed countries, transfer of marketing technology from developed to less-developed countries is suggested. The book discusses the problems connected with such transfer.

The book puts its main emphasis on the following areas of study:

- The contribution that marketing can make to economic development.

- The possible existence of stages of marketing development at different levels of economic development.

- The role of the market economy and of market structure in economic development.

- The applicability of advanced marketing technology and know-how from the West as a stimulator of economic development in LDCs.

- The application of marketing technology transfer to economic development goals. A methodology for evaluating stages of economic development and identifying appropriate types of marketing technology transfer is also developed.

- Marketing strategy for economic development. In particular, contribution of channels of distribution and consumerism policies to economic development is delineated.

- For orderly decision-making purposes both at micro (firm) and macro (country) levels, there is a need for marketing research. Marketing research techniques and processes facilitate the economic development process. The last chapter deals with this important issue in relation to less-developed countries.

It must be pointed out at the outset that the main emphasis of this book is on less-developed countries. This group of countries has shown a tremendous growth during the last two decades. In aggregate terms, while the LDCs have seen their GDP grow by 3.2 percent annually between 1950 and 1980, the middle-income LDCs have attained a rise of 3.1 percent annually. On the other hand, low-income LDCs attained a growth rate of only 1.3 percent during this period.[1]

Although LDCs make up three-fourths of the world's population, they consume less than one-fourth of its resources. "More than 700 million people are classified as destitute; it is estimated that 70 percent of the children suffer from malnutrition; as many as 300 million people are physically or mentally retarded as a result of inadequate diets."[2]

Marketing as a scientific decision-making tool can play an important role in the economic development of LDCs. As such, marketing techniques and know-how used as input for socioeconomic development need to be adapted to the prevailing conditions of the particular country. Marketing can be used effectively as an engine for the country's accelerated economic development, irrespective of the sectors of the economy involved. In order to accelerate the economic development process in LDCs, more emphasis on marketing is needed in economic development plans. This kind of planning will enable public policymakers as well as private firms to find out what people's needs and desires are. This kind of approach will bring about a highly accurate match between what is produced and what is demanded in LDCs, leading to effective utilization of scarce resources. What LDCs need most is to widen their markets, both at home and abroad; by giving further impetus to the overall economic developmental effort. In this process, marketing will be the important catalyst.

NOTES

1. S. Sinclair, "The State of the Third World in 1982," *Third World Economic Handbook*, (London: Euromonitor Publications Limited, 1982), p. 3.
2. L. A. Tavis, "Multinationals As Foreign Agents of Change in the Third World," *Business Horizons* 26, no. 5 (September–October 1983): 2.

Acknowledgments

This book is the happy outcome of the author's enduring interest in the relationship between economic development and the marketing process, and the interactions between them. The point of view presented here stems from two decades of study, teaching, scholarly research, and practical experience. The insights contained herein were gained in a number of developed countries of the rich North as well as in less-developed countries of the poor South.

During the preparation and completion of this project, the author has received the constant assistance and encouragement of Mount Saint Vincent University administration. In particular, Dr. Susan Clark, Dean of Human and Professional Studies, and Dr. Wayne B. Ingalls, Director for Research and Special Projects, were a constant source of encouragement.

I thank Ms. Barbara Leffel, Praeger economics editor, for her foresight in realizing the importance of the subject area. Her extraordinary help, cooperation, encouragement, and understanding have facilitated the project completion immensely. I am also thankful to Praeger Publishers Inc. for undertaking projects of this nature, thereby filling the void in the international marketing literature.

Projects of this nature cannot be completed without the enthusiastic support of a number of assistants. I would like to acknowledge the help and assistance of Gail McNeil for editing the manuscript and offering very useful stylistic changes. Randall Brooks of Saint Mary's University diligently prepared the artwork, for which I am thankful. Special thanks go to staff members of Mount Saint Vincent University typing pool for word-processing the manuscript with a tremendous sense of responsibility.

My sincere thanks and appreciation go to my wife Glynis and daughters Öykü, Övgü, and Elif, for being very understanding and tolerant during the completion of this project. As always, they were a constant source of encouragement and support.

Needless to say, the author is solely responsible for any errors or omissions in this volume.

1

Marketing and Economic Development Interface

WHAT IS ECONOMIC DEVELOPMENT?

A great deal has been written on the subject of the economic development process. But there are still problems in the conceptualization and measurement of what constitutes economic development. Narver and Savitt[1] offered two approaches to the solution of this problem. The first one is a cross-sectional view of the economic development process in which a single country is compared against others on a number of pre-established criteria. The biggest problem with this approach is the lack of comparable data bases, especially among less-developed countries. A second approach is to assess a country's progress in economic development from a given starting point to some future time period—a longitudinal approach. The problem with this approach is that what happened in the past may not necessarily happen in the future. In other words, a linear model of explanation may not always be accurate for orderly decision-making purposes.

Rostow[2] has developed a concept of stages of economic development to provide a systematic theory of the economic growth of nations. He identified five stages of economic development:[3]

1. *Traditional society.* In this society, economic change and improvements are not sufficient to increase output per capita. A high proportion of resources is in agriculture. Little economic exchange in organized markets takes place. The level of per capita product is low.

2. *Transitional society.* This society forms contacts with outside cultures, which partially removes the effect of custom on the social structure, the political system, and production methods. There is increased productivity in agriculture.

3. *Takeoff stage.* Nations experience an accelerated growth rate. Productive improvements lead to expansion in the leading sectors, causing increased requirements and creating external economies for other sectors. An enormous increase takes place in the capital stock of a country at this stage. This society would generate sufficient capital for the key sectors and have a high rate of plough-back of profits to finance the supplementary growth sectors stimulated.

4. *Technological maturity.* This is the effective application of modern technology to the full range of a society's economic activity. New leading sectors gather importance, replacing the leading sectors of the takeoff stage.

5. *High mass consumption.* One of the most important results of technological maturity is the pronounced rise of income per capita to levels that provide purchasing power beyond the basic necessities of food, shelter, and clothing. This surplus income can be used in a number of ways.

Generally, the economic growth of less-developed countries is always viewed in terms of the patterns gone through by developed countries of the West. Although Rostow's classification of the stages of economic growth may be an excellent model for showing how developed countries of the West have grown, one should be careful in its use as a predictive model for less-developed countries.[4] Douglas identified four stages in the economic development process.[5] Although these stages are similar to the five stages identified by Rostow, there are certain slight differences. The specific characteristics of the stages are: the level of real per capita income achieved, the level of development relative to the maximum income in the most highly developed economy, and the rate of change in per capita income from year to year. The stages of economic development suggest a growth pattern for a nation's income per capita following an S-shaped growth curve as shown in Figure 1.1.

Economic development can be defined as the dynamic process whereby changes in social, political, and economic forces bring about improvements in per capita income. These improvements are distributed among different strata of the population.[6] Rogers defined economic development as a sub-part of the greater process of social change—the process by which alteration occurs in the structure and function of a social system.[7]

Samli and Mentzer presented the economic development process as a continuum through time.[8] They assessed the degree of economic development and the particular technological needs of each country. They used a multi-attribute methodology for evaluating the stage of a country's

FIGURE 1.1   Economic Development Process

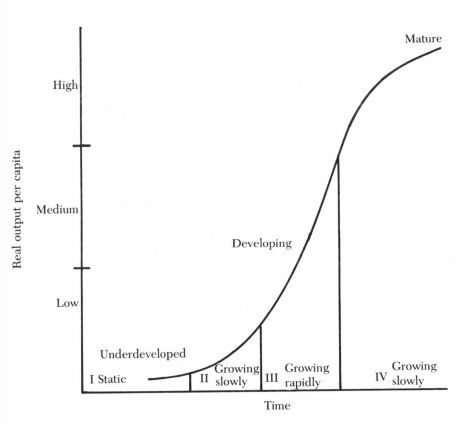

Source: Figure 21.1, "Periods of Economic Growth" (p. 601) from ECONOMICS OF MARKETING by Edna Douglas Copyright © 1975 by Edna Douglas. Reprinted by permission of Harper & Row, Publishers, Inc.

economic development.[9] The factors listed on the left hand side of Table 1.1 are those necessary for a smooth economic development process. For instance, Romanian scholars contend that marketing contributes strongly to economic development in the areas of an improved distribution system, an improved marketing information system, and an improved information dissemination system and better consumer motivation.[10] It must be pointed out here that factor emphasis in each country will vary not only in importance but also in order.

The "stages of growth" thesis developed by Rostow states that wealthier nations move upward and forward in a "take off" stage, pass through a

TABLE 1.1. Evaluation of Stage of Economic Development

Factor	Stage of development				
	Very good	Good	Average	Poor	Very poor
National economy Trade	Totally national trade systems[a]	—	—	—	Individual self-sufficient economic units (i.e., tribes)
Production	Totally national production systems[a]	—	—	—	Totally cottage industries
Standardization Production	Standardized parts—assembly line operations	—	—	—	Unstandardized parts—hand-made production
Production design	Nationally accepted product norms and standards of design	—	—	—	Localized norms and designs
Purchasing	Standard contracts	—	—	—	Transaction specific negotiation
Transportation systems Network	Nationally coordinated highway, rail, air, pipe, and water systems[a]	—	—	—	No transportation network
Rolling stock	Modern transportation equipment	—	—	—	Primitive equipment

Carriers	Coordinated transportation management	—	—	—	No professional carriers
Storage systems Facilities	Modern, specialized facilities and location analysis	—	—	—	No facilities
Management	Coordinated storage activity between facilities	—	—	—	No coordination
Mass communication	Modern, coordinated national systems[a]	—	—	—	No system
Marketing knowledge	Application of marketing concept and philosophies	—	—	—	No knowledge of marketing concept
Decision-maker amenability to marketing	Receptive to new marketing ideas	—	—	—	Negative to marketing ideas
Technology distribution institutions[b]	Formal offices for technology transfer exist	—	—	—	No formal offices for technology transfer exist

[a]Implies national in scope, not necessarily nationally controlled.
[b]For example, patent offices, professional associations, retailer/wholesaler associations, chambers of commerce, the academic community.

Source: A. Coskun Samli and John T. Mentzer, "A Model for Marketing in Economic Development," *Columbia Journal of World Business* 16, no. 3 (Fall 1981): 97. Reprinted with permission.

"maturity stage," and into a stage of "high mass consumption."[11] Based on these stages, countries of the world could be classified into: developed and less developed. This is, of course, the conventional economic development model. Dawson proposes a few new perspectives which include additional examples of nations that follow each approach, based on their stated economic development policies (see Table 1.2).[12] In their pursuit of economic development, less-developed countries of the world would be engaged in certain activities in congruence with the selected model of economic development. These activities are summarized as follows:

- Develop organizational capacity to monitor development approaches
- Reassess corporate goals, objectives, and programs
- Develop marketing strategies for each development mode
- Cultivate skill in applied anthropology
- Maintain a long-run profit perspective
- Become agents of attitude change[13]

The desire for economic development and growth may be the single most important environmental factor to which the marketer needs to adjust his task. As part of the marketing environment, economic development presents a two-sided challenge. First of all, a study of the general aspects of economic development is needed to gain some appreciation for the economic milieu within less-developed countries. A country's aspirations for economic development and marketing's assigned role in such expectations need to be studied in order to gain some appreciation for the marketing environment in a less-developed country. Second, the state of economic development should be studied with respect to market potential. This should include the present level of economic achievement attained by the country and its economic growth potential (see Table 1.3).

It is stated that less-developed countries have placed too much emphasis on GNP, growth rates, production, and investment. As a result, consumption has lost its place as the goal of production. Less-developed countries need an economic plan that places primary emphasis on increased consumption.[14]

Recently, Loeb introduced five very important ingredients of a nation's recipe for success in economic development pursuits.[15] He stated that countries will grow and prosper only if they meet the following conditions:

A rich, modern, highly productive agricultural base that provides a nation the capacity to feed its own people and export for economic gain and political leverage.

An abundant base of energy-bearing raw materials including oil, natural gas, and coal.

A strong base of raw materials that are not energy related, such as iron ore, copper, lead, asbestos, etc.

An advanced, modern, automated, highly developed technology in industry.

An educated, motivated, skilled, and highly sophisticated population.

Of the 157 members of the United Nations only the United States, Canada, and Australia meet all of the five criteria mentioned above. All of these have rich agriculture, abundant energy and non-energy resources, advanced industrial technology, and skilled, educated populations.[16]

DIFFERENT PHASES OF ECONOMIC DEVELOPMENT

In recent years, interest in the role of marketing in economic development has grown. Most governments and policymakers of less-developed countries have come to realize the importance of marketing along with production, finance, and investment improvements. There are several issues one could consider when analyzing the role of marketing in economic development. These are summarized as follows:[17]

a. In most cases economic development debates are centered on the existence or absence of a free market for economic activities rather than being concerned with the market for goods and services and its characteristics.

b. One of the tasks of marketing is to make consumption dynamic. This desire on the part of LDCs leads to an increased emphasis on production for the market rather than on the development of a capital base.

c. It is stated that the high costs of marketing inefficiencies in the channel system and the limited scale of operations of firms in LDCs hinder the contribution of marketing to economic development. There are conflicting views, however, on how distribution channels can be made more efficient and effective by reducing the number of intermediaries.

d. Marketing is also labeled as the most important "multiplier" of the economic development process. As such, it mobilizes latent economic

TABLE 1.2. A Comparison of Six Approaches to Development

Model	Cornerstones of development policy	Prominent examples (recent, current, or potential)
Stages of growth (conventional)	Massive industrialization High technology High mass consumption External economic power and influence	United States, Soviet Union, Great Britain, France, West Germany, Japan
Isolationism	Total economic self-sufficiency Freedom from superpower domination Preservation of indigenous culture Rigid central planning and control	Albania, Algeria, Burma, China, Cuba, Iran, Kampuchea, Uganda
Basic needs	Redistribution of income Health, education, and welfare of the masses Boosting agricultural productivity Central planning and control	China, Colombia, Costa Rica, Gabon, Malawi, Mali, Peru, Sri Lanka, Tanzania

Appropriate technology	Evolutionary progress toward local/ regional self-reliance Decentralized decision making Small, simple, labor-intensive manufacture and handicraft Rural-based agro-industrial culture	Bangladesh, Bhutan, Ethiopia, Ghana, India, Indonesia, Philippines
Calculative collaboration	Greater share of international economy Maximum exploitation of natural-resource base Preservation of national/regional ideology and culture Selective industrialization and infrastructure modernization	Brazil, Egypt, Jordan, Kenya, Lebanon, Liberia, Mexico, Saudi Arabia, Syria, Venezuela, Zaire
De-development	Rectifying uneven patterns of development Reducing foreign energy dependence Eliminating economic excess or waste Satisfying deeper range of human needs	United States, Soviet Union, Japan

Source: Reprinted by permission from BUSINESS Magazine. "Facing the New Realities of International Development," by Leslie M. Dawson, January–February 1981. Copyright © 1981 by the College of Business Administration, Georgia State University, Atlanta.

TABLE 1.3. The Stages of Economic Development

Different stages	Socioeconomic characteristics	Examples
Industrialized countries	• High literacy • Modern technology • High per capita GNP	The United States, Canada, Japan, the Soviet Union
Developing countries	• Rising education • Improving technology • Low per capita GNP	Latin American countries
Less-developed countries	• Low literacy • Limited technology • Extremely low per capita GNP	Countries of Africa and South Asia

Source: Compiled by the author.

energy and fully contributes to the development of managers and much needed entrepreneurs in the economy of a less-developed country.

Despite this renewed interest in the role of marketing in economic development, its role will change in response to development taking place in the economy as a whole as well as in sectoral areas. From this, one can postulate that marketing in a particular society passes through a number of stages, performing a variety of roles and tasks that correspond to the general level of economic development of the country. This is to say that the role of marketing in underdeveloped countries will be quite different from its role in countries with more mature and advanced economies. As a result, we need to understand: the phases of economic development that different countries pass through; and the impact that each economic development phase or stage has on demand for various classes and brands of products and services. For instance, marketing agencies increase consumer wants by stimulating demand in less-developed countries. Copulsky[18] outlines five phases of the economic development process:

    I. The Pre-Industrial or Commercial Phase

        There is very limited use of advanced machinery, no elaborate transformation of materials, and few specialized employees. As primitive as the country may be, however, there are transportation, commerce, and exchange systems. Example: some African countries.

II. The Primary Manufacturing Phase
As a result of surplus capacity, resources are developed for exports. In most cases, this involves the processing of raw materials in agriculture, fisheries, and mining. Example: some oil-exporting countries of the Persian Gulf and North Africa.

III. Production of Non-Durable and Semi-Durable Consumer Finished Goods
Use of small-scale industries, which necessitates low investment and labor-intensive technologies, is evident. This approach encourages local manufactures because of the availability of their own raw materials. Product examples are paints, drugs, and textiles. Example: resource-rich developing countries of Africa and Latin America.

IV. Initiation of the Production of Capital and Consumer Durable Goods
A manufacturing industry is developed to a certain level, although it is, in most cases, oriented toward import substitution for such products as automobiles, refrigerators, or farm machinery. In this phase of the economy, the manufacturing sector shifts increasingly from finished non-durable and semi-durable consumer goods to capital goods and consumer durable goods. Examples: Brazil, Singapore, Spain, and Turkey.

V. Exports of Manufactured Products
With the establishment of an industrial base in the economy, the export of manufactured products becomes very significant. Increased efficiency and productivity bring about much needed efficiency in total industries and lead to global competitiveness. Examples: Italy, Ireland.

During the evolutionary pattern of development of marketing arrangements, traditional marketing systems are characterized by large numbers of small enterprises with relatively small capital investments. The initial effects of economic development show themselves mainly at a retail level. For instance, as the purchasing power of consumers increases, retailers have greater opportunities to expand their businesses and increase turnover and profits.

In the course of economic development, there is a tendency to make more use of capital and technology and to increase the scale of operations. When marketing operations depend mainly on human labor with few capital investments in plant and equipment, there is not much advantage in beginning operations on a larger scale. If this is the case, small businesses under the close personal direction of the proprietor are likely to do better. When mechanical equipment is used for a number of business activities and a higher turnover is desirable, the advantages of scale become more apparent.

Greater coordination and integration constitute another feature of marketing development, especially in the more advanced stages of the economic development process. As the size of fixed investments grows, the enterprises and institutions in the marketing system of a country find it increasingly advantageous to plan their operations well in advance and to secure their relationships with their trading partners. Through forward and backward linkages they aim to assure themselves of supplies and markets and reduce their risks.

It is stated by Emlen that production may be the door to economic development and growth in less-developed countries, but marketing is the key element that starts the development process moving.[19] Despite this contention, marketing has traditionally been treated as the forgotten and neglected area of economic activity and thinking in less-developed countries. Although marketing has a low profile in the economic development efforts of these countries, the contribution that marketing knowledge can make to the internal strength of these countries is significant. Marketing could become the most effective stimulator of economic development activity through two inherent, interrelated forces. These are: its ability to develop a group of entrepreneurs and managers who would be the motivating force behind improvement; and its contribution as a systematic discipline that lends itself to an expeditious teaching and learning process.

It must be pointed out here that mere transplantation of Western methods, techniques, and marketing know-how is not enough to ensure their automatic acceptance and easy implementation. As a result, all technology transfer must be closely integrated with the cultural and socioeconomic framework of the society into which it is introduced. The traditional socioeconomic and cultural patterns of less-developed countries may provide an environment for the application of modern marketing, but only after its adaptation to the sociological complex of the recipient country. This topic is discussed further in Chapter 4.

Marketing strategies used by companies as well as by public policy-makers at each stage of the economic development phase will vary from country to country, depending on the availability or nonavailability of resources. Some less-developed countries have scarce natural resources; others are lacking in technology, finance, and manpower resources. Firms and governments as well as consumers of these countries are forced to respond progressively and productively to the changing economic environment. A number of possible marketing strategies are suggested by Hanna, Kizilbash, and Smart for both private and public businesses faced with economic, technological, or managerial scarcities.[20] Under the conditions of economic scarcity mentioned above, the government may assume a more activist role by regulating the market and setting quotas. Consumer buying habits, spending behavior, and purchase motives will change, as will the nature and magnitude of competition.

The behavior of the firm will be affected by the nature and extent of government regulations. For example, government regulations may force the firm to reconsider its pricing, inventory, and advertising policies. As a result of conditions of scarcity, changes in the purchasing patterns of organizational buyers and final consumers will emerge. To this end, in the industrial goods market we will see a trend toward stockpiling and a move toward resolving procurement problems. Companies will try to obtain long-range purchasing contracts and explore alternative sources of supply. In the consumer market, consumers will become more price sensitive, demand more value for their money, and become more interested in product information and safety as well as energy-saving products. Consumers will become less interested in product model changes and show more interest in product durability. They will attempt to stretch their limited financial resources over a long period of time until conditions of scarcity are over. Finally, competition among firms becomes less vigorous and their competitive marketing strategies move in a different direction. For instance, in most cases firms show: (a) less reliance on price competition; (b) more inclination toward sharing of marketing resources; (c) increased efforts to integrate vertically to ensure a larger share of supplies, and to integrate horizontally to create economies in marketing and distribution; (d) a search for additional ways to reduce marketing costs even further; (e) a reactivation of bartering arrangements; and (f) less reliance on demand stimulation (creation) activities.[21]

WHAT IS MARKETING?

Marketing is defined as the process of planning and executing the conception, pricing, promotion, and distribution of ideas, goods, and services to create exchanges that satisfy individual and organizational objectives.[22] Irrespective of its level of development, every economic system, no matter how primitive or advanced, is suffused with marketing activities. These activities are carried out by private firms, government agencies, and individuals. It is not the existence of a market economy that makes marketing essential but the exchange of values and the processes that facilitate such activity.[23] As such, marketing as an activity is different from trading in three essential ways:

a. One of the most prominent functions of marketing is to determine what is in demand and to guide that demand into channels that will enable industry to operate at the highest possible level of productivity.

b. The second important task of marketing is to influence production in such a manner as to make it satisfy demand in the best possible way.

c. Marketing activity makes sure that market-oriented entrepreneurial activities are enhanced and rewarded.[24]

What is the position of marketing then in the economic system of which it is an indispensable part? In answering this question we will identify three basic types of activity: extractive or manufacturing activities; marketing activities; and consumption activities. Extractive processes are those that involve the withdrawal of natural resources. Marketing activities include those types of business activities that create time, place, and possession utilities. Finally, consumption involves the performance of activities that result in a reduction in the economic value or usefulness of a product (see Table 1.4).

TABLE 1.4. Role of Marketing in the Economic Development Process

Extraction/Manufacturing/Marketing	*Consumption*
Create economic value	Reduces economic value
Improve industrial and commercial bases of an economy	Increases standards of living in a society.

Source: Compiled by the author.

The marketing sector of an economy consists of different specialized institutions that vary from country to country and add economic value to the products. Marketing institutions serve as an economic bridge between manufacturing and consumption. Despite its contemporary importance, marketing is treated as a subordinate kind of activity by Rostow:

> ... down to the present day it is difficult to get development economists and policy makers to accord to problems of efficiency in distribution the same attention they give automatically to problems of production, investment, and finance.[25]

So far, marketing is one of the most overlooked activities in the economic development process. As such, it is, as an institutional form of activity, alien to many economies. As a result, developmental activity is hampered in most cases. Why has there been a minimal concern for marketing, especially in most less-developed countries? The answer to this question can be given partially with reference to the primary concern of the developmental planners of these countries. In these countries the major concern has always been with the processes of manufacturing, capital formation, and industrialization. Production is the shortest route to economic development in LDCs.

In most less-developed countries the technical side of the industrialization process is given greater emphasis and the role of marketing in this process is ignored. The industrialization process and the development of a marketing system should complement each other. An improved marketing system in a less-developed country facilitates efficient use of scarce economic resources and helps smooth the flow of need-satisfying goods and services in domestic as well as in foreign markets. As such, marketing is a complex process that embraces the entire system of markets, prices, institutions, and the activities necessary to guide the efficient and orderly matching of supply and demand.

There are many discrepancies or gaps between what is produced by companies and what is demanded by consumers. For orderly economic development and increased standards of living in any country, these apparent discrepancies need adjustment. In less-developed countries, there are gaps in time, space, form, and possession between need-satisfying goods and the way in which demand is expressed for them. The main reason for these gaps is the lack of information and the absence of institutional forms that would normally perform the needed marketing functions. In less-developed countries there may be substantial production capacity and enough resources to complete transactions but an absence of exchange because a lack of communication between buyers and sellers creates problems. To the extent to which marketing is able to bridge these gaps, it can contribute to the socioeconomic development of less-developed countries. Through this process marketing can become the allocator of scarce resources in a less-developed economy.[26] Certain development-related marketing activities are pursued in less-developed countries, and particular problems result. This interface of development-related problems and marketing systems of a less-developed country is shown in Figure 1.2.

EARLIER TREATMENTS OF
MARKETING—PASSIVE INTERACTION

Marketing is a process that facilitates the planning, promotion, distribution, and servicing of the goods and services desired by the citizens of

FIGURE 1.2. Interface of Marketing Institutions and Economic Development—Related Problems

Source: John V. Petrov, "The Role of Marketing in a Developing Society," *Optimum* 7, 4 (1976): 30. Reproduced by permission of the Minister of Supply and Services Canada.

a nation. According to this concept, a private or public enterprise must cater to the needs and desires of the citizens while at the same time meeting the organizational objectives of the company (to make profit). Under the modern marketing concept, the consumers (citizens) become the focal point of most economic and business decisions. Production activities are geared to producing need-satisfying goods and services. Needs are determined through market research. Finance is organized to provide the capital required to produce and facilitate the sale of desired products. The marketing concept indicates that consumer orientation at a profit should be the backbone for the planning and execution of most business activities.

Marketing activity plays an active role in facilitating the economic development process. Development is measured by a number of performance variables. The presence or absence of these dimensions (factors) in a given country shows clearly the level of marketing and economic development as well as the interfaces between them.

The distribution of the goods produced during the development process tends to be neglected in the relevant literature. In particular, the efficiency of the distributive trade has not received enough attention in LDCs themselves. What are the causes of this neglect? There are certain reasons one could consider:

a. In LDCs, traders are widely regarded as mere "parasites" and as such, trade has a low esteem as a profession.

b. In many LDCs trade, especially wholesale trade, is dominated by ethnic minorities.

c. Because of negative attitudes toward trade, LDC government policymakers tend to underestimate its contribution to the national economy. In most cases, trade accounts for some 20 percent of the GNP of these countries.

Despite the neglect of distribution and marketing, Hirsch states that improvements in the method or scope of distribution in any economic system can aid in economic development by leading to a more efficient use of existing productive resources.[27] It can result in an expansion of market size, which can lead to economies of scale and eventually to mass production. Another advantage of efficient distribution is that it reduces a community's need to keep working capital tied up in storing goods for future consumption.

Rao has distinguished six structural dimensions that have an impact on marketing and economic development.[28] These are:

a. Physical facilities that are the basic infrastructure that is crucial to a market-oriented economy

b. Institutional facilities for the exchange of goods and for financial assistance

c. Market accessibility

d. Technology transfer

e. Behavioral factors needed in economic development. These factors can be positively influenced by the structure of the economic and social system prevailing in a nation.

f. Regulation. Governments in less developed nations, through regulation, assume active leadership roles in structuring environments conducive to economic development and growth. The impact of these different structural dimensions is shown in Figure 1.3.

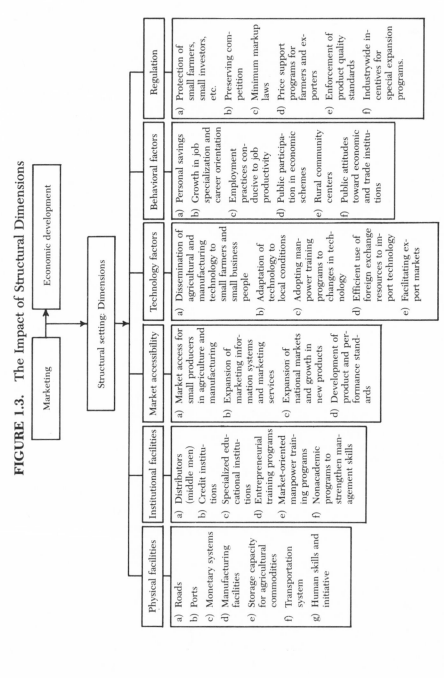

FIGURE 1.3. The Impact of Structural Dimensions

Marketing → Economic development

Structural setting: Dimensions

Physical facilities
a) Roads
b) Ports
c) Monetary systems
d) Manufacturing facilities
e) Storage capacity for agricultural commodities
f) Transportation system
g) Human skills and initiative

Institutional facilities
a) Distributors (middle men)
b) Credit institutions
c) Specialized educational institutions
d) Entrepreneurial training programs
e) Market-oriented manpower training programs
f) Nonacademic programs to strengthen management skills

Market accessibility
a) Market access for small producers in agriculture and manufacturing
b) Expansion of marketing information systems and marketing services
c) Expansion of national markets and growth in new products
d) Development of product and performance standards

Technology factors
a) Dissemination of agricultural and manufacturing technology to small farmers and small business people
b) Adaptation of technology to local conditions
c) Adopting manpower training programs to changes in technology
d) Efficient use of foreign exchange resources to import technology
e) Facilitating export markets

Behavioral factors
a) Personal savings
b) Growth in job specialization and career orientation
c) Employment practices conducive to job productivity
d) Public participation in economic schemes
e) Rural community centers
f) Public attitudes toward economic and trade institutions

Regulation
a) Protection of small farmers, small investors, etc.
b) Preserving competition
c) Minimum markup laws
d) Price support programs for farmers and exporters
e) Enforcement of product quality standards
f) Industrywide incentives for special expansion programs.

Source: Tanniru R. Rao, "Marketing and Economic Development," *Marketing & Management Digest* Vol. 8 No. 1 (January 1976): 17. Reprinted with permission.

The environmental changes in marketing that accompany the process of economic development involve related improvements in structure, product variety and volume, and management. An appropriate analytical approach must necessarily include all of the three variables as well as their interaction. In supermarket development, for instance, it is argued that there is a certain interconnection between structural change, product innovation and variety, and managerial attitudes and goals. Marketing developments are integrated in the larger social and economic context. Will a sufficient number of residents be willing and able to change their established shopping patterns so that the newly established store can survive? Will the availability of food supplies be suitable to city dwellers of a less-developed economy?[29] It is further maintained that the transformation of marketing activities during the development process would require simultaneous and interrelated changes in the following:

a. *Structural variables.* In less-developed countries, the large wholesalers and the few large domestic manufacturers that are concentrated in city centers constitute the primary supply sources and provide a major focus of attention for most of marketing activity. Key structural dimensions are the number, size, and location of marketing outlets.

b. *Product variety and volume.* In an economic development context, product variety and volume are considered in three dimensions. These are: (i) horizontal—that is, variety and specialization within and among individual marketing establishments at the same functional level (e.g., specialized versus general store types of retailing); (ii) vertical—changes in variety and specialization from one marketing level to the next (e.g., the assortment function of middlemen); (iii) time—introduction of new products and changes in the relative importance of product groups over time.

c. *Managerial variables.* Role of managerial activities and attitudes, and the importance of goals, motivations, and socio-cultural variables in the economic development process. For instance, managerial behavior oriented toward high-margin and low-volume distribution channels fails to stimulate both production expansion and demand response, and thus serves as a powerful brake on the economic development process.[30]

The evolution of marketing in most societies has characteristically gone through the following four phases:

1. The complementary phase, where marketing is used essentially as a sales tool.

2. The integrating phase, where marketing functions assume command of all of the company's commercial activities.

3. The strategic phase, where marketing activity becomes the unifying guideline for all company activities.

4. The metaphysical phase, which is characterized by the transition of marketing from a strictly entrepreneurial tool to one where it assumes the dimensions of a social science. Objectives include the promotion of social interests far beyond those of the individual company or industrial sector.[31]

It is stated by Scherb that great progress has been made in the development of marketing techniques in Brazil.[32] At present, the great majority of Brazilian enterprises are still trying to move from phase 1 to phase 2. The switch from phase 2 to 3 has been achieved successfully by only a small number of firms, especially in the consumer goods field.

POSITIVE CONTRIBUTIONS OF MARKETING

Marketing is the performance of all business activities that direct the flow of need-satisfying goods and services from producer to consumer (or final user).[33] The set of activities performed necessitates the performance of certain functions, the importance of which varies from country to country. Technical functions are performed, such as assembling, sorting, cleaning, packing, storage, transporting, and processing. These technical functions go along with a group of economic functions such as buying, selling, pricing, financing, and promotion. In addition to the technical dimension, marketing also has a social side, determined principally by cultural factors prevailing in an environment.[34] What the Japanese have done, so far, is to marry the technical and social dimensions of marketing in the furtherance of economic development.

> Japan, Inc., [signifies] the close working relationships between government, business and labor.... More specifically, the role of the integrated trading companies, government supports and subsidies and businesses' easy access to the banks are key features of the Japanese political economy. Industry structure features include close ties between manufacturers and their principal suppliers and distributors, a comparatively cheap labor force, and labor unions that work with rather than against management. Many observers have characterized the Japanese people as intensely committed to the work ethic, dedicated to the achievement of individual and national success, and willing to accept delayed gratification as a prerequisite to economic development.[35]

During marketing, certain services are rendered, the value of the marketed product is determined, and transfer of ownership activity takes place. As a result, the marketing process allocates scarce resources of a society to its members. As such, the marketing process performs a co-ordinating function by steering supply and demand with respect to time, place, and form utilities.[36]

The marketing system gains increasing importance as a traditional society is transformed into a modern industrialized society. The increasing proportion of the population living in urban centers and rising levels of income necessitate more highly organized distribution channels for pro-cessing and distributing products. The increasing interdependence of major sectors of the economy requires an effective system of exchange to coordinate production and distribution of both agricultural and consumer goods.

In the industrialized societies of the West, a strong market economy has emerged as a result of mass production, distribution, consumption, and communication. In these economies, large-scale production is a result of large-scale consumption, and the demands of consumers are stimulated by mass communication. When we look at the less-developed countries of the world, most of these characteristics are lacking at this stage in their development. It is stated that the major problem is how to enlarge the scope and intensity of the market in these countries. Of course, it is hoped that the enlargement of markets will result in greater buying power, which will lead to an increased and improved supply of products (see Figure 1.4).

The creation of improved and increased supplies of need-satisfying goods and services will increase the productivity of the total economic system of a country through creation of time, place, and possession utilities.[37] It is further stated that

> A smoothly functioning marketing system conducive to economic growth necessitates the existence of these sub-systems. First a system of physical distribution activity creating time and place utilities; second a financial system making the distribution of goods possible, and hence creating possession utility; and finally there is the functional-communicative system of matching supply and demand. This is the integration of the wants, needs, and purchasing power of consumers with the overall productive capacity and resources of production. This is direct in-volvement in the creation of form and possession utilities.[38]

Of these three marketing subsystems, physical distribution activities are considered to be of prime importance for less-developed countries. To this end, it is advocated that multinational companies could become a medium

FIGURE 1.4. Marketing as Generator of Economic Utilities

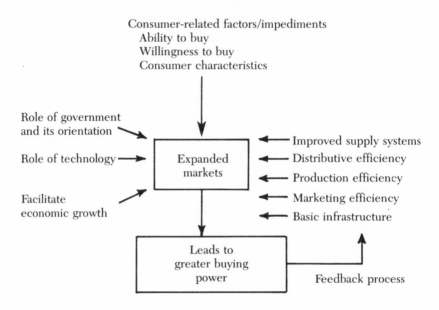

Source: Compiled by the author.

of transfer of Western marketing knowledge and techniques/concepts to less-developed countries, paying special attention to physical distribution improvements, which are of vital importance for these countries. Multinational corporations are not only transplanters of marketing know-how to less-developed countries, they are also transformers of attitudes toward economic development growth in general, and business in particular.[39]

Marketing is related to the process of development in three important ways. First, the marketing system serves as a major channel for the movement of capital. Second, the marketing system is a major tool for integrating the rural sector into the market economy. Third, marketing becomes an important sub-sector itself.[40]

An import-oriented marketing system is tailored to goods flowing from a foreign-based source of supply and is inadequate for marketing of local products. In an import-oriented marketing system, the locus lies near the consumer end of the marketing channel. Many marketing functions, such as sorting and assorting, selling, storage and warehousing, advertising and promotion, and financing, are performed by channel intermediaries. The establishment of domestic manufacturing of the import-substitution type invariably shifts the locus of the marketing functions to the production end of the channel.

Import-oriented marketing mechanisms are generally characterized by a lack of functional specialization. Intermediaries may simultaneously assume different functions such as importing, wholesaling, semi-whole-saling, and retailing. Thus, an intermediary does not see to a specific link in the channel, but to a range of other intermediaries. An import-oriented marketing mechanism usually works backward; consumers, retailers, and other intermediaries are always seeking goods. This situation arises from the tendency of importers to accelerate the flow of goods, and from the sporadic and uneven flow of imports.[41]

In view of the lack of functional specialization and excessive division of labor, a large number of people are engaged in the marketing process. Can existing import-oriented channels be effectively used in the distribution of domestic products? How can existing channels be adapted to local manufacturing? In most cases, the new firm adapts to the practices and operations of existing channels. Conflicts may occur between import-oriented channels and the needs of domestic manufacturing firms. These conflicts are summarized by Sherbini as follows:

a. Imports not only segment the domestic market, they may also fragment that market. Existing channels may not serve the needs of a domestic manufacturer who is contemplating nationwide distribution.

b. Import-oriented channels are generally characterized by a lack of functional specialization. Intermediaries generally assume certain functions such as importing, wholesaling, sub-wholesaling, and retailing. A domestic manufacturer would be interested in a chain type of channel where specific tasks can be assigned.

c. Lack of functional specialization is accompanied by a high degree of division of labor. Such tasks as financing, storage, warehousing, transportation, packing, sorting, and grading are often performed by separate agencies and intermediaries. Domestic manufacturing requires a greater integration of these tasks.

d. An import-oriented channel usually works backward; consumers, retailers, and other intermediaries are always seeking goods. On the other hand, domestic manufacturing ensures a steady stream of merchandise, requiring a smooth flow free from obstructions and stockpiles.

e. The variations in product specifications, resulting from different foreign origins, and in available supplies, lead to certain practices unfavorable for domestic manufacturing.

f. The credit system may differ considerably from that required by domestic manufacturing. Credit also plays a primary role in sustaining and regulating the flow of imports into domestic markets.

g. Because of the above inherent conflicts, some firms may develop new channels of distribution to serve more adequately the needs of domestic manufacturing. This has often created tension within existing marketing channels.[42]

Decision Model

The marketing process is defined as those activities performed by buyers and sellers for exchanging relevant market information in order to establish conditions of exchange and materialize legal and physical exchange of ownership. Micro marketing issues are those that are related to the management of the individual firm's factor procurement and product merchandising and distribution efforts. Micro-marketing efforts are primarily concerned with the individual firm's profit maximization through efficient factor procurement, final sale, and physical product distribution. Macro-marketing issues, on the other hand, are those related to the aggregate effect of government regulations, policies and actions, social customs, consumption patterns, and micro-marketing decisions of individual firms.[43]

For a proper allocation of resources and smooth distribution of need-satisfying goods and services in a national economy we need to construct a decision model. This model not only examines the activities of the individual marketing manager at the micro level, it also looks at the activities of the developmental planner at the macro level.[44] As shown in Figure 1.5, behavioral variables are also included in the system of relationships, based on the macro-functionalist view of the impact of the environment on the prevailing marketing system. A search for cause-and-effect relationships between the state of a marketing system and the level of economic development would facilitate prediction and the consequent decision-making process.[45]

The model developed in Figure 1.5 indicates the various micro-level changes impinging on the marketing system that are a prerequisite for changes of inputs into the behavior system of the marketing executive and public policymaker. The apparent possibilities for national economic growth are strongly conditioned by prevailing micro-environmental factors as well as by macro-institutional patterns. External factors, such as international market trends and terms of trade, define outer constraints on the growth of many countries.

So far, the focus of institutional analysis has been on a variety of social organizations that influence the economic process within a given country. In most less-developed countries, firms and government officials are preoccupied with production, and as such, organizations that facilitate the

FIGURE 1.5. Marketing System Improvement and Economic Development/Growth Interface

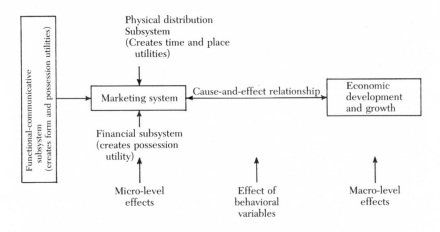

Source: Compiled by the author.

production process have a prominent place in the economy. As a result, company managers do not have an appreciation of marketing, which leads to company business policies that are poorly conceived and executed.

In most less-developed countries, given the current scarcity of resources and the tremendous development needs of the economy, the prime task for the economic system would be to allocate available resources effectively to the particular needs of the market. As a result of this effort, consumer welfare would be increased and greater value would be obtained by members of society.[46] With the apparent production orientation of most less-developed countries, available resources are not being used to meet the unfulfilled needs of the citizens, as very little attention is paid to consumer requirements. In most cases consumers are obliged to select whatever the producers offer.

To advance the economies of less-developed countries and to increase the prosperity of their industries, more attention will have to be paid to marketing. In particular, adoption and implementation of the consumer-oriented marketing concept is urgently needed. Basing their analysis on their findings in Peru, Glade and Udell suggested the following:

> Potential markets must be carefully studied to determine local needs, efficient distribution channels must be established to serve different regions, pricing policies frequently should be adapted to the low margin-high volume principle, and marketing communications should be used to

educate and expand markets that will support a more efficient system of production.

By emphasizing efficiency, a better allocation of resources, and the development of national markets, a higher standard of living and greater opportunities for employment and capital will be provided. In addition, the resulting efficiency and growth of national industries will provide a foundation for the development of industries that will be competitive in the international markets of the world.[47]

Marketing stimulates economic development, rather than being dependent on it. This is its formative character. Bartels offers further evidence:

- Through quality standardization, unified sales promotion, and rational price determination, agricultural markets are extended and production increased.
- Through improvement of storage and transportation facilities, economies in distribution are achieved, markets are expanded, and production is encouraged.
- Through market research and information services, producers better schedule and allocate offerings, realize more stable prices, avoid excess competition, and better serve markets.
- Through product testing, manufacturers determine the acceptability of products, better utilize resources, and avoid waste.
- Through presale packaging, producers mechanize production, distribution, and consumption processes, with resulting economies and efficiencies for all.
- Through strategic location of wholesale and retail establishments, growth of shopping centers, residential areas, and highway systems is effected.
- Through advertising and consumer credit, demand is stimulated, consumption patterns are changed, and markets are opened for new products and new entrepreneurs.
- Through improvement of in-store merchandising, shopping is facilitated and ideas conveyed for making personal living more convenient and enjoyable.[48]

It was also noted by Reed Moyer that marketing can contribute to economic development in a number of ways, as summarized below:

a. The marketing system can reduce risks by providing adequate and timely information flows.

b. Marketing activity can provide the organizational framework necessary in coordinating production and consumption activities and in rationing the supply of commodities to consumers in response to their expressed needs and wants.

c. Marketing institutions can be a source of entrepreneurial talent and capital for other sectors of the economy.

d. The marketing system can generate pecuniary and technological internal and external economies for producing firms as a result of the extension of their markets.

e. The marketing system may draw subsistence producers into the exchange economy.

f. Marketing institutions can increase the elasticities of supply and demand by making available new or improved products that buyers may find desirable.

g. Marketing institutions can lower consumer costs by improving distribution efficiency through technological innovation, more intensive resource use, and less spoilage.

h. The marketing system can reduce transaction and exchange costs between producers and consumers.[49]

NOTES

1. J. C. Narver and Ronald Savitt, *The Marketing Economy: An Analytical Approach* (New York: Holt, Rinehart and Winston, 1971).

2. W. W. Rostow, *The Stages of Economic Growth*, 2d ed., (London: Cambridge University Press, 1971).

3. Rostow, *The Stages of Economic Growth.*

4. N.N. Barish and M. Verhulst, *Management Sciences in the Emerging Countries: New Tools for Economic Development* (London: Pergamon Press, 1965).

5. Edna Douglas, "Marketing and Economic Development," in *Economics of Marketing* (New York: Harper and Row, 1975).

6. Kelly Harrison, *Development, Unemployment, and Marketing in Latin America*, Occasional Paper no. 2, Latin American Studies Center, Michigan State University (April 1972): 11.

7. E. M. Rogers, *Modernization Among Peasants: The Impact of Communication* (New York: Holt, Rinehart & Winston, 1969).

8. A. Coskun Samli and J. T. Mentzer, "A Model for Marketing in Economic Development," *Columbia Journal of World Business* 16, no. 3 (Fall 1981): 96.

9. Ibid

10. A Coskum Samli, *Marketing and Distribution Systems in Eastern European Economies* (New York: Praeger, 1978).

11.W. W. Rostow, *The Stages of Economic Growth* (London: Cambridge University Press, 1960).

12. Leslie M. Dawson, "Facing the New Realities of International Development," *Business* 31, no. 1 (January–February 1981): 29–35.

13. Ibid., pp. 32–34.

14. R. Ferber (ed.), *Consumption and Income Distribution in Latin America* (Washington, D.C.: Brookings Institution/ECIEL, 1980).

15. Marshall Loeb, "For a Bigger Economic Pie, Stir in Five Ingredients," *Marketing News* (July 9, 1982): 9.

16. Ibid.

17. T. M. Weisenberger and D. Keith Humphries, "Marketing's Role in Economic Development," in *Proceedings of the Southern Marketing Association, Mississippi, 1976*, edited by Henry W. Nash and Donald P. Robin, pp. 17–19.

18. William Copulsky, "Forecasting Sales in Underdeveloped Countries," *Journal of Marketing* 24, no. 1 (July 1959): 36–40.

19. Woodruff J. Emlen, "Let's Export Marketing Know-How," *Harvard Business Review* 36, no. 6 (November–December 1958): 70–76.

20. Nessim Hanna, A. H. Kizilbash, and Albert Smart, "Marketing Strategy under Conditions of Economic Scarcity," *Journal of Marketing* 39 (January 1975): 63–80.

21. Ibid., pp. 63–64.

22. "AMA Board Approves New Marketing Definition," *Marketing News* 19, no. 5 (March 1, 1985): 1.

23. Ronald Savitt, *Marketing and Economic Development: The Case of Turkey* (School of Administrative Sciences, Bogazici University, Istanbul, Turkey, May 1973), pp. 2–3.

24. G. Muller-Heumann and R. Bohringer, "Stimulating Consumption—An Alternative," *Intereconomics* 11 (1973): 347.

25. Walt W. Rostow, "The Concept of a National Market and Its Economic Growth Implications," in *Proceedings of the American Marketing Association, Fall 1965*, p. 19.

26. Charles C. Slater, "Modern Marketing—The Biased Allocator of Resources," in *New Essays in Marketing Theory*, edited by George Fisk (Boston, MA: Allyn and Bacon, 1971), pp. 422–38.

27. L. V. Hirsch, "The Contribution of Marketing to Economic Development—A Generally Neglected Area," in *The Social Responsibility of Marketing, Proceedings of the 1961 Winter Conference of the American Marketing Association, Chicago, 1961*, edited by W. D. Stevens, pp. 413–18.

28. This part is summarized from Tanniru R. Rao, "Marketing and Economic Development," *Marketing and Management Digest* (January 1976): 16, 18.

29. Lee E. Preston, "Marketing Organization and Economic Development: Structure, Products, and Management," in *Vertical Marketing Systems* (Boston: Scott Foresman, 1970), pp. 116–34.

30. Ibid.

31. Otto H. Scherb, "Brazil Pursues Industrial Eminence," *Advertising Age* (May 12, 1980): 58.

32. Ibid.

33. George Fisk, *Marketing Systems* (New York: Harper & Row, 1967).

34. R. Bartels, "Are Domestic and International Marketing Dissimilar?" *Journal of Marketing* 32 (July 1968): 56–61.

35. P. Kotler and L. Fahey, "The World's Champion Marketers: The Japanese," The *Journal of Business Strategy* 3, no. 1 (Summer 1982): 4.

36. *Marketing and Rural Development* (German Foundation For International Development, Berlin, 1978), pp. A3–A4.

37. A. Coskun Samli, "Exportability of American Marketing Knowledge," *MSU Business Topics* 13, no. 4 (Autumn 1965): 34–42.

38. Ibid., pp. 36–37.

39. Hans B. Thorelli, "The Multinational Corporation As a Change Agent," *The Southern Journal of Business* 1, no. 3 (July 1966): 1–9.

40. *Marketing: A Dynamic Force For Rural Development* (German Foundation For International Development, Berlin, 1978), p. 21.

41. A. A. Sherbini, "Import-Oriented Marketing Mechanisms," *MSU Business Topics* (Spring 1978): 70-73.

42. A. A. Sherbini, "Marketing in the Industrialization of Underdeveloped Countries," *Journal of Marketing* 29 (January 1965): 30.

43. Harrison, *Development, Unemployment,* pp. 1-2.

44. Martin Pfaff, "The Marketing Function and Economic Development: An Approach to a Systematic Decision Model," *AMA Conference Proceedings, Fall Conference, Chicago, 1965,* pp. 46-47.

45. James E. Littlefield, "The Relationship of Marketing to Economic Development in Peru," *Southern Journal of Business* (July 1968): 1-14.

46. William P. Glade and J. G. Udell, "The Marketing Concept and Economic Development: Peru," *Journal of Inter-American Studies* 10, no. 4 (October 1968): 533-46.

47. Ibid., pp. 545-46.

48. Robert Bartels, "Marketing and Economic Development," in *Macro Marketing—Distribution Processes From a Societal Perspective, Proceedings of the Macro-Marketing Seminar, Colorado, August 15-18, 1976,* edited by Charles C. Slater, p. 213.

49. Reed Moyer, *Marketing in Economic Development,* Occasional Paper no. 1, (East Lansing, MI: Institute for International Business Studies, Michigan State University, 1965), pp. 7-19.

2
Marketing as the Prime Mover of Development Activity

INTRODUCTION

The discussion thus far has emphasized the fact that the industrialization process and the resultant economic development activity are ongoing processes. Similarly, industrialization and economic development both can be accelerated and/or facilitated by a smoothly running, effective marketing and distribution system. Such a system is necessary for industrialization and the economic development process. Thus, perhaps the most important aspect of marketing with regard to economic development will be marketing know-how transfer. Technology transfer without a corresponding transfer of skills is not likely to succeed. In addition to the transfer of expertise there are a number of other areas where marketing is likely to play a very important role in the economic development process.

So far, marketing activity has been closely associated with the industrialized countries of the West. It has been presented as an engine of growth. As such, marketing activity is linked with growth policies at both the microeconomic (individual firm) and macroeconomic (country) levels. In industrialized countries of the West, marketing activity aims at bridging the gap between buyer and seller, the two parties to an exchange process.[1]

Marketing in a developmental sense does play a number of important roles. It cultivates changes in public attitudes; brings about changes in the quality of life; encourages a modern way of living; increases the standard of living; strives to build efficient economic and social institutions and secures the satisfaction of the public, which is the primary recipient of national development. Accordingly, one can define marketing in a developmental sense as follows:

> Marketing is the design, organization and implementation of economic, and social programs to influence public participation in a nation's development. This involves techniques of marketing research, product planning, pricing, communication and distribution.[2]

In general terms, marketing makes a positive contribution to economic development. Its effect will be most apparent when

- the function of acquainting potential buyers and sellers as well as the transmittal of information concerning product quality are adequately performed;
- a minimal amount of resources is absorbed directly by institutions engaged in marketing activities;
- declines in import or domestic prices are rapidly transmitted throughout society and demand is stimulated for products with a high domestic and export growth potential or low import prices;
- in order to pass on the benefits of economic development and ameliorate the living standards of the population, institutions engaged in marketing activities are dispersed throughout the country.[3]

ROLE OF MARKETING IN DEVELOPED COUNTRIES

Developed countries have a set of problems different from those of the less-developed countries.[4] In both types of countries, naturally, marketing is still necessary to make the distribution of goods and services as efficient as possible. But this is no longer considered sufficient, perhaps because marketing today deals with more major and complex issues than it did, say, some two decades ago.[5] In other words, marketing's role in North America, for instance, is considered to be much broader than the traditional role envisaged some 40 years ago.[6] At least three vast areas are within the constraints of modern marketing as it deals with the consumer-citizen concept rather than the consumer concept alone. These are consumerism, ecology, and poverty. All three have tremendous impact on the economic development process.

The first and foremost economic concern of developed countries is to maintain their standards of living as they maintain the economic momentum that they have gained. The prevailing energy crisis, combined with the scarcity of certain raw materials and other resources, will make it more and more difficult for these countries to maintain their present economic status.

Developed countries in the past have tried to cooperate with less-developed countries primarily because they wanted to develop new markets for their products. However, these countries are likely to intensify their cooperative efforts with LDCs not only to develop new markets but to exchange the raw materials and other resources that the less-developed countries have and the developed countries need, in return for finished goods, technology transfer, and food. Marketing knowledge could be one of the exchange factors. If the necessary marketing skills are transferred, the developed countries, first, will benefit directly because they will receive valuable scarce commodities or fuels in return. But they will benefit indirectly as well.

ROLE OF MARKETING IN LESS-DEVELOPED COUNTRIES

The less-developed country, as it receives marketing know-how and knowledge, will first improve its efficiency in distribution. With the increased time and place utilities there will be an increased efficiency which will free more resources to be exchanged with their developed country counterparts.

Generally, the economic development process takes place within the institutional framework of a country. There are societal (macro) as well as institutional (micro) level goals. Optimum success takes place when societal and institutional goals promote higher levels of economic progress for the citizens of a country. In other words, there is agreement between micro and macro forces. In Figure 2.1 macro (societal) goals are shown on the x-axis and institutional (micro) goals on the y-axis. The straight line (OZ) indicates economic development progress, which is measured by increased physical output. In zone I, both society's agent and the business institutions involved work together to achieve socially desirable goals. Having established these socially desirable goals, both public and private institutions work to serve the needs of the market in the best way possible.[7]

Although the Mexican government found it necessary to nationalize the petroleum industry and economically necessary to set up a public sector business enterprise to manage its petroleum interests, both government and institutions responded to the demands of the consumer and permitted others to service particular segments of this market. This was not an alteration in the basic philosophy about petroleum operations in

FIGURE 2.1. Marketing Adaptation for Economic Development

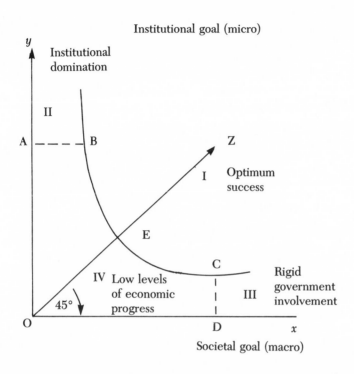

Source: Reprinted by permission of the publisher from "Opportunities for Marketing Growth in the Mexican Market," by Douglas L. Lamont, *The Southern Journal of Business,* 4, no. 2, p. 274. Copyright 1969 by Elsevier Science Publishing Co., Inc.

Mexico; rather, it was the adaptation process working at its best to meet the increasing demands of a growing market for gasoline. The distribution of gasoline to deficient regional areas and the improvement of retail services are but two of the many opportunities open to marketers in what before had been considered the sole province of those business institutions operating nationalized industries.[8]

These examples clearly show that marketing can make a major contribution to economic development. They show how marketing adaptation can bring profits to individual firms and at the same time meet societal objectives.

During the economic development process, certain marketing functions are performed at the individual firm level, which will result in certain macro societal benefits. Samli distinguishes a number of problem areas that can be corrected by properly performing appropriate marketing functions.[9] The six problem areas are: scarce resources, inappropriate products, lack of standardization, product waste, uninformed consumers, and misdirected distribution (see Table 2.1).

THE IMPROVEMENT OF MARKETING SYSTEMS FOR ECONOMIC DEVELOPMENT

The recent marketing systems literature suggests an evolutionary sequence of market development.[10] Most marketing systems studies advocate a move toward a capital-intensive type of system. Very little attention has been paid so far to the variability of marketing structures and the behavior of developed versus less-developed economic systems.[11]

In most countries, the path of marketing system development goes

TABLE 2.1. Impact of Marketing Functions on Economic Development

Problem Areas	Corrective Marketing Functions	Impact on Economic Development
Scarce resources	Better marketing	Significant savings, greater economic efficiency
Inappropriate products	Careful product research	Increased form utility, significant savings in scarce resources
Lack of standardization	Establishing measurable, realistic, permanent standards	Improved production processes, reduced waste in production and resource utilization
Product waste	Better transportation and storage	Increased time and place utilities
Uninformed consumers	Better consumer education and better communication	Increased efficiency in possession utility
Products do not reach the people who need them the most	Better distribution function and better infrastructure	Increased time and place utilities, an overall increase in the society's economic well-being

Source: A. Coskun Samli, "The Necessary Micromarketing Functions in LDCs for Macro Benefits," in *Developments in Marketing Science*, edited by J. D. Lindquist (Kalamazoo, MI: Academy of Marketing Science 1984), pp. 154–55. Reprinted with permission.

simply from some version of "primitive" marketing (peasant exchange system) to some form of "modern" marketing (full-fledged commercialization). In their study, Forman and Riegelhaupt proposed five stages in the development of a marketing system of a country, starting with a labor-intensive stage where exchanges are exclusively horizontal and the predominant type of market is a local market place.[12] The marketing system moves to a capital-intensive stage where exchanges are largely vertical and the predominant type of market is urban consumer.

The marketing problems one would face at different stages of development in marketing systems would vary from country to country, depending on a host of environmental factors. After preliminary identification of marketing problems at different stages of the system's development, there is a need to define the problems in a clear-cut fashion. To this end, one has to pay particular attention to the following two areas: (a) the linkages of the particular problem with other activities in the marketing system, and (b) the readiness of the individuals and institutions principally involved to make the changes required.[13] As an example, if storage of perishables is a high-priority problem area, the kinds of linkages to be explored are shown in Figure 2.2. At a later stage, a checklist may be prepared in which each of these factors is evaluated. The priority marketing functions shown in Figure 2.3 are also evaluated.

Marketing activities convert the physical outputs of production establishments into sales revenues and user inventories or satisfactions. Irrespective of how marketing activities are organized and carried out, they contribute greatly to any economy because of their direct utilization of resources and their impact on other aspects of economic and social life. The economy of a country can be considered as a system of interrelated markets. As an example of this, the marketing system of Greece is depicted in Figure 2.4 in relation to marketing systems of other countries.[14] The boxes indicate the major functional activities through which materials and services flow into the economy. These show raw material production and importation, manufacturing (production), wholesale distribution, and retail distribution. All of the market flows directly associated with the movement of consumer goods into retail trade are marked with an "×" on the figure. All of the flows are interrelated in important ways. This figure shows the economy as a flow system operating through different markets, serving as a framework within which individual tasks are performed.[15]

Changes take place in marketing systems which, in turn, affect the level of economic development of a country. As a case example we will show the integrative effects of marketing system changes on the stages of development in Brazil. Forman and Riegelhaupt have distinguished five different stages in the process of rationalization of the marketing system in Brazil:[16]

FIGURE 2.2. Marketing System Improvements at Different Stages of Development

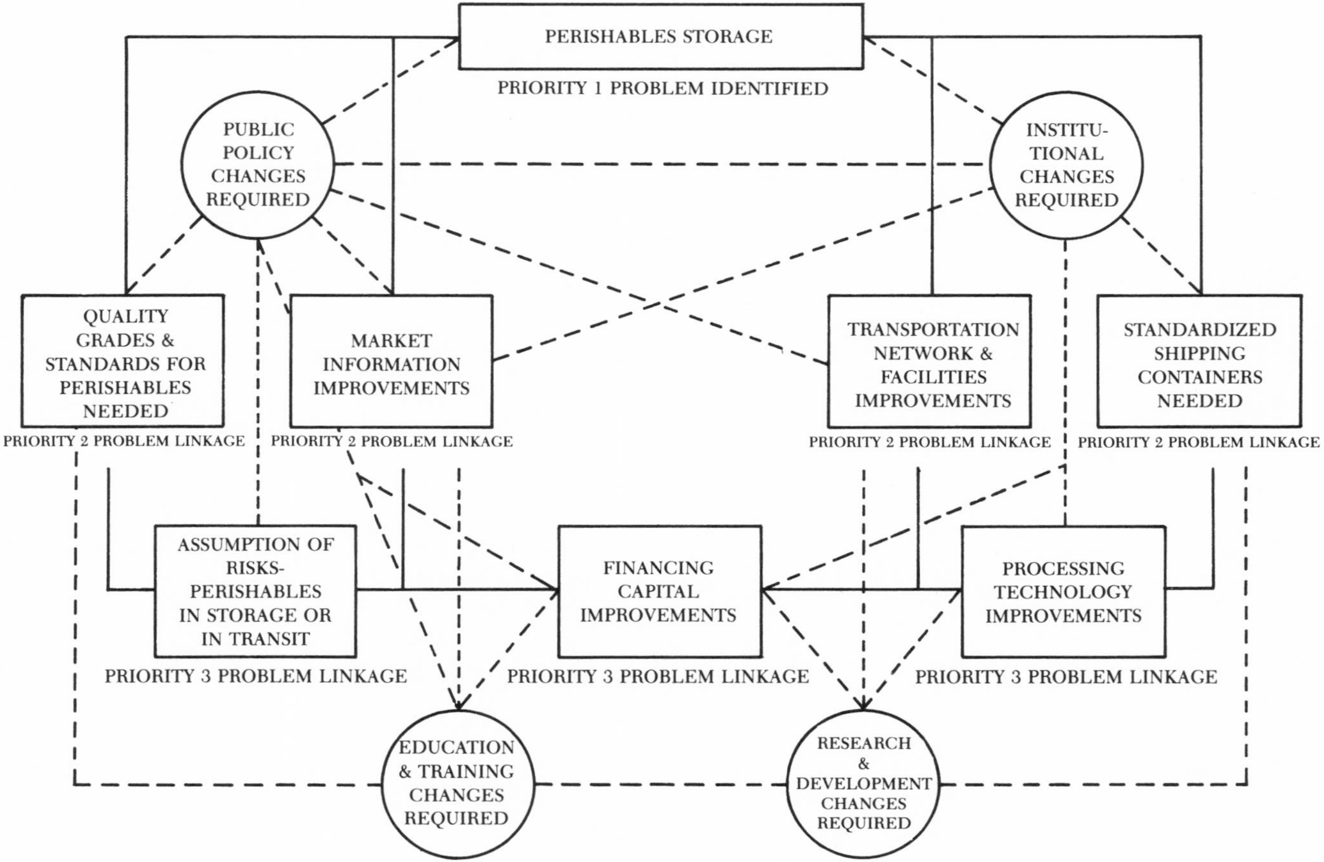

Source: Improving Marketing Systems in Developing Countries (Washington, D.C.: Economic Research Service, U.S. Department of

FIGURE 2.3. Marketing System Improvements: Problem Linkage Example

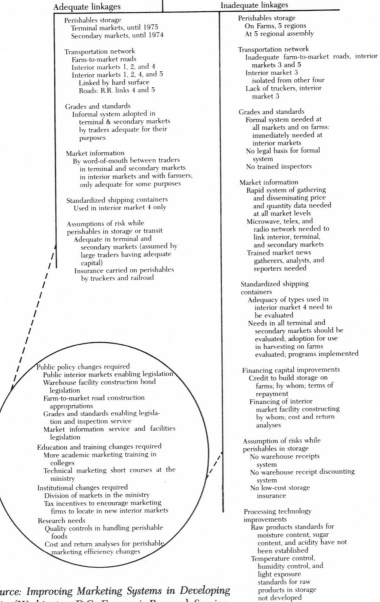

Storage of perishables

Adequate linkages	Inadequate linkages

Perishables storage
  Terminal markets, until 1975
  Secondary markets, until 1974
	Perishables storage
	  On Farms, 5 regions
	  At 5 regional assembly

Transportation network
  Farm-to-market roads
  Interior markets 1, 2, and 4
  Interior markets 1, 2, 4, and 5
    Linked by hard surface
    Roads: R.R. links 4 and 5
	Transportation network
	  Inadequate farm-to-market roads, interior
	    markets 3 and 5
	  Interior market 3
	    isolated from other four
	  Lack of truckers, interior
	    market 3

Grades and standards
  Informal system adopted in
    terminal & secondary markets
    by traders adequate for their
    purposes
	Grades and standards
	  Formal system needed at
	    all markets and on farms;
	    immediately needed at
	    interior markets
	  No legal basis for formal
	    system
	  No trained inspectors

Market information
  By word-of-mouth between traders
    in terminal and secondary markets
    in interior markets and with farmers;
    only adequate for some purposes
	Market information
	  Rapid system of gathering
	    and disseminating price
	    and quantity data needed
	    at all market levels
	  Microwave, telex, and
	    radio network needed to
	    link interior, terminal,
	    and secondary markets
	  Trained market news
	    gatherers, analysts, and
	    reporters needed

Standardized shipping containers
  Used in interior market 4 only
	Standardized shipping
	containers
	  Adequacy of types used in
	    interior market 4 need to
	    be evaluated
	  Needs in all terminal and
	    secondary markets should be
	    evaluated; adoption for use
	    in harvesting on farms
	    evaluated; programs implemented

Assumptions of risk while
perishables in storage or transit
  Adequate in terminal and
    secondary markets (assumed by
    large traders having adequate
    capital)
  Insurance carried on perishables
    by truckers and railroad
	Financing capital improvements
	  Credit to build storage on
	    farms; by whom; terms of
	    repayment
	  Financing of interior
	    market facility constructing
	    by whom; cost and return
	    analyses

Public policy changes required
  Public interior markets enabling legislation
  Warehouse facility construction bond
    legislation
  Farm-to-market road construction
    appropriations
  Grades and standards enabling legisla-
    tion and inspection service
  Market information service and facilities
    legislation
Education and training changes required
  More academic marketing training in
    colleges
  Technical marketing short courses at the
    ministry
Institutional changes required
  Division of markets in the ministry
  Tax incentives to encourage marketing
    firms to locate in new interior markets
Research needs
  Quality controls in handling perishable
    foods
  Cost and return analyses for perishable
    marketing efficiency changes
	Assumption of risks while
	perishables in storage
	  No warehouse receipts
	    system
	  No warehouse receipt discounting
	    system
	  No low-cost storage
	    insurance
	
	Processing technology
	improvements
	  Raw products standards for
	    moisture content, sugar
	    content, and acidity have not
	    been established
	  Temperature control,
	    humidity control, and
	    light exposure
	    standards for raw
	    products in storage
	    not developed

Source: Improving Marketing Systems in Developing Countries (Washington, D.C.: Economic Research Service, U.S. Department of Agriculture, February 1972), p. 24. Reprinted with permission.

FIGURE 2.4. The Marketing System in Greece

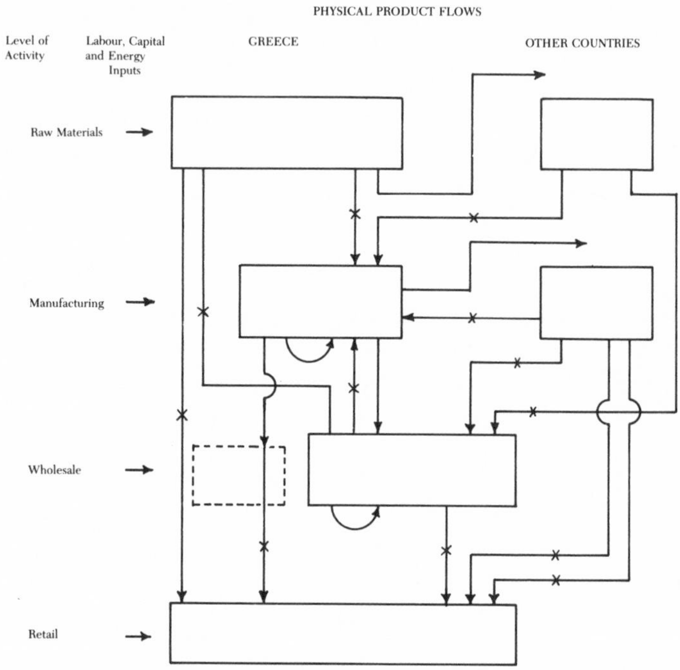

PHYSICAL PRODUCT FLOWS

Source: Lee E. Preston, *Consumer Goods Marketing in a Developing Economy* (Athens, Greece: Center of Planning and Economic Research, 1968); p. 30. Reprinted with permission.

Stage 1: The peasant retails his own goods in the local marketplace.

Stage 2: The incipient upward flow of goods through peasants who sell to middlemen. The first two stages are characterized by labor-intensive operations in both production and distribution areas.

Stage 3: Middlemen go to the source to buy in larger quantities and sell either in the marketplace or to wholesalers.

Stage 4: Wholesalers begin to bypass the middlemen and go directly to the peasant producer.

Stage 5: a. The prevailing tendency in Brazil is for wholesalers operating in highly capitalized economies of scale to want to deal directly with large-scale producers who assure a steady and continuous supply of food staples at a central delivery point.

b. Another form of supplying urban areas with quantities of foodstuffs grown on small individual plots is through marketing cooperatives.

c. Peasants group themselves into cooperatives for the production and sale of goods to wholesalers (see Table 2.2).[17]

TABLE 2.2. Stages in the Marketing System during the Economic Development Process

Stage	Participants	Predominant types of markets	Marketing inputs	Production inputs
1.	Peasant producer-consumer	Local marketplace	Labor intensive	Labor intensive
2.	Peasant producer-middlemen-consumer	Local marketplace and distribution fair	Labor intensive	Labor intensive
3.	Peasant producer-middlemen-wholesaler and consumer	Distribution fair with increased growth in local marketplace	Increased capitalization through wholesaling	Labor intensive
4.	Peasant producer-wholesaler-consumer	Distribution fair and urban consumers' market	Increased capitalization on all levels of distribution	Labor intensive
5.	Alternatives			
	a) Large-scale producers-wholesaler-consumers	Urban consumers' market	Capital intensive	Capital intensive
	b) Peasant producer-wholesaler-middlemen-consumers	Marketing cooperatives for urban areas	Capital intensive	Capital intensive
	c) Large scale producers-peasant producer-wholesaler-consumer	Urban consumers' market	Capital intensive	Capital intensive through voluntary cooperation

Source: Shepard Forman and Joyce F. Riegelhaupt, "Market Place and Marketing System: Toward a Theory of Peasant Economic Integration," *Comparative Studies in Society and History* 12 (1970): 208. Reprinted with permission.

As can be seen, marketing systems are in a process of continuous change as the economic development process takes place. Sustained growth requires a continuous search for methods and ways of increasing performance of the various elements of the marketing system. Barriers to improved marketing performance develop within the marketing system. The individual company, given its position in the system, cannot by itself alter the marketing system to achieve improved performance. Improved performance necessitates effective coordination of the specialized activities performed by individual participants. Failures in coordination of marketing activities of individual firms become effective barriers to the economic development process.

Marketing Efficiency

The dynamics of marketing system improvement during the development process has received little attention in the marketing literature. A number of studies have looked at marketing system efficiency.[18] Smith analyzed marketing system improvements undergoing rapid development.[19] The author divided the period of marketing system development into three stages:

a. Oligopsony and centralization
b. Trucks, credit, and decentralization
c. Product differentiation

Throughout these three distinct stages the performance and efficiency of the marketing system in Brazil was related to inputs supplied by other sectors such as transportation, credit, storage, and communications facilities. Smith further suggested that

> Marketing should, in the normal course of events, contribute positively to the development process. Growth should reduce marketing costs, which, in turn, should stimulate production necessary for further growth.
> A corollary, however, is that the large cost reductions will be concentrated in the earlier stages of growth, as the economy moves from a poor to reasonably adequate infrastructure and financial networks.[20]

Marketing efficiency signifies the movement of goods from producers to consumers at the lowest cost consistent with provision of the services both desire and are able to pay for.[21] In general terms, marketing efficiency is envisaged with the following strategic dimensions:[22]

Prices: Cost and profit margins approach the level that is just sufficient to reward investment at the going rate.

Size and number of firms: All marketing activities are undertaken by enterprises which are fully informed of factors relevant to these business activities and which operate on the most efficient scale.

Service provided: The quality of the service is neither too high nor too low in relation to cost and consumer desires.

Analysis of efficiency by comparison of channels is complicated by differences in the nature and value of the services provided. Institutions may stimulate or impede economic development by their influence on the direct calculation of costs and benefits, the relationships between production and marketing, the order of economic relationships, the knowledge of economic opportunities, and society's motivations and values.[23]

In general, business firms can improve efficiency and as a result make a positive contribution to economic development whenever

a. The function of bringing potential buyers and sellers together and spreading information concerning product quality is adequately performed.

b. A minimum quantity of resources is absorbed directly by the small firms engaged in economic activities.

c. Declines in import or domestic prices are rapidly transmitted throughout society and demand is stimulated for products with a high domestic and export growth potential or low import prices.

d. Small firms are dispersed throughout the country in order to pass on the benefits of economic development and ameliorate the living standards of the population.[24]

Warrack analyzed two separate components of marketing efficiency: operational efficiency and exchange efficiency.[25] Each efficiency component is examined in terms of costs and pricing. When the marketing process creates form, space, time, and possession utilities, certain costs are involved. Operational efficiency is dependent on marketing cost analysis, and marketing cost depends on marketing organization and a proper marketing logistics system (see Figure 2.5). Marketing organization determines the way physical facilities are organized. These physical facilities are of two types. The first one is a functional organization responsible for "who deals with whom" during the marketing system performance. The second one is a spatial organization that consists of a set of geographic locations comprising different industries whose number and size may vary. Marketing logistics factors create time, place, and possession

FIGURE 2.5. The Determinants of Operational Efficiency in Marketing Systems

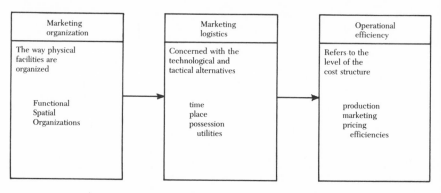

Marketing organization	Marketing logistics	Operational efficiency
The way physical facilities are organized	Concerned with the technological and tactical alternatives	Refers to the level of the cost structure
Functional Spatial Organizations	time place possession utilities	production marketing pricing efficiencies

Source: Adapted from A. A. Warrack, "A Conceptual Framework for Analysis of Market Efficiency," *Journal of Agricultural Economics* 20, no. 3 (1968): 12.

utilities, and as such they are conditioned by the conduct of marketing organizations. Although the marketing organization determines the workings of marketing logistics, the components of marketing logistics would determine the marketing cost structure in the creation of utilities. Operational efficiency is indicated by the cost structure. High costs imply low efficiency in the generation of utility-creating marketing services.[26]

The second component of marketing efficiency is exchange efficiency, which has two determinants. These are market structure and competitive strategy. The first one describes characteristics of a marketing system that exercises strategic influence on competition and the pricing system within a given market (see Figure 2.6). It is pointed out that as market structure deviates from the specification of an ideal market system, market power accrues to individual firms in the industry. Exchange efficiency refers to the relationship between costs and prices. When there is more deviation from perfect competition and higher market power, there will be a wider differential between costs and prices. In most cases, higher market power implies lower exchange efficiency and vice versa.[27]

When designing efficient marketing programs, two basic elements should be regarded as strategic for success. These are participation and facilities. The necessary and achievable degree of participation by target consumer groups in the design and implementation of efficient marketing programs varies according to socio-political conditions. *Facilities* means the amount and level of technical services and material inputs provided.[28] Both elements could form a basic typology for planning market improvement, and greater efficiency (see Figure 2.7). A country, or more realistically, an

FIGURE 2.6. The Determinants of Exchange Efficiency in Marketing Systems

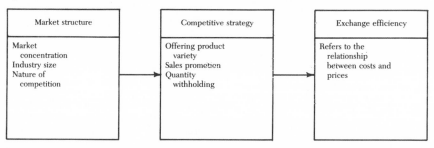

Market structure	Competitive strategy	Exchange efficiency
Market concentration Industry size Nature of competition	Offering product variety Sales promotion Quantity withholding	Refers to the relationship between costs and prices

Source: Adapted from A. A. Warrack, "A Conceptual Framework for Analysis of Market Efficiency," *Journal of Agricultural Economics* 20, no. 3 (1968): 14.

area within a country, may then be seen to support one of the following situations:

a. low participation and low facilities (e.g., Ethiopia prior to land reform)
b. low participation and high facilities (e.g., parts of Brazil)
c. high participation and low facilities (e.g., Tanzania, cattle marketing in the Sahel, and Ethiopia after land reform)
d. high participation and high facilities (e.g., Republic of South Korea)

FIGURE 2.7. Market Improvement for Efficiency

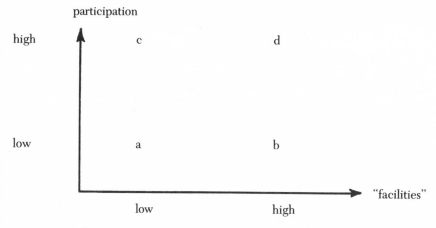

Source: Marketing: A Dynamic Force For Rural Development (Berlin: German Foundation For International Development, 1978), p. 36. Reprinted with permission.

A great deal of efforts to improve food marketing in less-developed countries has been directed toward improving the efficiency of the physical movement of products from rural areas to consuming centers in urban areas. In most cases, institutional reforms and marketing facility projects were designed to reduce marketing costs, improve product acceptability, and expand consumption and production of food.[29]

The strategy, as suggested above, was to design and implement a set of interrelated programs that would remove or reduce the barriers to improved market performance. A conceptual model summarizing a comprehensive set of food marketing system efficiencies is shown in Table 2.3. The sequence of changes in food system processes indicates the potential dynamics of market efficiency whereby benefits can be shared by producers as well as consumers.[30]

Various components of a marketing system have an impact on the economic development process. Of course, the impact of marketing system changes on the economy of a country is difficult to measure. Slater developed a model for inducing the internal market development of a less-developed economy.[31] Griggs states:

> It is first necessary to obtain as precise a description as possible of the existing marketing channels for moving domestically produced food products to the urban markets in order to identify major channel members. The identified channel members are studied to determine what factors they feel inhibit them from bringing more products through the market channel. These factors could include uncertainty about future prices or the level of future demand. Only after the marketing channel members' attitudes toward risk and uncertainty are ascertained is it effective to take the second step—introduction of selected marketing reforms designed to reduce or spread marketing risks in order to induce expansion of marketing participation.[32]

Improvements in the marketing system of a country will have certain economic consequences. First of all, the economic impact needs to be viewed as a collection of interrelated forces, each having an influence on the other. Second, the change in the marketing system needs to be measured in terms of the effects it has on the other sectors in the marketing system.

During the economic development process, marketing institutions and organizations of a private or public nature are concerned with a number of issues: the differences between the marketing characteristics of different types of products, the variability of marketing chains, the relationships between the scales of production and consumption and the structure of marketing chains, and the relationships between different

TABLE 2.3. A Conceptual Model Showing a Series of Interrelated Food Marketing System Reforms and Expected Linkages to Stimulate Economic Growth and Development

Sequence of changes in food system processes	Fomenting actions seemingly needed to foster change	Potential points of entry in national food system reform process
Reduce marketing costs in urban areas for locally produced food products Lower food prices increase effective income Increase effective urban demand for food and consumer goods and related marketing services	Capital and technical assistance to foster improvements in efficiency of traditional urban marketers Timely introduction of infrastructures as a tool to stimulate improvement in channel performance More effective public facilitative and regulatory programs	Urban food distribution components
Increased food production and agricultural production specialization	Additional and more appropriate agricultural production extension efforts	
Increased rural incomes and market participation on both the supply and demand sides	Development of appropriate packages of inputs Effective market information and price stabilization programs Supervised credit programs	Rural food production components
Increased rural and urban demand for organization and coordination services of commodity subsystems	Foster backward vertical coordination of food marketing Capital and technical assistance to rural assemblers and transporters	Rural assembly market components

(continued)

TABLE 2.3. (*Continued*)

Sequence of changes in food system processes	Fomenting actions seemingly needed to foster change	Potential points of entry in national food system reform process
Increased rural demand for improved physical distribution services (i.e., assembly activities)	Improve public storage, roads, exchange rules, grades	
Increased rural demand for: Farm inputs Purchased food Rural- and urban-produced consumer goods Marketing services related to the above three	Improve rural distribution services and lower costs for: Farm inputs Purchased food Consumer goods	Rural distribution components for Purchased food Farm inputs Consumer goods
Increased demand and employment in industry and related service sectors Increased income leading to increased demand for food and consumer goods	Use of appropriate technologies in production processes Develop more appropriate products for local market demand characteristics Lower costs of mass distribution to rural and urban areas	Rural and urban industrial and services components

Source: Marketing and Rural Development (Berlin: German Foundation for International Development, 1978), pp. N5–N6. Reprinted with permission.

types of marketing reform. As an example of this, interregional marketing processes in Ecuador are described in Figure 2.8.

Designing an effective production-distribution system should be viewed as an evolutionary process of development. The appropriate marketing system would depend on the economic reality of a particular time and place and is related to the stages in the economic development process. The needs and potentials of the marketing system would vary not only from product to product but also from country to country. A model

FIGURE 2.8. A Graphical Model of the Stages of Interregional Trade

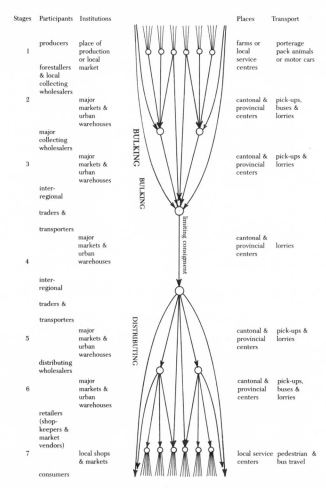

Stages	Participants	Institutions		Places	Transport
1	producers	place of production or local market		farms or local service centres	porterage pack animals or motor cars
	forestallers & local collecting wholesalers				
2		major markets & urban warehouses		cantonal & provincial centers	pick-ups, buses & lorries
	major collecting wholesalers				
3		major markets & urban warehouses	BULKING	cantonal & provincial centers	pick-ups & lorries
	inter-regional		BULKING		
	traders &				
	transporters				
4		major markets & urban warehouses	limiting consignment	cantonal & provincial centers	lorries
	inter-regional				
	traders &				
	transporters				
5		major markets & urban warehouses	DISTRIBUTING	cantonal & provincial centers	pick-ups & lorries
	distributing wholesalers		DISTRIBUTING		
6		major markets & urban warehouses		cantonal & provincial centers	pick-ups, buses & lorries
	retailers (shop-keepers & market vendors)				
7		local shops & markets		local service centers	pedestrian & bus travel
	consumers				

The length and breadth of the arrows are approximately proportional to the distance travelled and the volume of each consignment.

Source: R.J. Bromley, "Interregional Marketing and Alternative Reform Strategies in Ecuador," *European Journal of Marketing* 8, no. 3 (1978): 247. Reprinted with permission.

showing induced economic development through marketing system improvement is illustrated in Figure 2.9.

This prescribed production distribution system would identify for a country the vertical linkages and sequences from producers to final consumers. It would also diagnose the barriers to improved performance of the marketing system. A coordinated set of programs and policies designed

FIGURE 2.9. Inducing Internal National Market Development

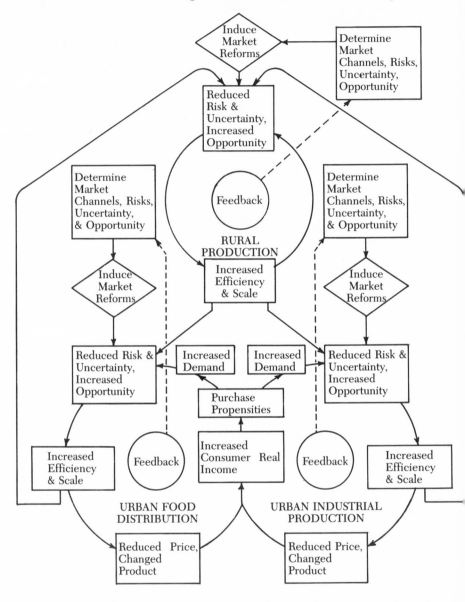

Source: James D. Shaffer, "Designing Agricultural Marketing Systems in Developing Countries," paper presented at the Agricultural Marketing Conference in Katmandu, Nepal, February 21–24, 1972, p. 28. Reprinted with permission.

to shape the production distribution system should be guided by a set of overriding goals. These goals, of course, need to be established by public policymakers in each country. It is, however, very useful to develop a set of general objectives for those institutions participating in the planning and coordinating of an orderly marketing program. Such a set of goals and policies for food marketing are suggested by Shaffer[33] as follows:

a. To assure an abundant and reliable supply of food at economical prices. To stimulate the production and distribution of food, which will result in nutritionally adequate diets for all.

b. To facilitate and promote the production and distribution of that combination of foods and related services which best reflects the preferences and needs of consumers and the real relative costs of production.

c. To create incentives for increased productivity in each activity of the total system of food production and distribution (especially to provide farmers with reliable markets, reducing uncertainty, thus stimulating production and creating incentives to produce those commodities demanded by consumers).

d. To stimulate the development of opportunities for productive and rewarding employment and promote the development of a productive labor force.

e. To stimulate the development of a fair and equitable exchange system. To especially ensure that the consequences of government policies and programs are fair and equitable.

f. To discourage uneconomic uses and debasement of natural resources and the environment.

g. To encourage socially desirable population settlement patterns.

h. To encourage a sense of belonging and effectiveness among participants in the system.[34]

STAGES OF MARKET DEVELOPMENT

The nature of the market system depends very much on the characteristics of the country whose market is being examined. In most cases, the size of the population, the size of the trading area, the density of population, the development of communications and transportation networks, the amount of goods produced and their variety, and the degree of specialization all contribute to development of markets. These factors create the needs that a market system tries to fulfill and provide the framework within which the market system operates.[35]

A whole new family of nations, labeled the "advanced less-developed countries," is emerging. Included in this family are South Korea, Malaysia,

Singapore, Thailand, Nigeria, the Ivory Coast, Venezuela, and Kuwait. They are not only growing in wealth and education, they will also require more of what Western companies can produce and market. Of these, Singapore, South Korea, and Taiwan are the most promising. It is essential, however, that marketers in developed countries recognize the changes taking place in these societies and target their products and/or services to specific markets and regions of the less-developed world. As a result, we need to look at not only market systems but also stages of market development in the countries concerned.

There are socioeconomic, governmental, technological, and cultural differences among the countries of the less-developed world. The emergence of these countries in a world of vastly different stages of market and technological development calls for a new organizational arrangement. Because of this apparent trend, firms in developed countries should be reorganized to respond to the most important challenges of the less-developed country.

One approach that may prove to be extremely useful is the organization of less-developed countries by stages of market development or on the basis of their approach to development.[36] A stages-of-market development organization assembles and clusters the countries of the less-developed world and their systems into different categories that reflect similar market conditions.

In relation to market size, location, periodicity, and development, the market systems in the highlands of a country show characteristics distinctly different from those in the core areas. Market systems in less-developed countries are not developed properly and in most cases are in a state of rapid change. Changes taking place in market systems in Latin America are illustrated in Figure 2.10 by Symanski and Bromley.[37]

> The nature of individual market systems can be explained by the four interdependent clusters of variables in the ecological complex. Population, technology, and general economic organization form the primary clusters, and environment assumes a secondary role. Market organization, treated as a subcluster of variables within the cluster of socioeconomic organization, can be considered as a series of dependent variables which change according to changes in the independent variables of population, technology, general socioeconomic organization and environment. Through a process of circular and cumulative causation, changes in the independent variables can lead to permanent and comparatively magnified alterations in market organization.

In the above case, changes in the market systems are initiated by improvements in transport technology or reorganization, or improvement of transport services. The changes tend to be self-reinforcing through

FIGURE 2.10. Changes in Market Systems Stimulated by Transport Improvements

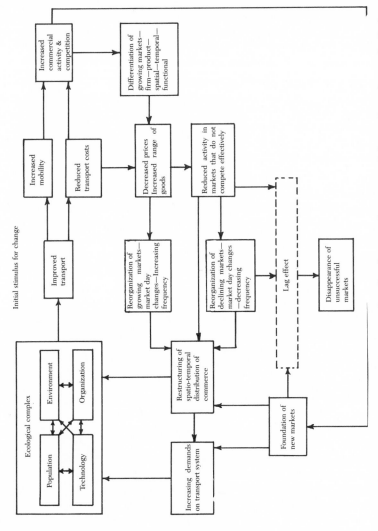

Source: Richard Symanski and R.J. Bromley, "Market Development and the Ecological Complex," *The Professional Geographer* 26, no. 4 (November 1974): 385. Reprinted with permission.

positive feedback. The readjusted market system places more demands on the transportation system and this may lead to further transport improvements.[38]

It is shown that improvements in the market system can have a great impact on the economic development process. The market system can be used as an educational tool for integrating individuals into the process of industrialization more effectively. Improvements in the coordination of the market produce economic benefits in terms of lower marketing costs arising from gains in physical, facilitative, and managerial efficiency.

As a country progresses along the economic development continuum, the service sector of its economy expands and prospers in relation to its production sector. In line with this development, the total resources devoted to service industries tends to increase. As a result, marketing operations become more extensive and complex to meet ever increasing consumer demand for a greater variety of products and more attractive services. This, in turn, means increased standards of living.

Market development, like economic development, must be based on division of labor into specialized functions, and the growth of the market economy reflects this specialization. Of course, this progressive specialization must be associated with an expansion of the marketing system and its capacity to move supplies between different areas and market segments. For instance, urban market development generally relies on marketing channels capable of providing a flow of products of all kinds from different areas.

Generally, economic development creates higher incomes, causing consumers to seek a different variety of products and make their purchases in different ways. Consumers demand far more services and better retailing institutions. They are also increasingly prepared to pay for such improvements. Because of increased and improved profit margins, it becomes profitable for the marketing enterprises to provide them.

One could easily say that the economic development process is associated with increases in marketing expenditures in relation to production costs. It can be said that value added by marketing factors does increase faster than value added by primary production factors. Table 2.4 depicts the relationship between marketing and economic development.

As depicted in Table 2.4, in the early stages of economic development there is a shift from a subsistence economy to one in which production is offered for sale. Later there are lower production costs due to greater efficiency. Increases in the services provided by the marketing sector lead to quality improvement, better processing and packing, and wider distribution. During the process of economic development, the cost of extra services and processes is offset by improved efficiency in transport, storage, handling, and general organization.[39] At the advanced stage of

TABLE 2.4. Sectoral Changes and Level of Economic Development

Stage of economic development	Production costs	Marketing sector improvement	Productivity and efficiency	Consumer consumption behavior
Early	High	Low	Low	Hand to mouth
Medium	Lower	Progressive increase	Greater	Improved consumption
Advanced	Medium	High	Highest	Conspicuous consumption

Source: Compiled by the author.

economic development, as a community becomes wealthier consumer demand for quality, variety, appearance, and convenience leads to a greater outlay for marketing services for the same volume of products.

There must be a balance in the development of production, marketing, and market outlets. Modern marketing systems such as those found in the United States or Western Europe can develop only where there is a mass demand for quality products and services. In less-developed countries, the economic environment sets limits to the investments and innovations that are immediately justified. In most less-developed countries, investments and improvements in the marketing system lag behind, so that inadequate marketing arrangements become a serious constraint on the development of production and consumption.

It is stated that inadequate marketing systems in less-developed countries hinder industry development.

This may, of course, be due to shortcomings in the country's basic infrastructure (e.g., roads and communications), or to special political problems. The situation may be aggravated by some aspects of government policies or regulations and by a lack of certain central services the marketing system cannot provide for itself. The important point is that marketing arrangements and marketing enterprises are very much affected by government investments, economic measures and services. Sound policies and programmes for marketing improvements are therefore essential if the marketing system is to make its full contribution to the development of production and consumption, and promote change and progress instead of retarding them.[40]

MARKETING AS A POSITIVE FORCE IN DEVELOPMENT

In market-oriented economies, a marketing system not only links producers and consumers, it also makes an active, positive contribution to the economic development process. For instance, marketing enterprises seek to increase their turnover and sales, and their efforts promote economic activity in both the production and service sectors.

It is pointed out that a dynamic marketing system continually seeks to promote sales and consumption. It also works for the introduction of new product forms to enlarge the market and new services to increase turnover. To this end, new methods based on modern technology are introduced whenever it is thought they will increase the scope of company operations. For instance, recent technical innovations in the areas of transportation, physical distribution, and materials handling have transformed the scale and scope of marketing services and thus have created a whole range of new economic activities.

> A good marketing system not only stimulates consumption, but also generates increased production by seeking out extra supplies. If the pricing system works well, it produces suitable incentives to meet the consumers' needs more accurately in terms of types, qualities and times of supply. Production is thus adapted to the needs of consumers in response to price "signals" transmitted by the marketing system. The more highly developed industries tailor output to the preferences of the consumer markets served, particularly in terms of standardization of types and qualities.[41]

Government policymakers in less-developed countries are faced with a variety of alternatives to foster economic growth. Some attempt to stimulate development by strictly utilizing domestic resources. Others attempt to import the capital and technology from foreign investors or pursue a program that falls between the two alternatives.[42] Irrespective of the development program pursued, the following steps need to be undertaken:

a. Some research needs to be done on the problems existing in a nation that might be solved by economic development.
b. There must be a series of decisions on the means to solve these problems.
c. There must be a specification of a plan designed to achieve given objectives.

Modern marketing technology can help promote economic and social growth in less-developed countries of the world. It helps bridge the widening gap between rich and poor countries in the following situations:

a. The market mechanism, particularly in less-developed countries, fails to establish and maintain a balance between agricultural and industrial production, and is unable to foster a "territorially balanced" growth of the production system.

b. The dominant vehicle for economic and social growth will be innovation appropriate to the developing countries, which should employ additional labor as justified by savings in capital. This means that industrial processes of small productivity, used today in the industrialized countries, must in greater measure than in the past be transferred to less-developed countries.

c. Intervention by the state is needed to accelerate capital accumulation and to allocate it properly, not only in less-developed countries but also in underdeveloped areas of industrialized countries.

d. The character of a free market system should be maintained in less-developed countries to preserve and develop entrepreneurial vigor.[43]

When considering the role of marketing in economic development in less-developed countries, it is generally necessary to draw examples from other countries that are at the same level of economic development. Comparative analysis can be made among less-developed countries to find out similarities and differences. What can be gained from an examination of the marketing activities of different less-developed economies is the solution of specific problems that may have some common bases. To this end, it would be extremely valuable to construct a framework that would allow comparisons of less-developed countries on the basis of accepted criteria.

Irrespective of its level of development, every country has a marketing system that consists of a variety of institutions and facilitative agencies through which goods and services are channeled to satisfy final consumers. In every marketing system buyers and sellers seek satisfaction through the efficient transfer of goods and services. Having said this, we must also point out the fact that the organization and performance of marketing activities do show differences in centrally planned socialist economies versus less-developed economies or developed economies of the West.

Douglas and Wind looked at the possible relationships between marketing strategies used by companies and the environmental conditions surrounding company practices.[44] In particular, they asked:

To what extent are specific environmental conditions, such as the level of economic development and cultural patterns, associated with certain marketing practices?

How similar are marketing practices of firms within a given environment and is there a typical pattern of marketing practices within a country?

To what extent can differences in marketing practices in a given environment be explained in terms of specific firm characteristics such as size or managerial attitudes?

Countries, first of all, were classified according to their level of economic and technological development. By looking at the characteristics of the selected countries five different levels of development were identified. The study results indicated that there was no direct relationship between the environmental factors considered and marketing practices of companies. Countries of similar levels of development did not tend to have similar marketing practices.[45]

APPROPRIATE TECHNOLOGY FOR ECONOMIC DEVELOPMENT

Most less-developed countries have relatively recent experiences in planning their economic development efforts. The key to marketing products and services to these countries is to know and understand the phases of economic development these countries pass through and the impact that each phase has on demand for various classes of products. These countries are eager to acquire products that are appropriate to their own situations and needs.[46] Appropriateness has four dimensions for these countries:

a. *Appropriateness for goals:* Does the technology support the goals of the development policy?

b. *Appropriateness of product:* Is the final product of service delivered useful, acceptable, and affordable for the intended users?

c. *Appropriateness for process:* Does the production process make economic use of inputs?

d. *Cultural and environmental appropriateness:* Are the production processes, the products delivered, and the institutional arrangements compatible with the local environmental and cultural setting?

The five-year economic development plans used by most less-developed countries not only determine the appropriateness of products and technology, they are also used for the allocation of expenditures. An economic development plan prepared for a less-developed country comprises at least the following elements:

a. Strategy for industrial development.

b. Specific objectives and targets of the plan, particularly those concerning national products and employment.

c. An investment program for the governmental and public sectors, showing the allocations of developmental expenditures to the principal sectors.

d. Forecasts of planned investments in the private sector, and an indication of the policies adopted by the government for orienting and steering these investments into the desired fields through appropriate measures governing fiscal policy, foreign trade, foreign exchange, and foreign investments.

e. A financial budget giving the resources and expenditures of the governmental, public and private sectors, and of both domestic and foreign exchange.

f. A detailed account of sectoral development programs giving the planned projects in every sector and some basic information about every project.

g. A statement of basic policies and measures of implementation that will be carried out in order to effect changes favorable for development in the economic, social, and administrative spheres, such as labor legislation, agrarian reform, and education and training programs.

It is stated that an intermediate technology is one that is compatible with the economic goals and objectives of less-developed countries. An appropriate technology should:

a. Meet the technical needs of the production situation by: (i) using local materials and power resources, (ii) minimizing the content of imported materials, (iii) ensuring that the product will be produced in adequate quantity and acceptable quality for existing or potential markets, and (iv) ensuring that the product can be conveyed to market by available transportation without deterioration and in sufficient quantity and with adequate regularity to encourage demand.

b. Meet the social requirements of the production situation by: (i) using existing or easily transferable skills and avoiding complicated, time-consuming, and costly retraining, (ii) offering continuing or expanding job prospects, (iii) minimizing the displacement of labor and the creation of more unemployed or underemployed, and (iv) minimizing social or cultural disruption by increasing production and productivity by successive small increments rather than by larger single steps.

c. Meet the economic requirements of the production situation by: (i) minimizing the capital demand from local or national resources, (ii) minimizing foreign exchange requirements, (iii) ensuring that capital is used in a way that is compatible with local, regional, and national economic plans, (iv) ensuring that the main economic benefit returns to the producers and is not captured by a new class of middlemen, and (v) obtaining greater integration of producers into the monetary system.[47]

There are three methods of developing an appropriate technology for less-developed countries:[48]

a. The first is to modify existing practices, at the technical or economic level, so that production may be increased or diversified without large demands being made on resources or on the structure of local society.

b. The second is to revive and introduce an older, well-tried technology from an earlier stage of development of a different economy.

c. The third is to invent a new technology, or change the scale of a modern technology, to meet the needs of a particular situation. For instance, a number of Western companies married the high-tech elements of their products with products or services designed to meet the needs of poor, undereducated users in less-developed countries of Africa, Asia, and Latin America. Appropriate technology presents a growing market opportunity for small-sized companies in the industrialized countries. By offering appropriate technology, Western firms try to bridge the product gap between sophisticated Western technology and more primitive local goods. The purpose of this approach is to combine the best features of Western technology with local needs and resources to fill the gap and at the same time meet the basic needs of the poor.[49]

Companies have experienced considerable difficulties with the application of appropriate technology, especially in less-developed countries. For instance, bureaucratic constraints in India have proven more formidable than anticipated. There are other important constraints on the participation of private companies in the development and spread of appropriate technologies. Some examples are illustrated as follows:

- Lack of information on opportunities and markets for appropriate technology
- Lack of experience in managing programs that involve numerous small farmers and entrepreneurs
- Lack of support systems (training, services, spare parts) to help users minimize the risks inherent in new technology
- A legacy of local and governmental suspicion toward both appropriate technology and foreign involvement.[50]

It is suggested by Baron and Ginneken[51] that the economic and institutional environments in most less-developed countries favor the introduction of capital-intensive techniques of production relative to the actual availabilities of capital and labor.[52] A "benign cycle" model is developed as an alternative. According to this, a more egalitarian distribution of income is brought about by consolidating more purchasing power in the hands of lower-income LDC consumers. This, in turn, will increase the demand for products manufactured by labor-intensive methods. The incomes generated through additional employment opportunities among the poor will have the effect of further income redistribution, resulting in more equal income distribution (see Figure 2.11).

Technology Transfer and Economic Development

Since the early 1960s, most of the less-developed countries have looked to advanced countries of the West as a source of improved

FIGURE 2.11. Appropriate Technology and Economic Development

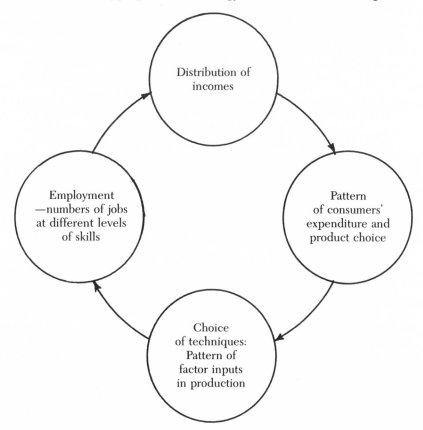

Source: C. Baron and M. van Ginneken, "Appropriate Products and Egalitarian Development," *International Labor Review* 212, no. 6 (November–December 1982): 673. Reprinted with permission.

technology and marketing knowledge. The argument in favor of technology transfer is that LDCs will produce goods for export, enabling them to import the products they need for their economic development.

In certain cases economic considerations are not the only policy guidelines. Pride or defense considerations may cause some less-developed countries to try to develop their own technology. In such a case, the technology should be developed through licensing agreements, as licensing of the product would make much more economic sense than other methods of technology transfer. Japan, for instance, developed its technology through an extensive use of licensing agreements.[53] The Japanese have been very successful at observing and imitating technologies in a variety of industries. Less-developed countries could learn a lot from the Japanese experience of technology transfer at a low cost.

The choice of technology not only has an effect on economic development and growth, it also has important side effects for other variables. In general, technologies used in developed countries are based on different factor proportions and resource endowments. In particular, most new technologies are capital-intensive in nature and thus may not totally be appropriate for many less-developed countries. As a solution to this dilemma, some LDCs, such as South Korea and Singapore, have combined their abundant and inexpensive labor with the technical know-how and marketing expertise of the multinational enterprise, thus achieving their industrialization and economic development objectives in an optimal way. This has been true in labor-intensive industries, such as electronics.[54]

Is technology developed in advanced countries of the West really appropriate to the economic development and industrialization prerequisites of less-developed countries? Some conflicting views have been expressed on this issue. We can summarize them as follows:

a. The first problem is that the products are inappropriate to the developmental needs of less-developed countries.[55]

b. Because of technical rigidities, capital-intensive methods cannot be adapted to differing circumstances of less-developed countries. For instance, in manufacturing industries such as chemicals, pharmaceuticals, or metal or oil refining, possibililties for substitution are limited.[56]

c. It is suggested by some that governments should try to encourage the selection of technology appropriate for the level of development of the country. One serious drawback to this approach, of course, is that priorities of government at times may not be in harmony with the country's economic development needs.[57]

Having examined the appropriateness of marketing technology transfer from developed to less-developed countries, we must emphasize the

TABLE 2.5. Four Stages of Marketing Technology Transfer

Stage I
  Determine rudimentary infrastructure necessary to initiate economic
    development
  Determine technology needs and international source for importation
Stage II
  Develop rudimentary transportation/storage system
  Redirect work force into infrastructure development activities
  Begin planning more advanced system
Stage III
  Plan more advanced transportation production and storage (TPS) system and
    import the necessary technology
  Plan mass communication system to augment TPS system and import technology
    to augment
Stage IV
  Establish criteria for evaluating TPS system and mass communication system as a
    whole
  Fine-tune infrastructure with imported technology, emphasizing marketing as a
    change agent
  Design system to export production/marketing infrastructure technology to
    culturally similar developing countries

Source: A. Coskun Samli, "Role of Marketing in Economic Development: What Should International Marketers Know?" in *International Marketing Management*, edited by Erdener Kaynak (New York: Praeger Special Studies, 1984), p. 48. Reprinted with permission.

fact that certain strategies are needed to transfer the marketing knowledge adequately. Samli and Mentzer have proposed a model to identify the specific steps of marketing technology transfer in various phases of the industrialization process.[58] This process entails a series of necessary steps as marketing technology imported by the less-developed country makes its special contribution to the country's economic development and growth. The model presented here provides a scheme for facilitating the movement of a country from a less-developed to a developed stage, and describes the functions within each stage necessary for movement to the next stage of economic development (see Table 2.5 and Figure 2.12).

    Generally, the economic development process involves the transformation of a traditional economy into a more modern, industrially based economy. As countries become more developed, marketing activities take on increasing importance as a coordinator and stimulator of economic activity. Effective and efficient marketing systems are not likely to emerge automatically during the development process, hence public policies and programs are needed to facilitate marketing changes. A systematic assessment of market system performance in relation to development goals is a

FIGURE 2.12. A Model of Technology Transfer to Less-Developed Countries

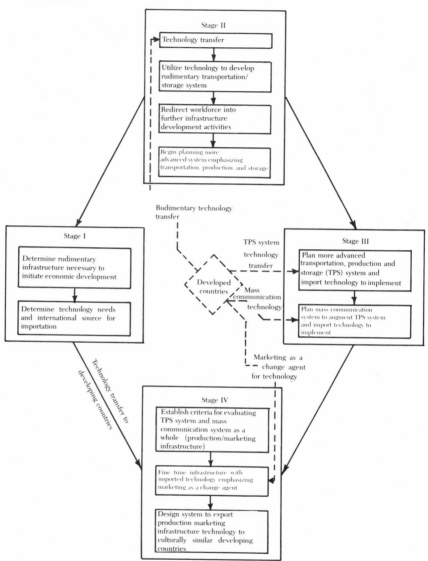

In this figure, the term "technology transfer" is limited to marketing technology transfer.

Source: A. Coskun Samli and John T. Mentzer, "A Model for Marketing in Economic Development," *Columbia Journal of World Business* 16, no. 3 (Fall 1981): 95. Reprinted with permission.

necessary prerequisite to marketing improvement programs. Although there are general strategies for improving marketing system performance in a given country, specific programs and strategies need to be carefully adapted to economic conditions in particular countries.[59]

Resistance to Technology Transfer

Although modern technology is of paramount importance for the development of third-world countries, there are still certain barriers to its smooth transfer. These are summarized as follows:

a. A particular technology may not be adopted because in the eyes of the members of the transferring nation, the disadvantages of technology transfer far outweigh its perceived advantages.

b. At times, output-increasing technology is not accepted by local people because its introduction would require the abandonment of certain traditional customs, habits, or forms of behavior.

c. A new technology may be rejected because of the fear that it would interfere with traditional social or kinship relations.

d. Along with the impact of social-structural relations on the transfer of new technology or techniques, there is the refusal to adopt output-increasing technology because its introduction threatens the established power or prestige of certain privileged groups in a country.[60]

Having discussed some of the inherent problems one may encounter in technology transfer from developed to less-developed economies, we can summarize the factors involved in the smooth transfer of technology.[61]

a. As much as possible, new technology should be adopted to the organizational and institutional principles of the recipient country.

b. Whenever and wherever possible, optimum use of local norms, values, and customs should be made.

c. An effort must be made to single out the person or persons who are most suitable for the transfer of technology. Personnel who have had some experience with the new technology in the source country should be given first priority.

d. When a new technology is introduced, the recipient country's culture and the interdependence of its integral parts should be considered. In particular, the source country should be aware of the function the new technology will play in the cultural whole and what other parts of social behavior will be affected by it.

NOTES

1. Michael J. Baker, "Marketing and Economic Growth," *Nigerian Journal of Marketing* 1 (February 1978): 3–8.

2. Tanniru R. Rao, "Developing Countries: Role of Marketing," *Marketing & Management Digest* (January 1976): 23.

3. John V. Petrof, "The Role of Marketing in a Developing Society," *Optimum* 7, no. 4 (1976): 29–30.

4. A. Coskun Samli, "The Future of Marketing in the Developed and Developing Countries: An Analysis of Contrast," *II Millimetro-Special* (Milan, Italy: 1973). pp. 12–21.

5. Eugene J. Kelley, *Marketing Planning and Competitive Strategy* (New Jersey: Prentice-Hall, 1972), p. 2; Philip Kotler, "What Consumerism Means for Marketers," *Harvard Business Review* (May–June, 1972): 52.

6. Philip Kotler and Sidney J. Levy, "Broadening the Concept of Marketing," *Journal of Marketing* (1969): 10–15.

7. Douglas L. Lamont, "Opportunities For Marketing Growth in the Mexican Market," *The Southern Journal of Business* 4, no. 2 (April 1969): 272–80.

8. Ibid., p. 272.

9. A. Coskun Samli, "The Necessary Micromarketing Functions in LDCs for Macro Benefits," in *Developments in Marketing Science*, edited by J. D. Lindquist (Kalamazoo, MI: Academy of Marketing Science, 1984): 153–55.

10. Erdener Kaynak and Ronald Savitt (eds.), *Comparative Marketing Systems* (New York: Praeger Special Studies, 1984).

11. Carol A. Smith, "Economics of Marketing Systems: Models from Economic Geography," *Annual Review of Anthropology* 3 (1974): 191.

12. S. Forman and J. F. Riegelhaupt, "Market Place and Marketing System: Toward a Theory of Peasant Economic Integration," *Comparative Studies in Society and History* 12 (1970): 188–212.

13. *Improving Marketing Systems in Developing Countries*, (Washington, D.C.: Economic Research Service, U.S. Department of Agriculture, February 1972), p. 20.

14. Lee E. Preston, *Consumer Goods Marketing in a Developing Economy* (Athens: Center of Planning and Economic Research, 1968), pp. 29–30.

15. Ibid., p. 30.

16. Forman and Riegelhaupt, "Market Place and Marketing Systems," pp. 207–209.

17. Ibid.

18. M. O. Farruk, "The Structure and Performance of the Rice Marketing System in East Pakistan," *Cornell International Agricultural Bulletin* (Ithaca, NY) no. 23 (1972); W. O. Jones, "Measuring the Effectiveness of Agricultural Marketing in Contributing to Economic Development: Some African Examples," *Food Research Institute Studies* 9, no. 3 (1970).

19. Gordon W. Smith, "Marketing and Economic Development: A Brazilian Case Study, 1930–1970," *Food Research Institute Studies* 12, no. 3, (1973): 179–98.

20. Ibid., p. 194.

21. John C. Abbott, "The Development of Marketing Institutions," in *Agricultural Development and Economic Growth*, edited by Herman M. Southworthy and Bruce F. Johnston (Ithaca, NY: Cornell University Press, 1967), pp. 364–97.

22. J. S. Bain, *Industrial Organization* (New York: John Wiley & Sons, 1959).

23. C. Wolf, "Institutions and Economic Development," *The American Economic Review* (December 1955).

24. John V. Petrof, "Small Business and Economic Development: The Case For Government Intervention," *Journal of Small Business Management* 18, no. 1 (January 1980): 52.

25. A. A. Warrack, "A Conceptual Framework For Analysis of Market Efficiency," *Journal of Agricultural Economics* 20, no. 3 (1968): 9–22.

26. Ibid., pp. 12–13.

27. Ibid., pp. 14–15.

28. *Marketing: A Dynamic Force For Rural Development* (Berlin: German Foundation For International Development, 1978), pp. 36–37.

29. Alvaro Silva, *Evaluation of Food Market Reform: CORABASTOS-Bogota* Ph.D. thesis, Michigan State University, East Lansing, 1976.

30. James D. Shaffer, "Designing Agricultural Marketing Systems in Developing Countries," paper presented at the Agricultural Marketing Conference in Kathmandu, Nepal, February 21-24, 1972, pp. 30–31.

31. Charles Slater, "Marketing Processes in Developing Latin American Societies," *Journal of Marketing* (July 1968): 50–55.

32. John E. Griggs, "Marketing in Economic Development," in *Evaluating Marketing Change: An Application of Systems Theory*, MSU International Business and Economic Studies, Michigan State University, East Lansing, 1970, p. 11.

33. Shaffer, "Designing Agricultural Marketing."

34. *Marketing and Rural Development* (Berlin: German Foundation For International Development, 1978), pp. N3–N4.

35. Alice Dewey, *Peasant Marketing in Java* (New York: The Free Press of Glencoe, 1962).

36. Leslie M. Dawson, "Opportunities for Small Business in Third World Markets," *American Journal of Small Business* 7, no. 1 (July– September 1982): 20.

37. Richard Symanski and R. J. Bromley, "Market Development and the Ecological Complex," *The Professional Geographer* 26, no. 4 (November 1974): 382–88.

38. Ibid., p. 384.

39. M. G. Fenn, *Marketing Livestock and Meat*, FOA Marketing Guide no. 3, Rome, 1977, pp. 5–6.

40. Ibid., p. 14.

41. Ibid., pp. 9–10.

42. Gordon A. DiPaolo, *Marketing Strategy for Economic Development* (New York: Dunellen, 1976), pp. 113–14.

43. *Marketing Management and Strategy for the Developing World* (New York: United Nations Industrial Development Organization, 1975), p. 38.

44. Susan P. Douglas and Yoram Wind, "Environmental Factors and Marketing Practices," *European Journal of Marketing* 7, no. 3 (Winter 1973-1974): 155–65.

45. Ibid., p. 163.

46. Vern Terpstra, "On Marketing Appropriate Products in Developing Countries," *Journal of International Marketing* 1, no. 1 (1981): 3; and IBRD, "An Appropriate Technology in World Bank Activities," July 19, 1976, p. 19.

47. T. A. Lawand, "Intermediate Technology—Its Practical Application," *Cooperation Canada*, no. 15 (July–August, 1974): 9–10.

48. H. Dickinson, "Dissemination of Appropriate Technologies," paper presented at the International Workshop in Development and Dissemination of Appropriate Technologies in Rural Areas, held in Kumasi, Ghana, July 1972.

49. Henry R. Norman and Patricia Blair, "The Coming Growth in 'Appropriate Technology,'" *Harvard Business Review* 60, no. 6 (November–December 1982): 62–65, 68.

50. Ibid., p. 66.

51. C. Baron and M. van Ginneken, "Appropriate Products and Egalitarian Development," *International Labor Review*, vol. 212, no. 6 (November–December, 1982), pp. 670–74.

52. *Marketing Management*, p. 30.

53. Yair Aharoni, *Markets, Planning and Development: The Private and Public Sectors in Economic Development* (Cambridge, MA: Ballinger, 1977), pp. 176–77.

54. Ibid., p. 178.

55. C. Cooper (ed.), "Science, Technology and Production in Underdeveloped Countries: An Introduction," *The Journal of Developmental Studies* 9, no. 1 (October 1972): 1-18.

56. R. J. Eckaus, "The Factor Proportions Problem in Underdeveloped Areas," *American Economic Review* 45, no. 4 (September 1955): 539-65; A. F. Ewing, *Industry in Africa* (London: Oxford University Press, 1968), pp. 12-13.

57. W. P. Strassman, *Technological Change in Economic Development* (Ithaca, NY: Cornell University Press, 1966); and F. Stewart, "Choice of Technique in Developing Countries," *The Journal of Development Studies* 9, no. 1 (October 1972): 99-122.

58. A Coskun Samli and J. T. Mentzer, "A Model For Marketing in Economic Development," *Columbia Journal of World Business* 16, no. 3 (Fall 1981): 91-101.

59. Harold M. Riley, *Improving Internal Marketing Systems As Part of National Development Systems,* Occasional Paper no. 3, Latin American Studies Center, Michigan State University, May 1972, p. 1.

60. B. F. Hoselitz, "Problems of Adapting and Communicating Modern Techniques to Less-Developed Areas," *Economic Development and Cultural Change* 2, no. 1 (January 1965): 255-61.

61. Ibid., pp. 264-67.

3
Operationalizing the Relationship Between Marketing and Economic Development

INTRODUCTION

An increasing number of marketing scholars and practitioners of development from government and industry have suggested that a major difficulty in the economic development of less-developed countries is that very little attention has been paid, so far, to the problems and opportunities of marketing. Peter Drucker noted that "in these countries, marketing is often neglected in favor of the more 'productive' field of manufacturing."[1] He further asserted that marketing is the most effective engine of economic development in that it contributes to the needs of developing countries through rapid development of entrepreneurs and managers for mobilizing latent economic resources. Drucker cites several reasons to support his thesis:

a. The development of a marketing system makes possible economic integration and the fullest utilization of whatever assets and productive capacity an economy already possesses.

b. Latent demand is converted into effective demand.

c. Marketing contributes to the foremost need of less-developed countries. Economic development is the result of the purposeful, responsible, risk-taking action of entrepreneurs and managers.

d. Marketing is a systematic discipline based on generalized, theoretical concepts, and so can therefore be taught.

The author gratefully acknowledges the contribution of Ben Issa Hudanah in the preparation of this section.

e. Marketing develops standards for products, services, conduct integrity, reliability, and foresight. It also develops a concern for the basic long-run impact of decisions on consumers, the economy, and society.[2]

In most LDCs, marketing is the least developed part of the economic system. This proposition seems to be closely related to an assumption that the marketing system of a country is essentially passive or adaptive in its relation to the economic system and the production aspects thereof. In less-developed countries the marketing function and process seem often to have been viewed, mistakenly, as a quasi-parasitic activity that is not a source of value in the total economic development process.[3] Possibly this attitude has developed over the years in part because resented expatriate minorities in less-developed countries have often tended to congregate in the marketing sectors of these economies and supposedly are making enormous profits.[4] In most LDCs, "economy of scarcity" conditions still prevail which necessitate and encourage more production and manufacturing.[5] However, application of marketing principles can facilitate the economic development of less-developed countries by permitting a more thorough evaluation of economic needs.

In recent years, interest in the role of marketing and economic development has grown. Social science literature on the subject suggests many marketing aspects that warrant the attention of economic planners.[6] It must be stated here that the most useful contributions to marketing in the development context so far have come from behavioral scientists. In studies of structural relationships between economic activities and cultural and social organizations, they have described and analyzed marketing systems of countries as well as the behavior of their consumers.

However, what has been written so far has been descriptive in nature or normative at best, dealing mainly with micro-marketing issues, and not with the larger societal (macro) role of marketing in the economic development of a country. As Petrof succinctly states, marketing makes a positive contribution to the economic development of a country when

a. The function of acquainting potential buyers and sellers as well as the transmittal of information concerning product quality is adequately performed.

b. A minimum amount of resources is absorbed directly by institutions engaged in marketing activities.

c. Declines in import or domestic prices are rapidly transmitted throughout society, and demand is stimulated for products with a high domestic and export growth potential or low import prices.

d. In order to pass on the benefits of economic development and ameliorate the living standards of the population, institutions engaged in marketing are dispersed throughout the country.[7]

The purpose of this chapter is to operationalize the relationship between the marketing system of a country and its economic development. To this end, first of all, characteristics of the marketing system in a less-developed country will be determined. Second, indicators of economic development will be highlighted. No agreement has so far been reached as to what constitutes "economic development." It is therefore essential that we come to an agreement on the parameters of economic development and how they should be measured. At a later stage an attempt will be made to establish causal relationships between marketing and economic development. It is also the argument of this chapter that certain marketing institutions contribute with varying degrees to the economic development process. The degree to which these institutions contribute to the level of economic development of LDCs will be examined in Chapter 4.

The study of the interface between marketing and economic development in an analytical manner is a comparatively new academic concern. A conceptual framework showing the relationship between marketing and economic development is indicated in Figure 3.1, which will be used as a point of conceptual reference in this study.

CONCEPTUAL FRAMEWORK

In recent years there has been a renewed interest in the role of marketing in the economic development process. Most of the studies undertaken so far can be classified into three broad categories, namely: normative conceptual development studies, comparative studies, and individual case studies.[8]

Normative studies have, for the most part, identified and described the importance of marketing in the economic development process. Comparative studies, on the other hand, examine the relationship between marketing and economic development across nations under varying environmental conditions and parameters. In most cases these studies try to isolate similarities and differences among nations at varying stages of economic development. Finally, the case study approach provides examples of applications of economic development programs to specific areas of marketing such as agriculture, industrialization, communication, and channels of distribution. It points out apparent relationships between various marketing functions, processes, and institutions and the economic development process.[9] Let us now discuss each of the above approaches

FIGURE 3.1. Marketing and Economic Development Interface

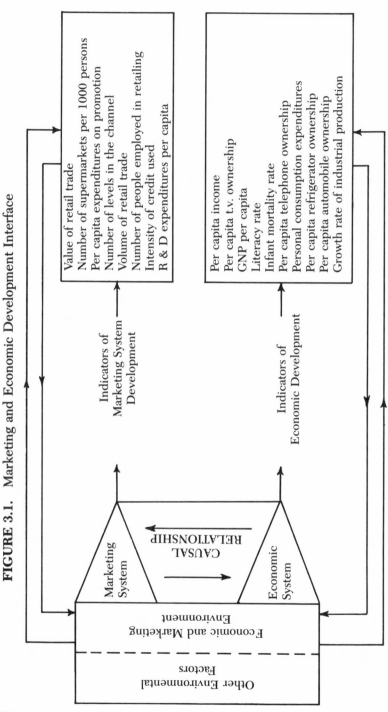

Value of retail trade
Number of supermarkets per 1000 persons
Per capita expenditures on promotion
Number of levels in the channel
Volume of retail trade
Number of people employed in retailing
Intensity of credit used
R & D expenditures per capita

Indicators of
Marketing System
Development

Per capita income
Per capita t.v. ownership
GNP per capita
Literacy rate
Infant mortality rate
Per capita telephone ownership
Personal consumption expenditures
Per capita refrigerator ownership
Per capita automobile ownership
Growth rate of industrial production

Indicators of
Economic Development

Marketing System

CAUSAL
RELATIONSHIP

Economic System

Economic and Marketing Environment

Other Environmental Factors

Source: Compiled by the author.

before trying to operationalize, in an integrative manner, the relationship between marketing and economic development.

IMPORTANCE OF MARKETING IN
ECONOMIC DEVELOPMENT (NORMATIVE STUDIES)

Traditionally, marketing activity and the practice of middlemen in LDCs have not been favorably valued.[10] The prevailing view among government planners and businesspeople of these countries is that the middlemen are parasitic and serve no useful function in the economy, which is oriented toward increasing production or manufacturing output. High gross profit margins are usually cited as reflecting the inefficiency of marketing intermediaries. Little attention is given, however, to the relationship between higher margins and risks in the channels of distribution system, or to the fact that—by definition—low volumes necessitate higher margins to break even.[11] For instance, CONASUPA (Compania Nacional de Subsistencias Populares) in Mexico seeks to enhance purchasing power in rural areas by providing retail stores that sell staple goods at low and stable prices. These small stores sell many items below cost, disrupting the monopolistic and speculative positions that private retailers often have in isolated markets. To increase productivity of small farmers, CONASUPO crop purchasing and storage centers disseminate high-yield seeds and market information, and some offer training in modern farming techniques. By competing with, not replacing, private retailers, CONASUPO hopes to have a stabilizing effect on the overall marketplace (CONASUPO offers prices that are 15–20 percent less than those offered by privately owned stores, and uses federal funds to subsidize its operations).[12]

There are still weaknesses in marketing and economic theory in describing the role of marketing in economic development. There is, however, a critical need for clarification of this point since public policy in less-developed countries appears to be moving toward active public-sector involvement in national market systems. There is an implicit assumption in such a policy that marketing does have a potential role in fostering economic development.

A critical review of the marketing literature suggests that the subject of marketing in economic development has attracted few interested scholars.[13] What has been written so far has been descriptive, dealing with skeletons and not with the larger role of marketing in the economic and/or social development of a less-developed country. As a result, the dynamics of marketing during the development process of less-developed countries has so far received little attention in the marketing literature. Although several recent works have explored the workings of urban marketing systems[14] in less-developed countries, the economic analysis of marketing structures and the forces molding them is much rarer.[15] The obstacles to such research are formidable. Data on the distribution sector of the economy are among the poorest in less-developed countries, and it gets worse as one moves back in time.

Theory of Marketing and Economic Development

There are two schools of thought on the contribution of marketing to economic development. These are "determinist" and "activist," depending on each school's perception and evaluation of the causal role marketing plays in economic development. This distinction is in harmony with Bartels' classification of marketing as an "adaptive" function and a consequence of environmental circumstances, and a "formative" influence in stimulating the economic development of a country.[16] A classification matrix for the relationship between marketing and economic development is shown in Table 3.1.

Bartels argues that whether marketing is adaptive or formative in economic development, it definitely is a constructive force in that process.[17] Whether taking a determinist or activist approach there are theoretical implications of empirical and hypothesized relationships between the development of the market system in less-developed countries and measures of overall economic development.[18]

Marketing is not merely passive and adaptive. It is dynamic and stimulates the economic development process.[19] This is its formative character. A change in marketing system and/or practice, however, with its resulting influences on development can occur only as the environmental conditions in LDCs change. Rao suggested six basic structural dimensions without whose existence marketing's contribution to the process of economic development will be scanty and haphazard.[20] These dimensions are: physical facilities, institutional facilities, market accessibility, technology transfer, behavioral factors, and regulations. He further maintains that it is the role of the government in an LDC to assume active leadership in structuring an environment conducive to economic development.

Two means were suggested to accomplish the required change in thinking: at the operational level, by widespread education of businessmen in marketing principles; or from a higher administrative level, through impositions on operators of plans and policies for improvement of the entire marketing sector of the economy.[21] However, others would argue that changes in environmental conditions could be attributable to changes in marketing institutions and practices. The determinists attribute the development of marketing systems of a country to changes in the socio-

TABLE 3.1. Contribution of Marketing to Economic Development

		Determinists	*Activists*
	Form	Compare the environment for market activity with the complexity, functions, and efficiency of the market system in various countries	Examine the functions performed by various institutions in the channel
Nature			
Formative (active)		Integrated channel Matrix-type organization	Short channel Marketing function allocation toward end of channel
Developed country		Information systems include backward flows Level of marketing operations high Free market systems	Cost-plus pricing Pulling strategy utilized Channel members' financial interdependency low
Adaptive (passive) Less-developed country		Independent channel Functional-type organization Information systems include forward flows Level of marketing operations low Controlled market systems	Long channel Marketing function allocation toward beginning of channel Arbitrary pricing Pushing strategy utilized Channel members' financial interdependency high

Source: Compiled by the author.

economic, technological, and cultural envirnoment within which they exist. The tendency of the determinists is to compare the envirnoment for market activity and efficiency of the market system in various countries. For example, Wadinambiaratchi concluded that market channel structures reflect the stage of economic development of a less-developed country.[22] Using data on nine countries at different stages of economic development (on per capita income, per capita generation of electricity, percentage urban population, manufacturing as a percentage of GNP, and private consumption expenditure as a percentage of national income and infant mortality rates), he found that marketing channels appeared to reflect the stage of economic development of a country.

So far, a basic problem in marketing theory has been the determination of the relationship between marketing systems and market structures to economic development.[23] A major obstacle has been the inability to define precisely the terms of interest. The use of indicators of economic development varies by author. Marketing system development is also described and measured in numerous ways. It is then no surprise that a consensus has not been reached as to the nature of this relationship. As marketers move in the direction of focusing on the macro-level effects of marketing endeavors, the critical role of marketing systems in the economic development process will continue to be a central point of theoretical exploration.

There is a theory which states that the development of the marketing system of a country is closely related to the level of development of its marketing environment. It is postulated by Douglas that a certain pattern of marketing system and structure appears in terms of the size and organization of firms, managerial attitudes, channel structure, institutional types, and marketing orientation at different stages of environmental development, which also includes the stage of economic development of the country.[24]

MARKET AND MARKETING SYSTEM CHARACTERISTICS IN LESS-DEVELOPED COUNTRIES (COMPARATIVE STUDIES)

A market system is simply a set of interrelated and interdependent activities. For instance, the economy of a country can be viewed as a system of coordinated sequences of physical activities. Within an economic system, marketing activities involve physical transformation in attempting to create different utilities. The systems approach as such is an orientation that emphasizes the system or the interdependence of related activities within a given developing market.

Generally speaking, one of the greatest obstacles to economic development in less-developed countries is the unfavorable attitudes of people toward marketing and middlemen. For instance, considerable segments of the populations of these nations do not appreciate the economic values marketing activities create. The middleman is regarded as the one who follows a dishonorable profession. Westfall and Harper, for example, in a study on India, stated that the Indians regard middlemen as schemers trying to profit at the expense of the public;[25] the educational authorities in less-developed countries also neglect marketing education. An emphasis on technical education and the humanities has produced company executives who have little interest in marketing as a management function. Salesmen and sales managers are regarded as appendages of questionable value, while engineers and production managers have enjoyed higher prestige in society.[26]

Among the distinct characteristics of emerging nations, because of nonhomogeneity of the markets and marketing practices, is a common phenomenon of a "dual economy." A less-developed country may have one or more major cities where the standard and pattern of living differs significantly from the rest of the economy. Even within a particular region of a country there may be differences among different income groups. As experts of the Food and Agriculture Organization of the United Nations stated, "The appropriate marketing strategy or policy for a metropolis like Bangkok, Buenos Aires, Caior, or Manila may differ from that for the rest of the country. Actually, there may be more market similarities among modern urban enclaves in different (less-developed) countries than there are between urban and rural sectors in a given country."[27] Hill and Still pointed out that products targeted to urban markets in LDCs need only minimal changes from those marketed in developed countries.[28] Products aimed at both semi-urban and urban markets require more changes, and those aimed at national markets undergo further adaptations to accommodate the requirements of culturally diverse rural populations. Thus each firm should determine the influences of different sectors of the economy on its own operations.

There are certain factors that are critical to marketing system development at different stages of the economic process. These factors create the necessary conditions for marketing system development as outlined below (see Figure 3.2):

    a. Resources at the command of the society. All resources, natural and human-made, that are productively employed are appropriate to the analysis.

    b. Environmental conditions that affect the marketing system and the needs it must fulfill.

    c. Societal factors that influence the choice of one marketing pattern rather than another equally possible on purely economic terms.[29]

High rates of illiteracy and low per capita income are also common characteristics of less-developed countries, which tends to hinder the development of the markets and marketing practices of various companies. Even the oil-producing countries—the Middle East for instance—tend to share these characteristics despite the great opportunities generated from oil revenues for expanding industries and development. Stewart suggested

FIGURE 3.2. Factors Affecting Marketing in Any Society at Different Levels of Economic Development

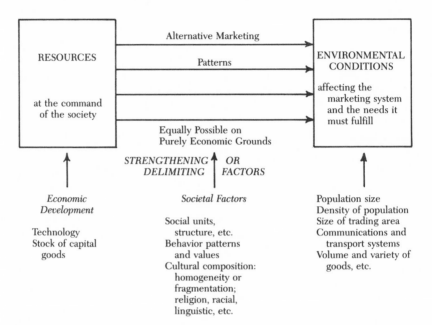

Source: B. Liander, V. Terpstra, M.Y. Yoshino, and A.A. Sherbini, *Comparative Analysis For International Marketing* (Boston, MA: Allyn and Bacon, 1967), p. 64. Reprinted with permission.

that the Middle East market is much narrower than the figures for oil revenues would suggest.[30] He also maintains that despite the oil revenues, large parts of the population in the area are not yet in the market at all. The distribution of income is extremely skewed, on both a geographical and a personal basis. That is to say that the ruling bodies, including royal families and their associates, enjoy a large portion of the country's wealth, and the big cities, where most of the business activities are concentrated, are better off geographically in the distribution of income than the rest of the country. Such a situation not only hinders the marketing opportunities of firms seeking wide distribution, but it also has certain implications for the concept of a "national market"; that is, the national market would be fragmented into various categories of consumers and small regional markets, and consequently the different marketing institutions would be operating and performing at a significantly different level of sophistication.

It has been argued that the marketing structure in a country reflects its stage of economic development. Erickson states that in marketing, as in other areas of social and economic activity, institutions and their activities do not arise simply by chance.[31] Rather they are a reflection of the particular environment in which they are operating. The institutions engaged in marketing and the methods used to market output reflect the environmental factors that are lumped together and called the market.

In most less-developed countries retail distribution is characterized by large numbers of little shops with small capital investment, low turnover, high margins, and high mortality. Most stores possess all these characteristics. The retailer could have the desired item in an hour, a day, or next week. The store layouts are generally haphazard; there is no stock control; and only the most elementary accounting records are kept.[32]

There is evidence that the structure of the retail channel is influenced by regional and economic factors in less-developed countries. Taylor, for instance, referring to Brazil says, "If the area in which the community is located is prosperous, two or three general stores may be found, but if the community is located in a depressed area, only one outlet serves the entire community. . . . the existence of the limited line stores is dependent on the size and economic level of the community. . . . in regions of lower economic level, the number of establishments follows the density of population in terms of purchasing power."[33] Two more studies confirmed this belief. First, Stewart, referring to the Middle-East, says that "product composition, of course, emanates primarily from the pattern of income distribution and tastes."[34] Second, Edward Marcus, referring to tropical Africa, says, " . . . in a market as changing as the African one, it becomes extremely important to keep in constant touch with the final consumer and to follow the impact of income changes on his taste for material goods."[35] Hirsch states that in many less-developed countries there is no clear-cut specialization of distribution activities either vertically by successive levels of distribution or horizontally by type of goods handled.[36] He maintains that this blurring of functions causes overlapping between the roles performed by channel agents rather than a shortening of the chain of distribution.

The marketing literature provides sufficient evidence that the present position of the channels of distribution in less-developed countries is at a natural stage of the evolution of the economy. Baker and El-Haddad emphasized that "marketing in a society passes through a number of stages assuming a variety of roles corresponding with the level of development of the economy."[37] One can therefore relate the present position of the distribution channels in the emerging nations to the evolutionary process of a non-monetary subsistence economy to a monetary one, and later from an economy of scarcity, where demand exceeds supply, to one of abundance, where supply of goods and services far exceeds the demand.

Such a sequence of development does not always follow in a balanced way with respect to every element of a marketing system. Slow development in the marketing channels, for instance, could slow the development of other elements in the marketing system, that is, marketing activities of manufacturers concerning levels of operations. New products developed may not find adequate channels of distribution. Manufacturers may lose some degree of control over marketing decisions.

Generally there are distinct differences in the marketing techniques and specific distribution methods used in different countries. These apparent variations tend to widen when LDC marketing systems are considered. This is possibly due to the fact that the economic value of marketing is not very much appreciated in less-developed countries. Some common characteristics, however, could still be pinpointed in these countries with respect to some if not all of the elements of their markets, marketing practices, and associated channels of distribution.[38]

Marketing institutions and techniques emerge in an economy from the country's experience. In other words, the institutions and the activities of today determine the type of institutions and activities of tomorrow. Thus, for a deeper understanding of the relationship between marketing and economic development in these countries, it is necessary to look at and explain the evolution of marketing practices at different stages of economic development.

ECONOMIC DEVELOPMENT AND MARKETING SYSTEM EVOLUTION (CASE STUDY APPROACH)

The available literature on economic development reveals that certain developments have taken place in the move from a primitive self-sufficient society to a highly developed country. There are five general levels of marketing development, as distinguished at different stages of the economic development process. These are:

Stage 1. Marketing, in its primitive way, can be seen in the most backward economy where the people are largely self-sufficient. They make their own clothes, grow their own food, and build their own houses and tools. There is no specialization or division of labor at this stage of development. There is little need for trade, which takes the form of bartering in the simplest way.

Stage 2. The second stage of marketing development is characterized by the emergence of small craftspeople and the *division of labor.* The craftspeople start concentrating on the production of the items in which they excel. As a result, each of those craftspeople starts producing more than he or she needs of some items and less of others, and this is the foundation of trade, which is the backbone of marketing activity.

Stage 3. As exchange begins to develop, primitive monetary systems take shape as small central markets emerge. Home handicrafts are slowly being replaced by small business firms with relatively small production levels. But no distinct specialized managerial functions are known to have been created.

Stage 4. This stage of the development of marketing witnesses the small producers beginning to manufacture their goods in larger quantities in anticipation of future orders. This is a decisive step toward marketing development. In this step, further division of labor occurs. Distinctions between a few managerial functions are made, but emphasis is still placed on production rather than marketing. Intermediaries between producers and consumers emerge to carry out the roles of middlemen. They carry out marketing functions to facilitate communication, buying, and selling. These intermediaries are allocated mainly on a geographical basis rather than by other consideration. Trading centers are also characteristic of this stage of development.

Stage 5. Modern marketing in Western Europe and the United States was born with the industrial revolution, when the words "surplus" and "overproduction" became increasingly common in the vocabulary of economists. The most significant development of marketing in this stage is the realization that there cannot be a high level of economic activity without a correspondingly high level of marketing activity.[39]

These five steps of marketing development do not show whether the marketing practices within individual firms follow the same or somehow similar lines of development. Let us now try to search for the most probable steps in the evolution of marketing practices at different stages of economic and marketing development of a less-developed country.

It is stated that subsistence economies are those in which an exchange mechanism is totally lacking. Whenever exchange takes place, it is sporadic. Peasant economies are those in which one segment of the population is totally dependent on others for procurement of its needs. Finally, commercial economies are those in which the entire population is dependent on exchange for all of its needs.[40]

Polanyi distinguished three major kinds of exchange, namely: operational exchange, decisional exchange, market exchange.[41]

> Operational exchange involves only locational movements of goods and services, with no accompanying appropriational movements. Appro-

priational movements of exchange may result either from "transactions" (circulation of goods) or from dispositions (administration of goods). A transaction is an appropriative movement as between hands; a disposition is a one-sided act of the hand.

Decisional exchange refers to appropriational movements of exchange at a set rate. In contrast, market exchange involves appropriational movements at a bargained rate.[42]

Table 3.2 shows different types of economies, along with various forms of exchange. Only the shaded alternatives are possible in reality in our contemporary world economies.

The marketing organization of firms is developed over a period of time. In the early nineteenth century, industrial firms, manufacturers, and commercial organizations did not know the principles of marketing organization and management as we know them today. Most of the early firms did not distinguish between marketing and other managerial functions simply because marketing had not been developed as a separate functional area within an organization.

Marketing management has been developing in European and North American business since the industrial revolution. Stanton suggested that marketing management in the United States has gone through three stages of development, and a fourth one is emerging.[43] Many small firms, even in

TABLE 3.2. The Economy–Exchange Matrix at Different Types of Economies

Forms of exchange / Type of economy	Decisional exchange		Market exchange	
	Reciprocative	Redistributive	Peripheral	Integrative
Subsistence	▨			
Peasant		▨	▨	
Commercial		▨		▨

Source: B. Liander, V. Terpstra, M.Y. Yoshino, and A.A. Sherbini, *Comparative Analysis For International Marketing* (Boston, MA: Allyn and Bacon, 1967), p. 158. Reprinted with permission.

the United States, are still in one of the earlier stages of marketing organization, and only a few have the most developed form of marketing organization and the outlook and philosophy that go with it.

A preliminary stage of marketing development was added to Stanton's four stages approach after a survey carried out in Peru.[44] The five stages of marketing maturation of manufacturing firms, therefore, range from a preliminary phase, where marketing is regarded as nothing more than a selling function, to a newly emerging phase where all short-term company policies are highly conditioned by marketing. The five stages of marketing development within business organizations are described below:

Stage 1. Small firms characterized by a general manager or president, relatively few workers and employees, no clear-cut functions separated from others (i.e. production, financing, and personnel are all functions performed by the president/owner of the firm). Marketing in its contemporary sense does not exist at this stage, but selling is the most evident marketing element. The manager of the firm generally makes all the decisions, except technical ones mainly involving production techniques.

Stage 2. Firms at this stage tend to have established departments for basic functions such as production, personnel, finance, purchasing, and selling. Still, the post of marketing manager is not recognized as a basic function. Instead the first sign of organizing the marketing activities takes the form of a sales department in which the sales manager is responsible for the field sales force; most other marketing activities are either still held by the general manager or are spread throughout the firm. Marketing, therefore, does not mean much more than selling in the first two stages described above.

Stage 3. As a further development, due to expanding production, the firms at this stage start encountering marketing problems, that is, more difficulties in selling their produce. They become aware of the importance of grouping the marketing activities under one marketing executive, who is still called the sales manager. The sales manager at this stage has little influence on production planning, packaging, or new product development. These functions are still under the control of the production manager.

Stage 4. The first sign of market orientation emerges at this stage, with the establishment and full recognition of a marketing department. The marketing manager takes over all the marketing activities in a fully integrated way. Other divisions attached to the marketing department, such as advertising, selling, and new product development are established within the marketing department. Aspects such as production planning, inventory control, and transportation are also influenced by the chief marketing executive. In some cases the chief marketing executive exercises wider influence over the entire organization of the firm. Long-term company policies are conditioned by marketing.

Stage 5. As management of the firm realizes what marketing orientation promise for the fulfillment of overall corporate objectives, marketing becomes the basic driving force for the entire firm. Both short- and long-run policies of firms become highly conditioned by marketing philosophy. This stage is hardly represented on an organizational chart, as the dimensions of the new marketing concept expand beyond the boundaries of the marketing management within the firm. This stage is reached when attitudes of all company executives reflect the marketing concept. A few firms have fully reached this stage of marketing maturation in the emerging nations. Multinational firms from emerging less-developed economies are good examples of this.

It should be clear, however, that the evolutionary stages of development of marketing management described above do not imply the existence of a single sequential course of development through which all firms must pass in the organization and conduct of the marketing management function. The border between any one stage and another is certainly not rigid. The classification thus is taken here as a convenient scale of organizational possibilities which could indicate or identify different degrees of sophistication in undertaking various functions of marketing management.

In LDCs small family firms are the most dominant force in both the industrial and commercial sectors of these countries. Thus one would expect that the bulk of these small businesses fall into the first two stages of marketing development, while few have reached stages 3 and 4. What seems to be important is whether or not the firms are moving upward in the scale of development. Most important, however, is whether the newly established firms tend to start their activities in the first stage of the scale and evolve throughout the remaining stages, or start their activities elsewhere.

There seem to be three major factors that govern the evolution of a firm's marketing organization throughout the five stages mentioned earlier. These are: the impetus springing from the marketing discipline in terms of broadening the marketing concept; a major breakthrough in technological innovation with resulting impact on modernization of production and increased productivity of manufacturing firms; and a number of serious marketing problems may arise following increased output of manufacturing firms (e.g., difficulties in selling their increased output). Apparently the problem is purely a marketing one. Either the marketing sector was out of phase with industrialization and economic development or the supply exceeded the demand. In both cases the firms concerned were left with no choice other than the recognition of the role of marketing in their activities. Thus the situation is more likely to induce upward movement in the scale of marketing stages of development.

It is pointed out that marketing activity may change the entire tone of the existing economic system of less-developed countries without any change in methods of production, distribution, or income. Marketing, therefore, contributes to the development of higher standards for economic behavior, integrity, and product reliability in less-developed countries.[45] Bonaparte pointed out that the level of marketing performance in Liberia roughly parallels that country's stage of economic development.[46] Table 3.3 shows that most of the marketing activities in Liberia take place in stage Ib (surplus commodity producer) and in stage IIa (small-scale manufacturing). Certain items in stage IIb and III also have mass appeal.

Public policymakers of LDCs are interested in a plan of action that would produce systematic economic growth. A model was developed by Hunt which illustrates the relationship between marketing, production and economic development (see Figure 3.3).[47]

> Production and marketing are variables which expand according to efficiency and inputs. If production and marketing are in balance then each factor will expand at a comparable rate. The combined production and marketing activity then provides the energy that gives economic development its upward thrust.
>
> Those who are production oriented will insist production is the prime energizer, and that marketing activity and economic development naturally follow. There are many examples to prove this type of thinking brings disaster.[48]

OPERATIONALIZING THE RELATIONSHIP BETWEEN MARKETING AND ECONOMIC DEVELOPMENT

There are socioeconomic, cultural, and technological differences among LDCs. The emergence of LDCs at vastly different stages of market development in the same geographic region calls for a new organizational setup.[49]

One approach that may prove to be extremely useful is organization of countries by stages of market development. A stages-of-market-development organization assembles the LDCs in its system into groups that reflect similar market conditions.[50] Heenan and Keegan identified three kinds of less-developed countries: resource-rich less-developed countries, labor-rich, rapidly industrializing countries, and market-rich, rapidly industrializing countries.[51] There are significant differences among the three groups of countries, but they also share a certain commonality: a drive for rapid economic development. As an example, Arab economies could be

TABLE 3.3. The Marketing Process in Liberia

Stages	Substage	Examples	Marketing functions in Liberia
I. Agricultural and raw materials	(a) Self-sufficient	Villages in rural areas	None
	(b) Surplus commodity producer	Agricultural: Coffee, palm kernels, rice, cocoa, fruits (bananas, oranges, pineapples, etc.), and vegetables	Physical distribution
II. Manufacturing	(a) Small-scale	Furniture, biscuits, plastic wares, ice-cream, tiles, brooms and brushes, Liberian handicrafts (tie-dyed cloth, belts, masks and wood carvings and jewelry, etc.)	Demand creation Physical distribution
	(b) Intermediate-scale	Oil refinery, paint, fishing and fish processing, cigarettes, cement, and beer	Demand creation Physical distribution
III. Marketing	Mass distribution	Food shops, automobiles and tractors, shipping agents and brokers, hotels and supermarkets	Demand creation Physical distribution, market information

rketing titutions	Channel control	Primary orientation	Resources employed	Comments
e	Traditional authority— village chief	Subsistence	Labor, land	Labor intensive. No organized markets
l-scale traders, .arket women," d the Liberian oduce arketing rporation PMC)	Producers	Entrepreneurial Commercial	Labor, land, trans- portation	Labor and land intensive. Product specialization. Local markets (upcountry)
chants, whole- lers, intra- rican trade harlies"	Producers Middlemen	Entrepreneurial Commercial	Labor, land, technology, transporta- tion, capital	Labor intensive. National and regional markets. Import-oriented
lesalers, such as beria Refining mpany (LRC), esurado Group of mpanies, Liberia ement Corporation, rker Industries, onrovia Tobacco rporation, Mon- via Brewers lesalers.	Producers Middlemen	Production and Finance	Labor, land, capital, technology, transporta- tion	Capital and labor intensive. National markets Import-oriented
ease in speci- ized middlemen, ch as United States ading Company JSTC), Paterson ochonis & Co. ort-import	Retailers Producers	Sales Service	Labor, land, capital, technology, transporta- tion Communica- tion	National markets Capital and land intensive Import- oriented

Source: T. H. Bonaparte, *Marketing in Less-Developed Countries: A Case Analysis of Liberia* v York: Pace University Graduate School, Center for Applied Research, Monograph 15,), pp. 4–5. Reprinted with permission.

FIGURE 3.3. Relationship of Marketing, Production, and Economic Development

Marketing Activity

Source: L.J. Hunt, "Marketing Education in Developing Environments," in *AMA 1974 Combined Proceedings*, edited by R.C. Curhan (Chicago, IL, 1975), p. 643. Reprinted with permission.

classified as oil or non-oil countries.[52] Although useful, this classification is not sufficient. Further refinements are needed if the realities are to be appreciated. A better classification was suggested by Waterbury and El-Mallakh, which was also adopted by the United Nations organizations.[53] They classified, for instance, the Arabic countries into four economic groups:

Group I—Advanced Stage Countries

These countries are characterized by the abundance and predominance of oil (90 percent or more of government income), surplus of capital, very high per capita income, limited agriculture, relatively small population, and an acute shortage of indigenous skilled labor. These countries have generally similar political orientations and cultural make-ups. They are all conservative Muslim societies with strong links to the West, free economies, and easily accessible markets. The countries in this group are Saudi Arabia, Kuwait, the United Arab Emirates, and Qatar.

Group II—Intermediate Stage Countries

These countries, in addition to oil and capital, have a significant agricultural potential, a more diversified economic base, a slightly larger population, and a shortage of technical skills. These countries are politically more radical and very nationalistic, favoring strict state control over the economy and national resources. This group includes Algeria, Iraq, and Libya.

Group III—Growing Stage Countries

Here the significance of oil diminishes considerably or completely gives way to agriculture and industries. These countries are more populous but suffer from shortage of capital. With the exception of Syria they are regarded as pro-Western. They rely on aid from oil-rich states and other sources to finance their development and sustain their large populations. This group includes Egypt, Morocco, Sudan, Syria, and Tunisia.

Group IV—Static Countries

These are special cases, consisting of Lebanon and Jordan. The most important economic sector here is the service sector, followed by light industry and manufacture, and less agriculture. There is relative availability of skilled personnel and managerial talent. Until the war of 1975 Lebanon was the business center of the Arab world.

An example of the categories and country assignments that a policy-maker might utilize is shown in Table 3.4. In the selection of different regions, per capita income is used as a decision tool. Group I represents high-income, less-developed countries where per capita income is more than $3,000. Group II represents medium-income, less-developed countries where per capita income ranges between $1,000 and $3,000. Finally,

TABLE 3.4. Stages of Market Development

	Less-developed country groupings		
Selected regions	Underdeveloped Low Income Group III (beginning stage; less than $1,000 per capita income)	Developing Medium Income Group II (intermediate stage; between $1,000 to $3,000 per capita income)	Developed High Income Group I (advanced stage; more than $3,000 per capita income)
Middle East	North Yemen	Turkey	Saudi Arabia
Latin America and Caribbean	Haiti	Peru	Venezuela
Asia	Sri-Lanka	South Korea	Singapore

These countries are selected arbitrarily.
Source: Compiled by the author.

Group III represents low-income, less-developed countries where per capita income is less than $1,000.

The advantage of the stage-of-market-development organization is its ability to focus the efforts of the decision-makers on strategic problems and opportunities associated with the most significant dimensions of today's LDC environment. The important question for a decision-maker considering a market-stages organizational structure is whether the scale of company operations in markets at different stages of development is sufficient to justify the creation of separate organizational units.

Because of the many economic development indicators discussed in Figure 3.1 that affect the development of the marketing system of a less-developed country, it is necessary to establish objective guidelines for their evaluation. Indicators of economic development consist of seven factors: private consumption expenditure; passenger cars in use; telephones in use, GDP, per capita income, total number of people employed in the manufacturing sector, and average hourly wages in manufacturing. Indicators of marketing system development consist of per capita expenditure on promotion, value of retail trade, number of people employed in retailing, per capita R&D expenditures, number of supermarkets per 1,000 persons, intensity of credit used, and number of levels in the channel.[54] Indicators of economic as well as marketing system development are shown in Tables 3.5 and 3.6.

The first decision to be made is to combine indicators of economic development and marketing system development separately. The next step is to calculate the average group scores. The group score will represent an average of scores in three high-, three medium-, and three low-income less-developed countries. Indicators of economic and marketing system development were aggregated into indices and ranked (see Table 3.7). Certain interesting trends have emerged.

For instance, Saudi Arabia ranked first in terms of level of economic development but ranked only seventh in terms of level of marketing system development. To operationalize the relationship between marketing and economic development further tests were undertaken. In particular, an attempt was made to see if there was any relationship between marketing and economic development as far as the nine selected less-developed countries were concerned. A simple correlation analysis was performed to see if there were any relationships between marketing and economic development. A two-tail test at $\alpha = 0.05$ was utilized (Table 3.8).

The analysis revealed that because of the differences in marketing systems of the nine less-developed countries selected for this study, no association was found between marketing systems of countries and the level of economic development. At a later stage, because of its highest

TABLE 3.5. Indicators of Economic Development

Selected countries	ROW	Consump	Cars	Tels	GDP	Income	Manufac	Wages	Econindx
North Yemen	1	4.14	0.65	3.04	0.72	2.00	4.29	°	2.4733
Haiti	2	1.98	1.30	0.84	0.41	1.08	2.52	°	1.3550
Sri Lanka	3	2.07	2.60	1.01	1.12	1.15	12.55	0.025	2.9321
Turkey	4	7.42	4.87	6.93	14.65	5.04	14.12	0.190	7.6029
Peru	5	6.83	5.52	4.56	5.75	4.60	17.09	°	7.3917
South Korea	6	9.40	1.95	14.86	16.82	6.50	17.65	0.210	9.6271
Saudi Arabia	7	23.45	29.55	8.61	39.42	41.21	2.84	°	24.1800
Venezuela	8	20.48	31.82	12.67	17.81	17.90	10.34	0.410	15.9186
Singapore	9	24.21	21.75	47.47	3.30	20.50	18.60	0.170	19.4286

°Data for this indicator were not available.

Source: Compiled by the author, using the following sources: *UNESCO Statistical Yearbook 1982* (Paris, 1982); Vivian Carlip, W. Overstreet, and D. Linder, *Economic Handbook of the World: 1982* (New York: McGraw-Hill, 1982); *International Marketing Data and Statistics 1982* (London: Euromonitor Publications, 1982); *The World in Figures,* 2d ed (New York: Facts on File, 1978); and *Yearbook of Labour Statistics 1982,* (Geneva: International Labour Office, 1982).

TABLE 3.6. Indicators of Marketing System Development

Selected countries	ROW	Advert	Wholsale	Newspaper	Retail	Sales	R&D	Supermark	Markindx
North Yemen	1	0.00	15.14	1.20	1.58	1.42	0.00	0.0001	3.8680
Haiti	2	4.12	7.09	2.39	7.37	0.00	0.00	0.4000	4.2740
Sri Lanka	3	0.59	12.46	25.72	11.14	10.58	5.52	0.7900	9.5429
Turkey	4	5.16	10.94	5.38	20.54	13.80	9.46	11.8600	11.0200
Peru	5	6.44	11.77	6.10	22.39	0.00	1.51	7.9100	9.3533
South Korea	6	8.77	10.17	23.56	6.35	54.69	24.93	19.7600	21.1757
Saudi Arabia	7	7.71	8.33	0.96	1.20	0.00	0.00	15.8100	6.8020
Venezuela	8	32.46	6.33	21.29	19.27	15.33	47.02	39.5300	25.8900
Singapore	9	34.74	17.82	13.40	5.27	4.18	16.52	3.9500	13.6971

Sources: See Table 3.5 footnote.

TABLE 3.7. Indicators of Economic and Marketing System Development

Selected countries	Economic index	Selected countries	Marketing index
Advanced stage		Advanced stage	
Saudi Arabia	24.18	Venezuela	25.89
Singapore	19.43	South Korea	21.18
Venezuela	15.92	Singapore	13.70
Intermediate stage		Intermediate stage	
South Korea	9.63	Turkey	11.02
Turkey	7.60	Sri Lanka	9.54
Peru	7.39	Peru	9.35
Beginning stage		Beginning stage	
Sri Lanka	2.93	Saudi Arabia	6.80
North Yemen	2.47	Haiti	4.27
Haiti	1.36	North Yemen	3.86

Source: Compiled by the author.

ranking in the economic index but low ranking in the marketing system development index, Saudi Arabia was dropped from the analysis and a second correlation analysis was performed without Saudi Arabia. It is interesting to note that a high positive correlation of 0.722 emerged (see Table 3.9).

The findings of this study provide certain insights into the impact of level of economic development on marketing system development. This is to say that similar patterns of development do create similar levels of marketing development patterns, which is contrary to the earlier findings of Douglas and Wind.[55] The study results also showed a direct relationship between economic development factors and marketing system development factors, at least in so far as the specific factors examined and the eight less-developed countries (Saudi Arabia excluded) were concerned. In oil-rich countries like Saudi Arabia, economic planners have heavily focused on manufacturing investment projects to increase oil, petrochemical, and related industries' production capabilities. Most aspects of marketing, other than investments in basic transportation infrastructures, have usually been relegated to a secondary and adaptive role in the economic development process. Little attention, so far, has been directed toward improvement of the marketing system infrastructure.

It can be concluded that in countries at similar levels of development, firms will tend to have similar marketing practices. The high degree of similarity among countries at each stage of development suggests that

TABLE 3.8. Relationship between Marketing and Economic Development (All Nine Countries)

	Consump	Cars	Tels	GDP	Income	Manufac	Wages	Advert	Wholsale
Cars	0.926								
Tels	0.702	0.453							
GDP	0.615	0.636	-0.005						
Income	0.888	0.870	0.391	0.817					
Manufac	0.115	-0.087	0.525	-0.202	-0.199				
Wages	0.620	0.739	0.106	0.784	0.622	-0.326			
Advert	0.767	0.709	0.793	0.015	0.394	0.276	0.637		
Wholsale	0.017	-0.228	0.536	-0.486	-0.156	0.431	-0.631	0.253	
Newspaper	0.052	0.061	0.214	-0.106	-0.161	0.558	-0.073	0.245	-0.014
Retail	-0.162	-0.021	-0.201	-0.114	-0.322	0.456	0.443	-0.011	-0.260
Sales	-0.079	-0.222	-0.071	0.650	-0.105	0.478	0.141	-0.320	-0.469
R&D	0.634	0.749	0.211	0.692	0.649	-0.437	0.933	0.674	-0.578
Supermark	0.532	0.641	0.085	0.598	0.406	0.118	0.944	0.482	-0.584
Econindx	0.974	0.897	0.604	0.744	0.948	0.093	0.609	0.604	-0.044
Markindx	0.437	0.429	0.372	0.246	0.139	0.529	0.876	0.621	-0.250

	Newspaper	Retail	Sales	R&D	Supermark	Econindx
Retail	0.193					
Sales	0.519	-0.001				
R&D	0.460	-0.072	0.230			
Supermark	0.385	0.360	0.415	0.914		
Econindx	0.010	-0.176	0.037	0.608	0.509	
Markindx	0.736	0.361	0.577	0.971	0.842	0.366

Source: Compiled by the author.

TABLE 3.9. Relationship between Marketing and Economic Development (Saudi Arabia Excluded)

	Consump	Cars	Tels	GDP	Income	Manufac	Wages	Advert	Wholsale
Cars	0.899								
Tels	0.855	0.581							
GDP	0.400	0.400	0.087						
Income	0.997	0.922	0.839	0.383					
Manufac	0.475	0.233	0.564	0.404	0.442				
Wages	0.620	0.739	0.106	0.784	0.622	−0.326			
Advert	0.979	0.938	0.791	0.256	0.990	0.238	0.637		
Wholsale	0.194	−0.095	0.541	−0.474	0.160	0.352	−0.631	0.225	
Newspaper	0.307	0.339	0.205	0.405	0.322	0.464	−0.073	0.202	−0.135
Retail	0.071	0.275	−0.253	0.481	0.082	0.316	0.443	−0.105	−0.437
Sales	−0.079	−0.222	−0.071	0.650	−0.105	0.478	0.141	−0.320	−0.469
R&D	0.634	0.749	0.211	0.692	0.649	−0.437	0.933	0.674	−0.578
Supermark	0.542	0.680	0.095	0.879	0.549	0.212	0.944	0.505	−0.574
Econindx	0.984	0.855	0.857	0.475	0.976	0.615	0.609	0.940	0.193
Markindx	0.675	0.690	0.368	0.840	0.675	0.482	0.876	0.613	−0.344

	Newspaper	Retail	Sales	R&D	Supermark	Econindx
Retail	0.038	−0.001				
Sales	0.519	−0.072	0.230			
R&D	0.460	0.467	0.415	0.914		
Supermark	0.476	0.153	0.037	0.608	0.560	
Econindx	0.369	0.291	0.577	0.971	0.912	0.722
Markindx	0.716					

Source: Compiled by the author.

companies marketing their products to these countries can use standardized marketing practices.[56]

CONCLUSIONS

In general, the economic development process involves the transformation of resource-based economies into industrially based economies. With increased economic development, one would expect more specialization in labor, adoption of more scientific technologies, and the geographic separation of production and consumption. All of these changes necessitate the development of a more efficient marketing system.[57] With economic development, the proportion of consumer expenditures for marketing services tends to increase and the marketing system becomes more important as a coordinator of production and consumption activities.

Differences in per capita income need to be translated into differences in per capita consumption expenditures. If they are not, the association of economic development as measured by per capita income need not be translated into an association with per capita consumption and with the correlated differences in the structure of consumption. Hence it is important to examine the connection between per capita income and the uses of income, particularly its use for consumption.[58]

Throughout the economic development process, market opportunities are exploited and some are created by certain developments in the marketing environment (e.g., an increase in real per capita income—if translated into an increase of demand—provides a market opportunity for certain commodities and services). This means that the size of the market is increased and the firms concerned have to respond. Their response to the new situations depends on their abilities, constraints, and attitudes. It would be quite useful, therefore, to look at the environmental factors in terms of their impact on the structure of the market rather than their effect on individual firms. The response of individual firms to the new market situation would be the next step for further analysis.

The interest in the role that marketing system development can play in economic development arose as a result of a number of failures of economic development plans. The role of marketing in economic development will have to develop from the bottom up, by pulling together and making sense of the experiences, insights, and findings reported in studies of the past. It is expected that knowledge in this area is more likely to develop through theory-based field studies and not through "armchair-developed grand theories."[59]

Marketing is more essential for the development of less-developed countries than their developed counterparts. Because of this, development plans should contain marketing programs for the development and improvement of marketing systems of less-developed countries. Without improvements in the marketing sector of the economy there will not be real development in the whole economy. In this effort to integrate marketing into the economic development process of less-developed countries, the following steps need to be considered fully:

A. Despite the similarities between marketing systems and the economic development of less-developed countries, as reported in various studies, there is still no strong evidence to prove that there are two identical marketing systems in the world. The same could be said about marketing practices of different firms in a given country; that is to say, their responses to the economic environment can be expected to differ. Thus no consistent pattern of marketing response and practice emerges at a national level in less-developed countries.

B. There is much written about the impact of economic development on marketing structures and systems. Less is written about how these factors might be ascertained or how they can be related to each other. The time factor might be the key to understanding the relationship between economic environment and marketing development. Thus further study of the evolution of marketing structures and organizations over time, along with the level of economic development reached by a less-developed country, is required.

C. Western marketing techniques and institutions can be transferred to less-developed countries only with atttention to the social, economic, technological, and cultural differences between these two types of countries. The transformation of machinery and industrial factories does not necessarily mean that they will be associated with development of marketing techniques and practices, although identical products will be produced by this machinery in any country.

D. Socioeconomic and cultural variables are basic requirements for understanding and analyzing marketing practices. Therefore, certain factors should be selected to examine the marketing systems of less-developed countries. The criterion used to examine such factors will be their impact on the structure of the market in the first place. The next step is to examine the change in business structure and organization of marketing practices in different firms operating in the system.

E. The evolution of marketing organization of firms goes through different stages, starting from a primitive organization where the marketing function tends to be mixed with other basic functions, to a highly sophisticated marketing management where the philosophy tends to involve a concept of the whole business. An examination of how these stages of marketing organization emerge over a period of time at different levels of economic development, along with the change in the marketing environment and its impact on market structure, would constitute a comprehensive approach to the study of marketing development in a less-developed country.

F. In so far as the emerging nations are concerned, there is strong evidence to suggest that until businesspeople recognize the importance of marketing as a specialized managerial function that warrants specialists, it is unlikely that much effort will be made to establish more advanced marketing organizations. Thus, educational efforts concerning the role of marketing and the training of marketing specialists are essential to the future economic development process of the emerging nations.

NOTES

1. Peter F. Drucker, "Marketing and Economic Development," *Journal of Marketing* 23, no. 3 (January 1958): 255.

2. Ibid., pp. 252–59.

3. Reed Moyer, *Marketing in Economic Development* (East Lansing, MI: Michigan State University, 1965), p. 1.

4. Yair Aharoni, *Markets, Planning and Development* (Cambridge MA: Ballinger, 1977).

5. A. Coskun Samli, "The Future of Marketing in the Developed and Developing Countries: An Analysis of Contrast," *II Millimetro Special,* proceedings entitled "Consumption: The Marketing Role in the Future Society Development," Milan, Italy, 1973.

6. A. Coskun Samli and John T. Mentzer, "A Model for Marketing in Economic Development," *Columbia Journal of World Business* 16, no. 3 (Fall 1981): 91–101.

7. John V. Petrof, "Economic Development and Marketing," in *Selling to the Global Shopping Centre,* proceedings of the 1977 International Marketing Conference, edited by H. W. Berkman and J. K. Fenyo, *Academy of Marketing Science Journal* 5 (1977): 87–90.

8. F. S. Carter and R. Savitt, "A Resource Allocation Model for Integrating Marketing into Economic Development Plans," in *Proceedings of the 1983 World Marketing Congress,* Halifax, Nova Scotia, November 1983, edited by E. Kaynak, p. 80.

9. Ibid.

10. John E. Griggs, *Evaluating Market Change: An Application of Systems Theory,* (East Lansing, MI: MSU International Business and Economic Studies, Michigan State University, 1970), pp. 1–14.

11. Marye Tharp Hilger, "Theories of the Relationship between Marketing and Economic Development," in *Macro-Marketing, An Elaboration of Issues,* proceedings of the Macro-Marketing Seminar, University of Colorado, Boulder, Colorado, August 14–17, edited by Phillip D. White and Charles C. Slater, 1977, p. 333.

12. M. T. Hilger, "Consumer Perceptions of a Public Marketer in Mexico," *Columbia Journal of World Business* 15, no. 3 (Fall 1980): 75–82.

13. Robert Bartels, "Marketing and Economic Development," in *Macro-Marketing: Distributive Processes from a Societal Perspective,* edited by Charles Slater (Boulder, CO: Business Research Division, University of Colorado, 1976), pp. 211–17.

14. For a fuller treatment of this issue see Erdener Kaynak and Ronald Savitt, *Comparative Marketing Systems* (New York: Praeger, 1984).

15. Marye Tharp Hilger, "Factors Inhibiting the Development of Comparative Marketing," paper presented at the Macro-Marketing Annual Conference, Long Island, NY, 1982.

16. Hilger, "Theories of the Relationship," pp. 336–37.

17. Robert Bartels, *Global Development and Marketing* (Columbus, OH: Grid Publishing, 1981).

18. Bartels, *Global Development,* p. 212.

19. Hilger, "Theories of the Relationship."

20. Tanniru R. Rao, "Marketing and Economic Development," *Marketing and Management Digest* vol. 8, no. 1 (January 1976): 15–18.

21. Bartels, *Global Development.*

22. George H. Wadinambiaratchi, "Theories of Retail Development," *Social and Economic Studies* 4 (December 1972): 391–404.

23. Moyer, *Marketing in Economic Development.*

24. S. P. Douglas, "Patterns and Parallels of Marketing Structures in Several Countries," *MSU Business Topics* (Spring 1971): 38–48.

25. R. Westfall and W. Harper, Jr., "Marketing in India," *Journal of Marketing* 25 (October 1960): 11–17.

26. Ugur Yavas, "Marketing Research Usage By Domestic and Foreign Manufacturing Firms in Turkey," *Management International Review* 23 (1983): 59; Ugur Yavas and W. Daniel Rowntree, "The Transfer of Management Know-How to Turkey Through Graduate Business Education: Some Empirical Findings," *Management International Review* 20, no. 2 (1980): 56–64.

27. B. Liander, V. Terpstra, M. Y. Yoshino, and A. A. Sherbini, *Comparative Analysis for International Marketing* (Boston, MA: Allyn and Bacon, 1967).

28. J. S. Hill and R. R. Still, "Effects of Urbanization on Multinational Product Planning: Markets in Lesser-Developed Countries," *Columbia Journal of World Business* 19, no. 2 (Summer 1984): 62–67.

29. Liander, Terpstra, Yoshino, and Sherbini, *Comparative Analysis for International Marketing,* p. 63.

30. C. F. Stewart, "The Changing Middle-East Market," *Journal of Marketing* 25 (January 1961): 47–51.

31. L. G. Erickson, "Analyzing Brazilian Consumer Markets," *Business Topics* 11 (Summer 1963): 7–26.

32. Erdener Kaynak, "Food Retailing Systems in Developing Countries," *Hacettepe Bulletin of Social Sciences and Humanities* 8, nos. 1–2 (June–December 1976): 37–51.

33. Donald A. Taylor, "Marketing in Brazil," in *Marketing and Economic Development,* edited by Peter D. Bennett (Chicago, IL: American Marketing Association, 1965), pp. 110–15.

34. Stewart, "The Changing Middle-East Market."

35. E. Marcus, "Selling the Tropical African Market," *Journal of Marketing* 25 (July 1961): 25–31.

36. L. V. Hirsch, "The Contribution of Marketing to Economic Development: A Generally Neglected Area," in *The Social Responsibility of Marketing,* edited by W. D. Stevens (Chicago, IL: American Marketing Association, 1961), pp. 413–18.

37. Michael Baker and A. El-Haddad, "Marketing and Economic Development," in *Proceedings of the European Academy for Advanced Research in Marketing, X Annual Workshop,* Copenhagen, 25–27 March, 1981, edited by H. H. Larsen and S. Heede, pp. 1249–82.

38. George Wadinambiaratchi, "Channels of Distribution in Developing Economies," *Business Quarterly* 30, no. 4 (Winter 1965): 74–82.

39. Ben I. Hudanah, *Marketing Structure and Marketing Practices of the Libyan Food Manufacturing Industry,* Ph. D. dissertation, Cranfield Institute of Technology, Cranfield, Bedfordshire, 1975, pp. 24–29.

40. Ibid., p. 155.

41. Karl Polanyi, C. M. Arensberg, and H. W. Pearson (eds), *Trade and Market in the Early Empires* (Glencoe, IL: Free Press, 1957).

42. Liander, Terpstra, Yoshino, and Sherbini, "Comparative Analysis," p. 155.

43. William J. Stanton, *Fundamentals of Marketing* (New York: McGraw-Hill, 1972), pp. 12–18.

44. William Glade, W. Strong, J. Udell, and R. Littlefield, *Marketing in a Developing Nation* (Lexington MA: Heath Lexington Books, 1970).

45. Drucker, "Marketing and Economic Development," pp. 255–59.

46. T. H. Bonaparte, *Marketing in Less-Developed Countries: A Case Analysis of Liberia,* (New York: Pace University Graduate School, The Center for Applied Research, monograph 15, 1977), p. 6.

47. L. J. Hunt, "Marketing Education in Developing Environments," in *New Marketing for Social and Economic Progress,* (Chicago, IL: American Marketing Association, 1975), pp. 642–46.

48. Ibid., p. 643.

49. Erdener Kaynak and A Coskun Samli, "Marketing Practices in Less-Developed Countries," *Journal of Business Research* 13, no. 1 (March 1984): 5–18.

50. Nathaniel H. Leff, "Multinational Corporate Pricing Strategy in the Developing Countries," *Journal of International Business Studies* (Fall 1975): 55–64; and Erdener Kaynak, *Marketing in the Third World* (New York: Praeger Special Studies, 1982).

51. D. A. Heenan and W. J. Keegan, "The Rise of Third World Multinationals," *Harvard Business Review* 57 (January–February 1979): 101–109.

52. A. M. Elbashier and J. R. Nicholls, *Export Marketing to the Arab World* (London: Graham & Trotman, 1982), pp. 7–8.

53. J. Waterbury and R. El-Mallakh, *The Middle East in the Coming Decade* (New York: McGraw-Hill, 1978).

54. For an excellent conceptual framework in selecting indicators see Helen Hughes, "Industrialization and Development: A Stocktaking," *Industry and Development,* no. 2 (1980): 1–27.

55. Susan P. Douglas and Yoram Wind, "Environmental Factors and Marketing Practices," *European Journal of Marketing* 7, no. 3 (Winter 1973–74): 155–65.

56. Erdener Kaynak and Lionel A. Mitchell, "An Analysis of Marketing Strategies Used in Diverse Cultures," *Journal of Advertising Research* 21, no. 3 (June 1981): 25–32.

57. Kelly Harrison, D. Henley, H. Riley, and J. Shaffer, *Improving Food Marketing Systems in Developing Countries,* Research Report no. 6 (East Lansing, MI: Latin American Studies Center, Michigan State University, November 1974), p. 2.

58. Ben Issa Hudanah, *Marketing Structure and Marketing Practices,* p. 24.

59. Arieh Goldman, "The Development and Implementation of a Marketing Based Economic Development Project in the Agricultural Sector—An Israeli Case," in *Comparative Marketing Systems,* edited by Erdener Kaynak and Ronald Savitt, (New York: Praeger, 1984), p. 53.

4
Channels of Distribution and the Economic Development Process

INTRODUCTION

The subject of channels of distribution has not yet been adequately developed in theory despite the fact that the subject has been one of the most frequently researched topics of marketing. The present world economic crisis, and cost and productivity consciousness in individual countries as well as across nations, make channels of distribution of paramount importance, both at firm (micro) and society (macro) levels.[1] This need has also stimulated a renewed interest in the relationship between channels of distribution and economic development. Among all distribution systems related research is gaining momentum as trade between countries at different stages of development increases at an accelerated rate. To be more effective in world markets today one must be more sensitive to the marketing decision areas where a significant percentage of total marketing costs occurs. This means being aware of the areas where distribution cost reductions and productivity improvements are possible and needed. As a result, North American and European companies have become more interested in the distribution systems of other countries.

The purpose of this chapter is to determine and evaluate the present state and likely developments of distribution systems in less-developed countries, and the relationship between channels of distribution and economic development. An attempt is also made to develop constructs and/or conceptual frameworks from which to study distribution systems across national boundaries. To this end, some working propositions/hypotheses are formulated in an effort to establish a sound base for studies in the field of cross-national distribution systems. The chapter will also equip North American and European managers with an in-depth understanding of the workings of LDC distribution systems in varying economic and environmental settings.

COMPARATIVE APPROACH

The comparative approach to distribution is concerned with the systematic detection, identification, classification, measurement, and interpretation of similarities and differences among various distributive institutions operating in LDCs.[2] However, comparison of distributive systems in these countries involves more than just locating similarities and differences, or discerning what is universal or unique among the varying systems.[3] The distinctions apparent in distributive processes and institutions must be interpreted in order to demonstrate the likely reasons for the similarities or differences of distributive systems of varying countries.[4] This, of course, is not an easy task.

The similarities or differences in distribution structures of countries, in most cases, are related to various environmental factors, in particular to a country's level of economic development.[5] In earlier works Cundiff and Wadinambiaratchi made this same connection. Their lag or stage hypothesis stated that distribution systems of less-developed countries look like the U.S. system at earlier periods of its development.[6] According to Cundiff: distributive innovations take place only in highly developed economic systems; an economic system's capacity to adopt distributive innovations successfully is directly related to its level of economic development; adaptation may be helped or hindered in countries where economic conditions are favorable to development; and aggressive firms can accelerate the adaptation process.[7] Contrary to this view, Douglas concluded that the development of marketing structure (including distribution) does not closely parallel that of the environment (including the economic environment).[8] At a later stage, Arndt found a relationship between channels of distribution structure and GNP per capita.[9] Goldman showed simplistic comparative associations between marketing and its economic environment.[10] Finally, Oritt and Hagan examined several different theories on the relationship between channels of distribution and the economic development process.[11]

The structure of retail distribution of a country changes along with the economic development process. Mittendorf identified three different retail distribution stages that are in harmony with the state of economic development of a country.[12] These stages are summarized below (see Figure 4.1).

Stage 1. The predominance of many small retailers and hawkers characterizes this stage. Wholesaling and retailing activities are undertaken by one enterprise. Example: tropical Africa.

FIGURE 4.1. Changes in Food Retailing and Wholesale in the Course of Economic Development in Developing Countries

Retailing (increasing role of food chains and declining role of public retail markets)

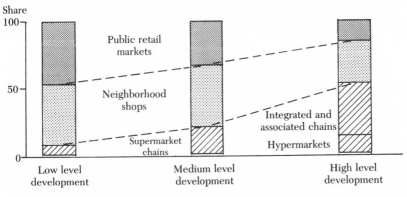

Wholesaling (declining role of wholesale markets and increasing direct shipments to food chains)

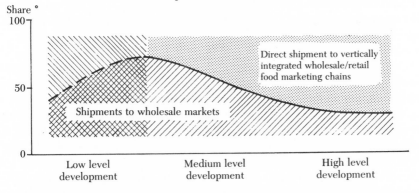

°Share of food passing through wholesale markets and direct shipments to food chains

Source: Hans J. Mittendorf, "The Challenge of Organizing City Food Marketing Systems in Developing Countries," *Zeitschrift für auslandische Landwirtschaft* 17, no. 4 (October–December 1978): 333. Reprinted by permission.

Stage 2. At this stage there are well-established traditional wholesalers who have an important function in the distribution of fruit, vegetables, and fish to a larger number of specialized retailers with a higher level of operation than what prevails in Stage 1. Example: many urban centers of Latin America, Mediterranean countries, and more highly developed Near and Far Eastern cities.

Stage 3. Associated with increased consumer income and GNP is the development of integrated and associated food chains. An increasing proportion of fruit and vegetables are purchased directly from packing stations and sent directly to the wholesale depots of food chains for redistribution directly to supermarkets, without passing through the wholesale market. At this stage, the traditional wholesale markets perform only a supplementary function in supplying highly seasonal and perishable food but not the bulk of the fruit and vegetables distributed.

One may easily question the wisdom of using a large number of environmental variables to explain similarities and differences in the distribution systems of different countries of the third world. After all, not every facet of the distribution system is affected significantly by the numerous elements in its economic, social, political, and cultural environments. It is thought that it would be wiser to use a relatively small but important number of environmental variables to explain similarities and/or differences between various distribution systems operating within the third world surroundings.[13] It must be pointed out here that the ultimate focus of the comparative analysis of distribution systems in LDCs should be on the distribution systems and their component parts per se rather than on the environment, otherwise one may end up comparing environments rather than the distribution systems operating within a particular environment.

Marketers generally believe that the economic development process is enhanced by placing high importance on distributive activities. Despite this contention, "whether markets pull development or lag behind it, it is evident that much planning in the area of economic development today neglects distribution."[14] It is believed that the channel structure of countries evolves along with the economic development process in harmony with the evolution of producers and channel intermediaries.[15] Before one considers the impact of economic development on distribution let us look at the structural characteristics of distribution systems.

STRUCTURAL CHARACTERISTICS OF DISTRIBUTIVE SYSTEMS

A distribution system in an LDC is an aggregate abstract concept; the basic units of such a system are the distributive units whose individual actions (performance of certain functions and processes) result in changes in the system. In these countries the availability of effective distributive institutions affects the economic development process. Figure 4.2 shows how the channels of distribution system effects the economic development process. This change and impact of the channels of distribution is summarized as follows:

FIGURE 4.2. Changes in Channels of Distribution for an Economic Development Program

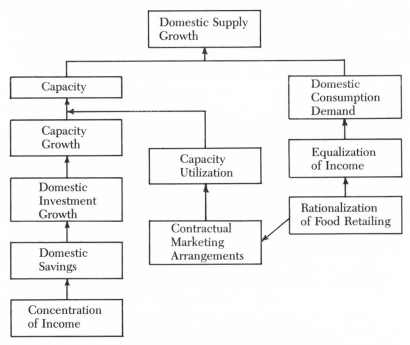

Note: \\ indicates this route not used in program (because of conflict with increasing domestic demand through income equalization)

Source: E. Jerome McCarthy, "Effective Marketing Institutions for Economic Development," in *Toward Scientific Marketing*, edited by Stephen A. Greyer (Chicago, IL: American Marketing Association, 1963 Proceedings, 1964), p. 63. Reprinted with permission.

a. Economic development is dependent on the growth of domestic supply through the growth of domestic demand (consumption).

b. The growth of domestic supply is also dependent on both the growth of capacity and the productive utilization of present capacity.

c. The growth of capacity is dependent on the growth of domestic investment, which in turn is dependent on the growth of domestic savings.

d. The growth of domestic savings is dependent on the increased concentration of income (because of a higher propensity to save in higher income classes).

e. The growth of domestic consumption (demand), however, is dependent on increased dispersion (equalization) of income (because of the higher propensity to consume in lower income classes).

f. Hence, one of the two determinants of economic growth—domestic demand growth—is in conflict with part (capacity growth) of the other one—supply growth.

g. Since in underdeveloped nations there is normally underutilization of capacity (e.g., high unemployment), and since the growth of domestic demand is not necessarily in conflict with increasing supply through better utilization of capacity (as it is with increasing capacity), then obviously the answer to increasing supply without reducing demand lies in increasing the productive use of present capacity.

h. The answer to simultaneously increasing the productive use of present capacity and consumption demand lies in rationalizing the food retail industry by inducing large-scale, low-margin, high-volume operations (supermarkets). Since so much of the market's income is spent on food, the lowering of food prices creates a real increase in the income of the masses. Increases in this income, as noted in (e), increase domestic consumption demand.

i. The rationalization of food retailing also provides the opportunity for such large-scale retailers to arrange for high-volume assured purchases from producers. Such contractual arrangements, by reducing the producer's risk (because of assured sales) and lowering his costs (because of the economics generated by high volume), induce increased utilization of his present capacity and hence supply, with minimum investment.

j. It would be helpful as well if public policy were directed toward improving market information, grading, transportation, public storage, and credit facilities. In addition, it is important that the portion of the labor force now redundant because of rationalization of food retailing be redeployed in a productive fashion.[16]

It is maintained that markets and channel structure are leading factors in the economic development process. The idea behind this thesis is that channels of distribution bring goods to marketplaces in the most effective and efficient way possible. If the channels are lacking or less satisfactory, markets will not materialize. Channels also stimulate the development of manufacturing and processing industries.[17]

Another group of scholars holds the view that the channel structure of a given country is a reflection of the stage of socioeconomic and technological development reached by that country. In his research on Latin America, Erickson conceded:

> In marketing, as in other areas of social and economic activity, institutions and methodology do not arise simply through chance. Rather,

they are a reflection of the particular environment in which they are found. The institutions which are engaged in marketing, and the methods used to market output, reflect the environmental factors which are lumped together and called the market.[18]

Prevailing marketing environmental factors in a country and stages of economic development reached are compared by Wadinambiaratchi:

The studies reviewed appear to substantiate the hypothesis that marketing channel structures reflect the stage of economic development.[19]

In most LDCs, there are distinctly different social systems that exist side by side and create different distributive arrangements and channel structures.[20] For instance, there is one channels-of-distribution arrangement for wealthier market segments where department stores and supermarkets serve the needs of consumers and another system of distribution for the lower-income masses who are catered to by corner stores, public markets, and itinerant retailers.[21] This model describes the market system in LDCs as the upper circuit of the dual economy having relatively few, but large and capital-intensive marketing firms that are organized along rational and formal lines. The lower circuit, by contrast, is said to include a multiplicity of small, capital-weak trade units that form long vertical and horizontal chains of distribution within this organizational structure, where family and personal relations are guiding principles. [22] Characteristics of stores serving the needs of the dual system in an LDC environment are shown in Table 4.1.

Similarities among distributive systems of LDCs exist not only in the case of modern institutions such as supermarkets but also in the case of traditional distributive outlets. Similarities among distributive systems are due to the same type of economic forces and distributive processes operating on and functions being performed by distributors, resulting in the appearance of similar distributive institutions and development paths.[23]

The organization and structure of the market for most products in LDCs is a function of certain economic variables, such as the size of the market; availability and nature of the goods; the size, productivity, and efficiency of production units; and their degree of specialization. These variables and their impact show basically similar patterns in LDCs at similar levels of development because these variables, in turn, are the products of a certain stage of economic development.[24]

The typical distributive establishment seen in LDCs is small scale and high in number of firms. This means that turnover in these distributive

TABLE 4.1. Characteristics of the Small and Large Food Stores of Istanbul

Underdeveloped food retail system *(Small food store–corner shop)*	*Developed food retail system* *(Large food store–self-service)*
Nonspecialization in the products held	Specialization in the products held
Most of the sales are on credit	Sale is made on cash-and-carry basis
Merchandise sold in store	Merchandise, pre-sold or self-sold
Stores have simple organizational set-ups	Stores have complex organizational set-ups
Price variations among stores	Fixed prices in all stores
Lack of advertising and brand promotion	Advertising and brand promotion used
Counter service exists	Self-service exists
High service level	Low service level
Personal selling	Impersonal selling
Stores mainly found in sparsely populated areas	Stores found in densely populated areas
Mostly organized as individual ownership	Mostly organized as partnership
Store size is usually less than 50 sq. m.	Store size is usually over 150 sq.m.
Most shops employ one or two persons	Most shops employ more than ten persons
Use old and traditional equipment	Use new and modern equipment
Most shops are open 90 hours a week	Most shops are open 50 hours a week
Use personal funds	Use shareholder funds
Intermediary suppliers used	Direct purchase from the producer
Frequency of purchases of supplies is high	Frequency of purchases of supplies is low
Maintain low stock level	Maintain high stock level
Lack of growth orientation	Growth oriented
Store owners mostly have primary education	Store employees mostly high-school graduates
Store owners mostly retired elderly people	Employees are middle-aged or young

Source: E. Kaynak, "Changes in the Food Retailing Institutions of Urban Turkey, The Istanbul Experience," *Studies in Development* 18 (Winter 1978): 63. Reprinted with permission.

outlets is low, the facilities where they operate are small, and the goods they handle are limited. Many of those found in small towns and neighborhood areas of cities are one-person shops, carrying very limited stock and doing no promotion. Large-scale distributive institutions are substantially concentrated in the major cities and serve mainly the needs of wealthier populations.[25]

The traditional type of distributive outlet that accounts for a major share of the available institutions in LDCs carries a poor assortment of products with uncertain quality and quantity. Under-stocking is common, and distributors offer few services and keep only the most elementary accounting records. These institutions generally provide an important form of unemployment relief for LDCs. Entry into the traditional type of distribution system is relatively easy because of the low investment and technical skills required. The result is a multiplicity of small distributive outlets characterized by poor management practices. These stores, in most cases, tend to operate with a minimum of space and the scale of operations is small. For this reason the distributor seeks high margins rather than volume to survive.[26] Despite these disadvantages, the present system of distributive outlets in LDCs, although inefficient in economic terms by Western standards, still maintains its existence because distributors are in a position to provide a great number of needed services. Foremost among these are credit and convenience in shopping. Moreover, these stores fill a social need in so far as the small shop is often the center of social life within the neighborhood.

ENVIRONMENT OF DISTRIBUTION SYSTEMS

Environment refers to what is external to the distribution system, and is neither directly controlling it, nor directly controlled by it. Various parts of the distributive environment are emphasized in different studies.[27] As a rule, comparisons are drawn within national and cultural divisions. Inter-cultural and inter-regional bases for comparison seem most natural for comparative distributive and marketing analysis.[28] The branches of marketing in which comparisons have been pursued at the international level have been concerned with the channels of distribution, especially those of wholesaling and retailing. The applicability of the comparative approach to the study of distribution requires recognition that the differences in distributive institutions and practices in various countries are as important as the similarities. Such contrasts are essential elements in a comparative analysis. For this reason, it is not adequate to simply describe distribution in another country. The critical element in comparative distribution in LDCs is the manner in which experience gained in developed countries is interpreted, related, and generalized through some sort of modified theory of distribution development.

The environment of a distribution system is a multidimensional concept consisting of the social, legal, economic, cultural, and physical characteristics of the markets in which distributors buy and sell.[29] Besides environmental factors, it has been hypothesized that past distributive behavior and the structure of individual distributors cause changes in the distribution system.[30] One of the most important relationships between the distribution system and the broader environment concerns the connection between the amount and type of distributive activity on one hand, and the many facets of distributive outlet and system efficiency on the other. Hence, the most appropriate starting point to investigate this relationship would be with the existing distributive structure in LDCs.

Unfortunately, few studies of this kind have been undertaken in LDCs; this makes a comparative distribution study particularly necessary. Second, most marketing scholars and practitioners, even the ones who have undertaken surveys in LDCs, have interpreted the prevalent distributive practices in terms of the socioeconomic conditions of the country in question.[31] This author does not question the effect of the socioeconomic factors on the distribution system prevailing in a country, but maintains that other environmental factors may affect the characteristics of distribution systems in LDCs. For example, the supplier environment, competition, and governmental legislation and actions might influence the development of an efficient distribution system, perhaps to a greater extent than the pure socioeconomic environment. Some of these studies stress technological and governmental aspects while others concentrate solely on socioeconomic variables such as family, education, income, and other demographic characteristics. Tremendous changes within which distributors of all kinds must operate are taking place in the broad environments of LDC distributive systems. As a result, a holistic approach to researching the relationship between the distribution system of a country and its environment is needed. This kind of analysis will produce a synergistic effect for an improved, mutually beneficial relationship between a distribution system and its various environmental factors.

However, the theory that the marketing system of a country is closely related to the development of its social, economic, and cultural environments is widely held by many scholars.[32] For instance, it is pointed out by Douglas that the precise nature of the relationship between environmental factors and the marketing system remains a matter of speculation.[33] A distribution system, for example, seeks basically to satisfy human needs, but the manner in which it functions varies widely among different societies. Furthermore, these variations are related to differences in the environment. Following from this, it can be hypothesized that under the influence of various environmental conditions, different patterns of distribution systems (in terms of type of institutions, processes, marketing practices, and organization of forms), managerial attitudes, and channel structure may be expected to emerge within different LDCs of the third world.

Distributive activities take place within the social, political, economic, and technological environments of a country. It is stated that environmental factors affect the marketing structure of a country through their impact on the individual firm. The prevailing economic conditions of a country, such as the availability or nonavailability of capital, manpower, and financial resources, determine the type of input available to firms as well as the organizational structure. Managerial attitudes are also affected by the marketing environment.[34] Size and organization of firms as well as managerial attitudes of their employees have an impact on the structure of the distribution system in a country. Thus, differences in the organizational and attitudinal characteristics of firms and in channel structure can be expected at different levels of economic development (see Figure 4.3).

MODERNIZATION OF DISTRIBUTION SYSTEMS

There is an urgent need for modernization of distributive systems in developing countries as a prerequisite to economic development. For instance, Rogers defines the modernization process as "the process by which individuals change from a traditional way of life to a more complex,

FIGURE 4.3. A Schema of the Relationships between Marketing Structure and the Marketing Environment

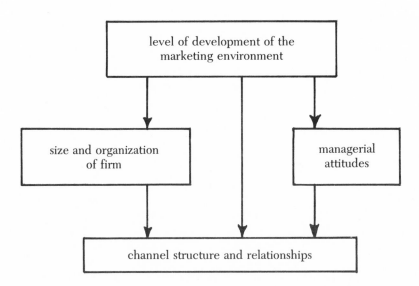

Source: Susan P. Douglas, "Patterns and Parallels of Marketing Structures in Several Countries," *MSU Business Topics* (Spring 1971): 39. Reprinted with permission.

technologically advanced and rapidly changing style of life."[35] He further provides a good description of the characteristics of LDC populations that hinder the industrialization process, and hence economic development activity. Some of the characteristics are summarized as follows:

Mutual distrust in interpersonal relations
Perceived limited good
Dependence on and hostility toward government authority
Familism
Lack of innovativeness
Fatalism
Limited aspirations
Lack of deferred gratification
Limited view of the world
Low empathy [36]

Who would lead the change and modernization efforts and how would they be handled? It is argued, for instance, that well-organized and coordinated markets and marketing systems can facilitate change, modernization, and the economic development process (see Figure 4.4).[37] Of the types of changes discussed here, the physical facilities and handling innovations are the ones that can be transferred easily from more developed countries. It must be pointed out here, however, that these are not necessarily the ones that would offer the greatest potential for improving the performance of a distribution system and hence facilitate the economic development process.[38]

Western distributive technology cannot simply be transferred to less-developed economies; it has to be adapted to the environment. Marketing is only one aspect of the total development process. There are certain problems inherent in adopting the distributive institutions of the West. One of the first problems is the lack of trained manpower for the job. Second, there has been little distribution planning. At times, items may be ready for distribution before marketing is ever considered and will consequently have a low probability of success. Product attributes are sometimes not carefully planned because consumer orientation has not become a way of life, and therefore many products do not correspond to market demand.

A lack of entrepreneurial talent in LDCs may make it difficult, if not impossible, to move directly into the development of modern distribution systems. One prerequisite of modern distributive institutions is a catchment area capable of supporting sizable merchandising operations. Structural changes in LDC markets have played an important part in the success of large distributive institutions. The ability to muster substantial capital

FIGURE 4.4. Modernization of Distributive Systems and Economic Development

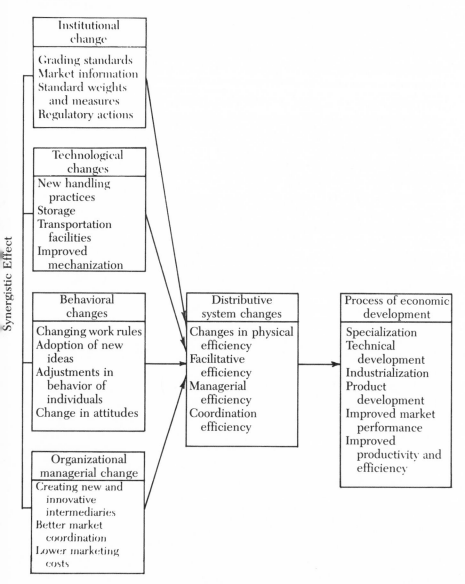

Source: Prepared by the author.

funds effectively is another prerequisite of modern distribution practices in LDCs.

It appears that continuous growth of the total market provides an opportunity for modern distributive institutions to take over an increasing share of the market without rapidly displacing a large number of traditional operations. Today, LDCs of the world are characterized by a continuous increase in income and population density. This constitutes an ever present source of pressure on distributive institutions in LDCs to develop new forms of marketing institutions to meet the increasing wants and needs of shoppers. This, in turn, helps the economic development process. The interaction taking place between the distribution system of LDCs and the surrounding environment is shown in Figure 4.5.

New distributive institutions are subject to several limitations: the number of potential customers, their incomes, and their social and economic makeup, all of which influence the types of institutions operating in LDCs. Each of these sets a different limit on the number of units demanded from the new distributive institution. Likewise, the number of units that could be set up in a given part of an LDC is subject to a variety of limitations—available managerial talent, financial resources, initiative, and capital. These are considered to be input variables, each of which sets a different limit on the number of units that could be operated profitably. It should be noted that the growth of the new distributive institution is, to a certain extent, contingent on easing the most restrictive input stimuli. As in any other distributive system, there is change and development in the LDC distributive system. This necessitates changes in all aspects of the marketing environment (social, economic, cultural, and operational) as well as the distribution system's response to them. Of course, such environmental changes are, to a large extent, beyond the control of the distribution system. For that reason, such environmental conditions should be taken into consideration while designing a marketing system. Certain characteristics of LDC consumers serve as a constraint on the development of modern distributive institutions, and only when certain changes occur does it become possible for these institutions to develop and prosper.

PREDICTIONS OF THE PATTERNS OF CHANGE

A number of studies have tried to predict the development of distribution channels in free market economies. The most common study examined changes in the structure of evolving channels of distribution.[39] It is stated that the number of levels in the channel, which are more

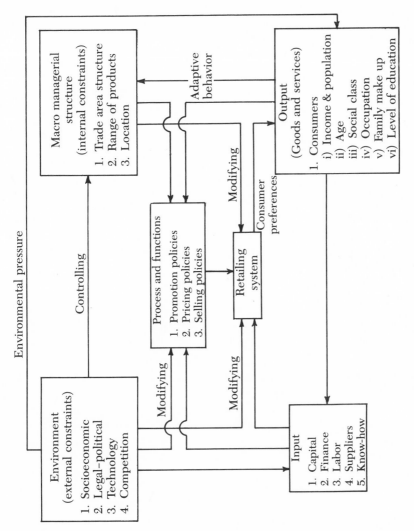

Source: Erdener Kaynak, "A Refined Approach to the Wheel of Retailing," *European Journal of Marketing* 13, no. 7 (1979): 242. Reprinted with permission.

numerous at the initial stages of the economic development process, tend to lessen with sophistication of the economy. Dannhaeuser contends that:

> the periodic market and itinerant peddler are replaced over time by the permanent marketplace which, in turn, loses its position as a market leader to the fragmented autonomous store system of distribution. The dominance of this type, finally, is displaced by that of the vertically integrated channel. This succession suggests another perspective of channel development. Here the nature of the contact points between the market levels receives attention. A line is drawn between those channels in which vertical coordination occurs via the price mechanism—each level is independent of the other—and the usually more recent one in which some type of vertical integration occurs. This may take the form of cross-level expansion of ownership or of contractual agreements, such as franchises.[40]

The channel modernization process takes different forms in different societies. For instance, in open economies with increased income and wealth the following channel modernization process takes place:

There is a steady reduction in the number of channel levels.
The internal organization of channel members loses its familistic idiom and becomes formalized along lines of modern management techniques.
Relations between trade units become depersonalized, standardized, and predictable.
Most important of all, vertical relations in the channel move from price mechanisms toward ownership and contractual control; vertical integration is increasingly resorted to.[41]

The evolution of marketing institutions in LDCs is a complex process that can be understood only by an analysis of the cultural, economic, and legal institutions that are presently at play. Unfortunately, very little is known about the evolution of marketing institutions in LDCs.[42] The premise of this proposition is that the structure of distribution systems is dependent on the characteristics of the societies these systems serve. That is, to some extent structural changes in distribution in an LDC may be due to changes in the economic, technological, social, and cultural environments of distributors. Moreover, there are differences in distributive structure among various environments within each LDC.

The findings of the empirical works undertaken by the author in a number of LDCs showed a distinct relationship between the main distributive functions performed, and institutional features and specific environmental forces within LDC markets. Certain patterns of distributive systems and institutions and their practices tend to correspond to the incidence and operations of certain factors occurring in the environment. The overall pattern is such that it looks as if these different envirnomental factors shape and set limits to the types of distributive institutions and practices that may exist within each LDC.

The environment contains certain operating conditions that limit the scope of the institutions' activity and affect their organizational structure. Factors such as income level, cultural attributes, consumer characteristics, and the structure of channels of distribution have a bearing on the market potential and thus the scale of the distributive institutions' operations (see Figure 4.6).

Modern distributive institutions and their operational methods can only be introduced when the forces in the environment permit. As long as the forces allow it, these institutions continue to exist. There cannot, then, be such a thing as the most appropriate or advanced distributive institutions and techniques, as what is most appropriate will vary from one economic system to another. A distributive system can be meaningfully "developed" or "underdeveloped," depending on whether the economic system in which it operates is developed or underdeveloped. If this is the case, the nature of the relationship can be stated in more specific terms than simply "developed" or "underdeveloped." If we can identify the stages of socioeconomic development, then we should be able to predict in general terms the kind of distribution pattern that is associated with given stages of economic development.[43] The effect of the environment on retail food distributors is shown in Figure 4.7.

FIGURE 4.6. Environmental Pressure on LDC Distribution Systems

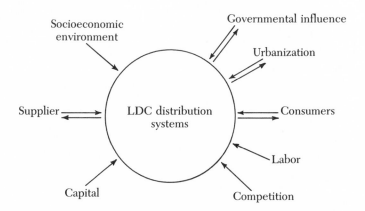

Source: Prepared by the author.

FIGURE 4.7. Systems Approach to Food Distribution

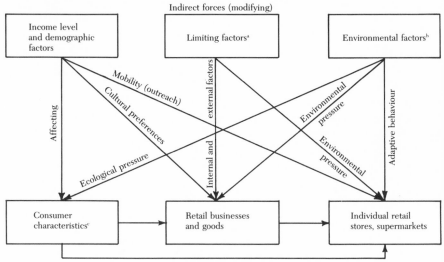

^aCapital, labor, financial resources, initiative, management talent, know-how, location, and site.

^bUrbanization, government, competition, suppliers, consumerism.

^cCulture, population makeup, income distribution, social class, family makeup, education.

Source: E. Kaynak, "Food Distribution Systems; Evolution in Latin America and the Middle East," *Food Policy* (May 1981): 87. Reprinted with permission.

Distributive institutions, methods, and techniques evolve with a changing social structure which in turn has evolving political, economic, and business components. Certain combinations of these produce specific social structures that create the need for certain distributive institutions and operational methods.[44] At respective points in the development of the LDC society, distributors are able and willing to offer a specific package of distributive institutions, methods, and techniques, and consumers are able and willing to accept that distributive package. LDCs with varying economic, political, social, and business conditions, have different societies, and therefore have different distributive systems. Even within the same LDC, regions with different combinations of conditions and therefore differing societies, have differing distribution systems. Thus, the distribution system changes with the environment.

It has been proposed by some that the environment dictates feasible changes in distribution systems and their operations.[45] The forces that shape the distributive environment are changes in the prevailing market

system and the evolution of socioeconomic and cultural conditions resulting from interactions between technology, sociopolitical setup, and the
available managerial talent with which goods are mobilized and allocated.

Several factors must be taken into consideration when assessing the
environment within which distributors of LDCs operate. Among these
factors are consumer-related impediments, the backward nature of the
supporting manufacturing industry, and the infrastructure as well as small
and inefficient distributive outlets. In order to be successful, distributive
institutions in LDCs must anticipate social, economic, and technological
trends as well as adapt to rapid and somewhat unpredictable changes in
the consumer market.

TRANSFER OF DISTRIBUTIVE TECHNOLOGY

The transfer of distributive institutions such as supermarkets from
developed to less-developed countries has been a topic of study for many
years. It was believed that the introduction of improved marketing institutions and methods would be an important element in the process of
economic development of less-developed countries.[46] Some scholars believe that advanced marketing techniques can be transferred from developed to less-developed economies on the premise that multinational
retailers can act as change agents in stimulating the spread of marketing
institutions and techniques.[47] These people believe that the small store is
an inefficient distributor and that retailing costs in developing countries
can be reduced significantly by fostering the appearance of large retail
stores. Consequently, many retail modernization programs in developing
countries are concerned with transforming the neighborhood stores into
large supermarkets.[48] Others believe that one should also take into account
the particular difficulties encountered when a marketing institution that
thrives in one economy is introduced into another society having quite
different economic and cultural characteristics.[49] Emerging nations un-
doubtedly can learn a great deal from developed countries whose marketing and distribution structures have had a longer period to develop.
None would deny, however, that less-developed economies have their own
special marketing needs and distribution focus. The conditions necessary
for successful operation of modern distributive institutions is simply
lacking in most of the less-developed countries.

It was postulated by Hollander that retailers from the richer nations
were urgently needed by the less-developed countries in order to offer
price and service competition to local middlemen, to stimulate local
production by helping to rationalize local sources of supply, and to make

new merchandise available as an incentive to indigenous labor.[50] Despite the marked spread of retailers and their innovative techniques across national boundaries in less-developed countries, one cannot overlook numerous instance of failures in such moves.[51]

The applicability or nonapplicability of foreign marketing innovations and know-how such as supermarketing and related marketing practices to less-developed countries is contingent on the conduciveness of environmental conditions. It is postulated here that the adoption of horizontal and vertical integration in retail distribution systems of less-developed countries may not achieve the desired results for the poorer consumers. An alternative approach (that is, strengthening and improvement of traditional retail systems) is a more appropriate course of action in those countries.

To overcome the deficiencies of the distribution systems in less-developed countries, the adoption of horizontal and vertical coordination and the introduction of modern, large-scale retail institutions into the distribution system of these countries has been recommended by some researchers.[52] Some people contend that the system should look more like the North American model. The criteria to support these normative models for less-developed countries are the improvements in transaction and market-structure productivity and efficiency that will come from the economies of large-scale distribution. These studies clearly recommend that large, modern, low-cost, multi-line, self-service supermarkets should be put into place alongside the traditional small, one- or two-person, single-line, high-cost shops.[53]

Studies have also indicated that the structure of a distribution system is a function of selected characteristics of the society it serves.[54] In North America, the retail innovations of this century are, to a large extent, a reflection of the changes in the retailers' environment. Retailing and marketing institutions are a function of the environmental factors of the period just past. Retailing practices may be said to be a function of the environmental factors of the same period. In less-developed countries of the world, the environmental factors affecting the operations of retailers are not the same as those in developed countries. For this reason, proper analysis of the different environmental conditions affecting any marketing institution and its operations need to be made before transferring any marketing technique or institution to less-developed countries of the world. The effect of environmental factors on distribution systems is shown in Figure 4.8.

Certain patterns of distribution systems and institutions and their practices tend to correspond with the incidence and operations of certain factors operating in the environment within which distributive institutions of all kinds are found. Such environmental conditions should be taken into

FIGURE 4.8. Environment–Food Retailing System Interface

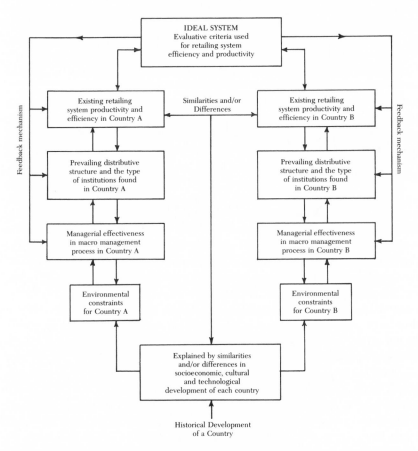

Source: Prepared by the author.

consideration and the necessary adaptations made when designing a distribution system for a less-developed country. Of all the environmental factors, the most significant is the consumer environment. Certain characteristics of the consumers of a less-developed country serve as a constraint on the development of modern distributive institutions such as supermarkets. Only when certain changes occur does it become possible for these institutions to develop and prosper.

When private enterprise introduces supermarkets in less-developed countries, it tends to place them in high-income areas simply because there is not enough buying power in low-income neighborhoods. Thus an institution which in North America caters adequately to the basic needs of the masses, becomes exclusive, bringing the benefits of mass marketing to those who least need them.[55] In most less-developed countries, there is not much concern on the part of the large food retail institutions operating in high-income areas with the needs and wants of consumers residing in lower-income areas.

The literature holds that a modern system of vertically integrated chains would provide substantial benefits through scale economies and self-service, and by bypassing clogged wholesale food markets.[56] It is difficult to transfer capital-intensive distributive techniques to less-developed countries with reasonable success. The United States, for example, has been an important nation for two centuries; it has abundant resources and expertise, and it received its human capital through immigration. Today, most of the less-developed countries, on the other hand, generally are short on resources and lack know-how. It is rather difficult to transfer U. S. marketing technology (supermarketing, which is a product of America's historical and economic conditions) to a completely dissimilar environment. For that reason, certain difficulties are inherent in transferring technology like supermarketing and horizontal integration from the United States to less-developed countries of the world.[57]

MANAGERIAL IMPLICATIONS

The method of organization and operational policies of distributive outlets and the spread of modern institutions in developed and less-developed countries show distinct differences. It is of the utmost importance to have some knowledge of the varying characteristics of modern distributive institutions operating in LDCs in relation to their changing socioeconomic environments.[58] The factors that affect modern distributive institutions and their operational methods in different environments and the underlying reasons for their appearance have been examined.

The examination of the distribution system in LDCs suggests that there are already innovative distributors attempting to achieve desired changes in the system. This attempt at change, although in its infancy in most LDCs, is occurring spontaneously.[59] It is reasonable, however, to expect that the more developed areas in these countries will undergo a more rapid process of modernization than the less-developed regions. The widespread diffusion of such modernization, then, becomes a major challenge for public policymakers in the less-developed countries.[60]

Small-scale distributive operations usually prevail at every stage of the production and distribution process in most LDC environments. At each stage, the result has been a proliferation of middlemen, each depending on high margins to offset low turnover. There has been little or no integration of the manufacturing and distribution functions, by which economies of larger-scale distribution might be realized and unduly long marketing channels eliminated. The scarcity of entrepreneurial ability and longer-term credit in distribution channels, outdated tax laws, and inadequate government regulation still inhibit the growth of distribution systems in most LDCs.[61]

The best way to design a distribution system in an LDC will be through modifying the existing distributive institutions. Existing public markets can be expected to play a useful part, especially in the less-developed regions of LDCs, but their importance will increasingly be confined to dealing in foodstuffs, such as fresh fruit and vegetables. The prospects of small distributors are quite different. The existing small distributors in LDCs cannot achieve the large volume of sales created by a program of reducing prices to generate more volume to enable further price reductions. The reason for this is that these stores are perceived as charging high prices, offering low-quality goods, and having no desirable attributes other than location convenience, the friendliness of the store personnel, and the offer of some credit facilities.[62]

There is ample opportunity for improvement in the distribution systems of LDCs. This may take three forms. The first is related to improvement in the physical appearance of marketplaces. The second is connected with improvements in distribution and marketing facilities, and the third is connected to the establishment of marketing extension services by government and semi-government agencies.[63]

Improvement in Physical Structure of Marketplaces

Some of the existing wholesale market areas need rebuilding in order to improve layout and physical appearance. Expansion of the market area is necessary to prevent overcrowding and congestion, which inhibit the free movement of buyers and sellers. There is also an increased need for storerooms in the market area in order to reduce the loss from physical damage, deterioration, and spoilage resulting from frequent handling and exposure to heat. How this can be realized in a vast majority of LDCs is discussed by Mittendorf.[64]

Marketing Facilities

The importance of adequate storage facilities to orderly distribution is questionable. If products could be stored safely, supplies would become steadier and product prices would tend to fluctuate less. The use of suitable containers is essential to the maintenance of the quality of most products. Thus it is necessary to encourage local industry in the manufacturing of tin, metal, and wood containers used in product packaging. Lack of suitable packaging materials has been responsible for loss of products at each level of the channels of distribution. The manner in which products are handled in distribution affects the maintenance of certain quality levels.

Some marketing services in LDCs can best be performed by the state, such as the establishment of grades and standards for products. One important limiting factor to the introduction of weights and measures is that most of the shoppers are illiterate. Second, most shoppers buy in very small quantities and weights, usually less than the weighted, prepackaged amount. For these reasons there may be opposition from some shoppers to the compulsory use of weights and measures in distribution.

One important means by which a reduction in marketing cost can be effected is to increase the scale of traders' business to an economic size. Many traders in the distribution system are too small to make optimum use of labor and equipment. Uneconomic, small-scale business tends to increase the per unit cost of distributing a commodity. It also leads to underutilization of equipment. The solution to this problem is the availability of credit facilities on such terms that channel members would be willing to borrow to expand their business.

Marketing Extension Services

Very few less-developed countries have a separate public organization for extension services in marketing. However, some extension is carried out within certain semiofficial organizations. There is a need for centralized responsibility in marketing extension work within government departments to deal specifically with distribution and marketing advisory, extension, and research work. A department of this nature in an LDC will serve a very useful purpose and will also facilitate the economic development process. The functions of a government marketing extension services department may be summarized as follows:

a. To conduct research and disseminate information on improvement of processing, preservation, storage, packaging, handling, and merchandizing of different products.

b. To provide and disseminate adequate market information that will enable the producer to make better decisions on what and when to manufacture, and where and how to sell it; to permit the middlemen or traders to make the right decision as to where and when to sell and to adjust their trading business to changes in supply of the products in which they deal.

c. To help expand markets for products through communication media; and to publish and distribute pamphlets and prepare programs to educate the public about the quality and availability of products.

d. To help to establish weights and measures, grades and standards, and the high level of sanitation required in the handling of food products.

CONCLUSIONS

With the background information obtained both by undertaking a comprehensive review of published material on distribution in LDCs and conducting empirical works in a number of less-developed countries of the third world, it is concluded that distribution needs vary among different LDCs at varying stages of economic development, even though they have certain common problems to tackle. These needs follow below.

How to Organize Total Distribution Systems

In LDCs policies are needed to ensure the orderly marketing of increased production as well as current short supplies of products. The total marketing system should be in a position to channel the present and increased production without depressing prices. An efficient marketing system in these countries would also require grades and standards, and price differentials for quality differences. Sufficient information and opportunity must be available for intermediaries to make appropriate marketing decisions. Increased and efficient commercial marketing of different products in LDCs will require new initiatives by governments of these countries and cooperation from the market participants. In many LDCs, marketing boards have been instituted as market-stabilizing agencies for particular commodities that are in short supply.[65] It will be very useful to find out how effective they have been. Their performance at different stages of economic development also needs to be delineated.

In LDCs the distribution problem is acute for a high proportion of the population. To overcome this problem, commercial distribution channels need to be supplemented by state-owned distributive outlets.[66] Although an improved distribution system for both the rural and urban populations ultimately depends on high education, increased productivity, and higher incomes, interim measures are needed. These measures could easily be instituted by marketing people. There is also an urgent need for active cooperation between the state and the private channel intermediaries.

Reducing the Losses in Moving Commodities
from Producer to the Ultimate Consumer

Losses (especially in food products) caused by inadequate storage and transportation contribute to food deficits in LDCs. As more foods are produced and moved to market for expanding urban populations, losses become larger. Another aspect of the problem is the food-marketing cost and efficiency in the physical handling of foodstuffs. There is no merit in substituting a capital-intensive operation for a labor-intensive one in most LDCs. An effort on the part of LDC public policy officials is needed to control and prevent large amounts of losses and spoilage.

Increasing the Processing and Preserving of Food

Processing is an important means of avoiding waste; it simplifies transportation of food products and spreads the period of consumption over a period of time. Hence, processing and preserving activities serve as a focal point for improvements in both supply and distribution channels.

Because of the problems associated with the large numbers of small suppliers that characterize LDCs, economies of scale in processing may not be realized, as small operations requiring less capital are quite suitable for the needs of these countries.

Desired Social and Behavioral Changes

There is a great waste of human resources in distribution systems in LDCs that are characterized by itinerant retailers, market stalls, and small retailers with small sales volumes. Changes in the distribution system must take these small traditional retailers into account, otherwise they will resist the ongoing change.

Social customs, individual attitudes, education, business institutions, methods of communication, and government influences and control differ markedly between the developed countries of the West and the less-developed countries. Modern distributive institutions and techniques cannot directly be transferred successfully to the LDCs without due regard for the different environmental factors. Even so, changes in distributive techniques and systems in the LDCs must be more gradual if they are to be successful.

Any distribution technology that is transplanted from one cultural and economic milieu to another would likely require local adaptation and change. Modern distributive methods are almost exclusively of a U.S. or West European origin, and their transfer to an underdeveloped environment encounters several serious barriers. Modern distribution methods provide improvements in productivity that can lead to improved marketing efficiency. It would seem, therefore, that improvements in distribution systems in LDCs can result from the increased use of modern distribution methods. Certainly many sparsely populated and low income urban areas can most efficiently be served by many small distributive outlets; but present large store operations can be extended to a large number of low-income, heavily populated, less-developed regions.

NOTES

1. Kemal Kurtulus, "The Present Status of Marketing Channels in Turkey," *Management International Review* 20, no. 4 (1980): 38–52.

2. E. Kaynak and R. Savitt, *Comparative Marketing Systems* (New York: Praeger, 1984).

3. Jean Boddewyn, "The Comparative Approach to the Study of Business Administration," *Academy of Management Journal* 8 (December 1965).

4. Erdener Kaynak, "Future Directions for Research in Comparative Marketing," *The Canadian Marketer* 11, no. 1 (1980): 23–28.

5. J. J. Boddewyn, "Comparative Marketing: Thirty Years Later," *Journal of International Business Studies* (Spring/Summer 1981): 70–71.

6. E. W. Cundiff, "Concepts in Comparative Retailing," *Journal of Marketing* 29 (January 1961): 59–63; G. Wadinambiaratchi, "Channels of Distribution in Developing Economies," *Business Quarterly* 30 (Winter 1965): 74–82.

7. Ibid.

8. Susan P. Douglas, "Patterns and Parallels of Marketing Structures in Several Countries," *MSU Business Topics* 19, no. 2 (Spring 1971): 38–48.

9. J. Arndt, "Temporal Lags in Comparative Retailing," *Journal of Marketing* (October 1972): 40–45.

10. A. Goldman, "Outreach of Consumers and the Modernization of Urban Food Retailing in Developing Countries," *Journal of Marketing* (October 1974): 8–16.

11. P. L. Oritt and A. J. Hagan, "Channels of Distribution and Economic Development," *Atlanta Economic Review* 27, no. 4 (July–August 1977): 40–44.

12. Hans J. Mittendorf, "The Challenge of Organizing City Food Marketing Systems in Developing Countries," *Zeitschrift für auslandische Landwirtschaft* 17, no. 4 (October–December 1978): 323–41.

13. Stanley J. Shapiro, "Comparative Marketing and Economic Development," in *Science in Marketing*, edited by George Schwartz (New York: John Wiley & Sons, 1965), pp. 398–429.

14. R. J. Holloway and R. S. Hancock, *Marketing in a Changing Environment* (New York: John Wiley & Sons, 1968), pp. 403–20.

15. E. J. McCarthy, "Effective Marketing Institutions for Economic Development," in *Toward Scientific Marketing*, edited by S. Greyser (Chicago, IL: American Marketing Association, 1964), p. 393.

16. Ibid., pp. 401–404.

17. N. R. Collins and R. H. Holton, "Programming Changes in Marketing in Planned Economic Development," *Kyklos* vol. 16, no. 1 (January 1963): 124; and McCarthy, "Effective Marketing," p. 146.

18. L. G. Erickson, "Analyzing Brazilian Consumer Markets," *MSU Business Topics* (Summer 1963): 13.

19. Wadinambiaratchi, "Channels of Distribution," p. 77.

20. J. H. Baeke, *Economics and Economic Policy of Dual Societies* (New York: Institute of Pacific Relations, 1953), pp. 3–5. Baeke calls this phenomenon "social dualism" (two socioeconomic, cultural, and consumption styles existing together in one nation). The two societies do not interact with each other and are separated by certain transitional forms.

21. E. Kaynak, "Food Retailing Systems in Developing Countries—The Case of Turkey," *Hacettepe Bulletin of Social Sciences and Humanities* 8, no. 1–2 (June–December 1976): 37–51.

22. N. Dannhaeuser, "The Role of the Neighborhood Store in Developing Economies: The Case of Dagupan City, Philippines," *The Journal of Developing Areas* 14 (January 1980): 157.

23. Arieh Goldman, *Developments and Change in Retail Systems*, Ph.D. thesis, University of California, Berkeley, 1970.

24. William H. Cunningham, R. M. Moore, and I. C. M. Cunningham, "Urban Markets in Industrializing Countries: The São Paulo Experience," *Journal of Marketing* 38 (April 1974): 2–12.

25. Joseph R. Guerin, "The Introduction of a New Food Marketing Institution in an Underdeveloped Economy: Supermarkets in Spain," *Food Research Institute Studies* 5, no. 3 (1965): 217–27.

26. Dov Izraeli, "Priorities for Research and Development in Marketing Systems for Developing Countries," Working Paper no. 209/274, April 1974, Tel Aviv University.

27. J. M. Carmen and R. M. March, "How Important for Marketing are Cultural Differences Between Similar Nations?" *Australian Marketing Researcher* 3, no. 1 (Summer 1979): 5–20; H. Hakason and B. Wootz, "Supplier Selection in an International Environment," *Journal of Marketing Research* (February 1975): 46–51.

28. Robert Green and Eric Langeard, "A Cross-National Comparison of Consumer Habits and Innovation Characteristics," *Journal of Marketing* (July 1975): 34–41; G. Harris, R. Still, and M. Crask, "A Comparison of Australian and U.S. Marketing Strategies," *Columbia Journal of World Business* (Summer 1978): 87–94; R. Hoover, R. Green, and J Saegert, "A Cross-National Study of Perceived Risk," *Journal of Marketing* (July 1978): 102–108.

29. Stanley C. Hollander, "Retailing: Cause or Effect?" in *Emerging Concepts in Marketing*, proceedings of the Winter Conference of the AMA, Chicago, 1963, edited by William S. Decker, p. 222.

30. Malcolm McNair, "Significant Trends and Developments in the Post War Period," in *Competitive Distribution in a Free High-Level Economy and Its Implications for the University*, edited by A. B. Smith (Pittsburgh, PA: University of Pittsburgh Press, 1965), pp. 1–25.

31. Robert Bartles, *Comparative Marketing: Wholesaling in Fifteen Countries* (Chicago, IL: Richard D. Irwin, 1963), pp. 1–6.

32. George Wadinambiaratchi, "Channels of Distribution in Developing Economies," *The Business Quarterly* 30 (Winter 1965): 74–82.

33. Douglas, "Patterns and Parallels."

34. Ibid., pp. 38–39.

35. E. M. Rogers, *Modernization Among Peasants: The Impact of Communication* (New York: Holt, Rinehart and Winston, 1969).

36. K. Harrison, *Development, Unemployment, and Marketing in Latin America*, Occasional Paper no. 2, Department of Agricultural Economics, Michigan State University, April 1972, p. 16.

37. D. S. Henley, "Marketing and Economic Integration in Developing Countries," in

Markets and Marketing in Developing Economies, edited by R. Moyer and S. C. Hollander (Chicago, IL: Richard D. Irwin, 1968), pp. 70-86.

38. Ibid., p. 21.

39. J. P. Gultinan, "Planned And Evolutionary Changes in Distribution Channels," *Journal of Retailing* 50 (1974): 79-91.

40. N. Dannhaeuser, "Evolution and Devolution of Downward Channel Integration in the Philippines," *Economic Development and Cultural Change*, 29, no. 3 (April 1981): 577.

41. Ibid., p. 578.

42. Erdener Kaynak, "A Refined Approach to the Wheel of Retailing," *European Journal of Marketing* 13, no. 7 (1979): 237-45; Dole A. Anderson, *Marketing Development—The Thailand Experience*, MSU International Business and Economic Studies, East Lansing, 1970, pp. 69-73.

43. G. Wadinambiaratchi, "Theories of Retail Development," *Social and Economic Studies* 4 (December 1972): 391-403.

44. F. Meissner,"Rise of Third World Demands Marketing be Stood on Its Head," *Marketing News*, October 6, 1978, p. 1.

45. Erdener Kaynak,"The Introduction of a Modern Food Retailing Institution to Less-Developed Economies: Problems and Opportunities," in *Marketing Channels: Domestic and International Perspectives*, edited by Michael G. Harvey and Robert F. Lusch (Norman, OK: University of Oklahoma, 1982), pp. 52-58.

46. Joseph R. Guerin, "The Introduction of a New Food Marketing Institution in an Underdeveloped Economy: Supermarkets in Spain," *Food Research Institute Studies* 5, no. 3 (1965): 217-27; and Charles C. Slater, "Market Channel Coordination and Economic Development," in *Vertical Marketing Systems*, edited by Louis P. Bucklin (Glenview, IL: Scott, Foresman & Co., 1970), pp. 141-42.

47. Hans B. Thorelli, "The Multinational Corporation as a Change Agent," *The Southern Journal of Business* 1, no. 3 (July 1966): 1-9; Arieh Goldman, "Stages in the Development of the Supermarket," *Journal of Retailing* (Winter 1975-1976): 202.

48. Arieh Goldman, "Growth of Large Food Stores in Developing Countries," *Journal of Retailing* 50, no. 2 (Summer 1974): 50.

49. Arieh Goldman, "Outreach of Consumers and the Modernization of Urban Food Retailing in Developing Countries," *Journal of Marketing* 38 (October 1974): 8-16; Louis P. Bucklin, "Improving Food Retailing in Developing Asian Countries," *Food Policy* (May 1977): 114-22.

50. Hollander, "Retailing: Cause or Effect?"

51. R. White, "Multinational Retailing: A Slow Advance?" *Retail and Distribution Management* 12, no. 2 (March-April 1984): 8-13; and William Applebaum, "Migros-Turk: A Case Study" (Boston, MA: Harvard Business School, 1975); and Mehmet Oluc, "Migros-Turk," *Journal of the Faculty of Economics* (Istanbul University, 1955-1956), pp. 231-49.

52. Harry A. Lipton, "The Impact of Double Digit Inflation upon the Modernization of the Retail Structure in Developed and Developing Economies," in *1975 Combined Proceedings*, edited by Edward M. Mazze, American Marketing Association series no. 37, 1976, p. 315.

53. David Appel, "The Supermarket: Early Development of an Institutional Innovation," *Journal of Retailing* 48 (Spring 1972): 39-52.

54. A. Graeme Cranch, "Modern Marketing Techniques Applied to Developing Countries," in *Marketing Education and the Real World and Dynamic Marketing in a Changing World*, edited by Boris W. Beeker, American Marketing Association, series no. 34, 1973, p. 183.

55. Meissner, "Rise of Third World," p. 1. See note 44.

56. Louis P. Bucklin, "Improving Food Retailing," p. 115. See note 49.

57. Dov Izraeli, "Priorities for Research and Development in Marketing Systems for Developing Countries," Working Paper no. 209/274, Tel Aviv University, Tel Aviv, April 1974, p. 9.

58. E. Kaynak, "Comparative Analysis of the Socio-Economic, Cultural and Regulatory Environments of Distributors in LDCs," *Singapore Management Review* 7, no. 1 (January 1985): 65-76.

59. Erdener Kaynak, "Food Distribution Systems: Evolution in Latin America and the Middle East," *Food Policy* 6, no. 2 (May 1981): 78-90.

60. Erdener Kaynak, "Government and Food Distribution in LDCs: The Turkish Experience," *Food Policy* 5, no. 2 (May 1980): 132-42.

61. Ugur Yavas, Erdener Kaynak, and E. Borak, "Food Shopping Orientations in an LDC; Some Lessons for Policy Makers," *Food Policy* 7, no. 2 (May 1982): 133-40.

62. Erdener Kaynak, "Shopping Practices for Food: Some Cross-Cultural Comparisons," in *Buyer Behavior*, edited by Michael J. Baker (Glasgow, Scotland: 1976, University of Strathclyde), pp. 107-41.

63. Kaynak, "Comparative Analysis," pp. 72-73. See note 58.

64. Hans J. Mittendorf, "Improvement of Wholesale Markets in Developing Countries," *International Fruit World* 2 (1981): 106-27.

65. Erza Sadan, "Use of Marketing Boards in Developed and Developing Countries," in *Agricultural Marketing for Developing Countries*, edited by D. Izraeli, D. N. Izraeli, and F. Meissner (New York: Halsted Press, 1976), pp. 65-75.

66. Vieka Linde, *Marketing in Developing Countries*, Marknadsventenskap, Göteborg, Sweden, 1980.

5
Consumerism and
Economic Development

INTRODUCTION

Consumerism is defined as a movement that seeks to increase the rights and powers of buyers in relation to sellers. So far, consumerism in developed Western countries, including the United States, Canada, France, Britain, Japan, and Sweden, has been concerned with such wide-ranging issues as the need for consumer choice, product/service information, consumer protection, and after-sales service and warranty.[1] Recent consumerism studies have primarily been descriptive. With the exception of one, none have attempted to develop a theoretical framework with solid historical antecedents for this social movement.[2]

Until now, very little attention has been devoted to consumerism issues in developing countries where the activity is still in its infancy or at an early stage of growth. In the future, an increasing amount of our trade will be conducted with developing countries. Government policymakers, consumer behavior researchers, and the business community must all be aware of and concerned about the growth of consumerism in these countries and its economic and social ramifications.[3]

In recent years, world markets have become more complex due to an increasing number and variety of products and services offered, and the changing magnitude and demands of consumers. This situation provides ideal conditions for the development of more systematic approaches for

An earlier version of this chapter appeared in Erdener Kaynak, "Some Thoughts of Consumerism in Developed and Less Developed Countries," *International Marketing Review*, vol. 2, no. 2 (Summer, 1985), pp. 15–30.

forecasting consumer demand in world markets. So far, marketers have found it difficult to come up with valid operational guidelines for consumer behavior in different socioeconomic and cultural environments. One can assume some differences in consumer demand patterns in different countries of the world because of the variances in their stages of economic development. As a result, one would expect different levels of consumerism activity.

Most of the marketing literature treats consumerism as a phenomenon that occurs only in developed countries. Consumerism in LDC environments has not been analyzed or discussed in much of the current literature. The reason for this void is the lack of an appropriate conceptual and methodological framework from which to study consumerism issues across nations and cultures. What is needed is a conceptualization of consumerism, with a comparison of relevant issues on an international basis. This is essential for model-building purposes. How do countries with different economic systems and different attitudes toward consumerism compare in both the frequency of consumer problems and the effectiveness of formal/ informal complaint-handling systems? Clearly, the answers to these questions are necessary if government regulators, consumers, marketing professionals, and consumer protection agencies are to develop policies to improve the functioning of market systems from the consumer's perspective, both within and across national and geopolitical boundaries.[4]

The purpose of this chapter is to develop conceptual frameworks and working propositions from which to study consumerism in multiple environments. Consumerism issues in developed versus LDC environments will be discussed and the implications for international trade and marketing elucidated. The influences that various socioeconomic, governmental, technological, and cultural environments have on consumerism at various times and in different places will be examined. In addition, the chapter will look at the influences that consumerism, in turn, exerts on its environments. The relative strength of these two influences (environment on consumerism and consumerism on environment) will then be evaluated.[5]

HISTORICAL PERSPECTIVES TO CONSUMERISM

Consumers first felt the need to unite more than two centuries ago, and in 1769 the first consumer cooperative society was formed in Scotland. This was followed in 1844 by a group of cooperative pioneers in Rochdale, who laid down certain general principles and policies that have survived until the present.[6] Much has happened since then, and today a new movement, consumerism, is spreading throughout the world, changing the rules for marketing and market systems in both developed and less-developed countries. From 1970 onward, the interest in consumerism on the part of consumer groups, business, government, and researchers has shown a tremendous growth due to the increased power of the consumer.[7]

Consumerism in this century has largely been viewed as an activity precipitated by excessive business power in buyer–seller relationships. It is believed that this traditional view of consumerism is declining, and a new consumerism is developing. This new consumerism attempts to reconcile traditional ideology with an evolving marketing environment.[8] Table 5.1 summarizes the main characteristics of traditional consumerism while presenting corresponding alternatives that incorporate the new trends in consumerism.

There are indications that consumerism, like other movements and innovations, develops along a particular life cycle. The following four

TABLE 5.1. Traditional versus Contemporary Consumerism

Traditional consumerism	New consumerism
Primarily concerned with conflicts of interest between consumers and business	Concerned with conflicts of interest between consumers and any other economic system participant, including business, government, unions, professional groups, and farmers
Primarily concerned with noneconomic issues (such as product safety and quality of health care) as opposed to economic issues (such as taxes and inflation)	Concerned with both noneconomic and economic issues depending on their relative importance at a given point in time
Emphasizes benefit rights (i.e., protection) approaches to consumer problems as opposed to opportunity rights (i.e., choice) approaches	Recognizes the advantages and disadvantages of both benefit and opportunity rights approaches depending on the issue and the groups affected
Views supporters of consumerism as a monolithic group	Views support for the movement as coming from groups with overlapping yet distinguishable approaches, some of which have not been encompassed by the traditional ideology

Source: R. J. Kroll and R. W. Stampfl, "The New Consumerism," in *Proceedings of the 27th Annual Conference of the American Council on Consumer Interests*, Minneapolis, Minnesota, April 8–11, 1981, edited by C. B. Meeks, p. 100. Reprinted with permission.

distinct stages have been identified: crystallization, organization, institutionalization, and conceptualization.[9] It is possible to position the various nations of the world on the life cycle by examining the extent of consumer information, protection legislation and public funding of consumer education programs, and the availability of consumer protection and government consumer agencies.[10] In addition to the existence of legislation, consumerism is manifested by an awareness by consumers of their rights and problems, and by public debate about such matters (see Figure 5.1).

Specific characteristics of each stage in the life cycle of consumerism activity are shown below:

Stage I (crystalization). At this initial stage the emphasis is on regulating the producer so as to foster competition. There is a high degree of market regulation, but no organized consumer movement of national status per se.

Stage II (organization). During this stage the consumer movement begins to organize itself in order to provide a consumer voice in legislation. In developed countries of the West, independent, voluntary consumer associations are formed. A good deal of emphasis is placed on: consumer education programs, comparative product testing, standard sizes, and informative labeling. Less-developed countries will likely reach for more aggressive forms of protection at this stage.

Stage III (institutionalization). Governments both at the local and central levels begin to intervene actively in markets on behalf of the consumer. Policies with regard to consumer affairs; competition; and trade marks, patents, copyrights and industrial property are established and used as blueprints.

Stage IV (conceptualization). This stage embraces consumer involvement in virtually all of the critical political, technological, social, and economic macro issues. There is complete consumer involvement with the broader policy issues affecting the masses rather than involvement only with traditional micro concerns. This critical stage of development has so far been attained by just nine countries.

Canada, the United States, and Sweden are believed to be the present forerunners in the consumerism movement as they have already reached the conceptualization stage. Canada, like other countries at the same stage of development, has a long history of consumer cooperatives, labor unions, and political organizations as well as voluntary consumer associations. Turkey is an example of a progressive developing country believed to be in the institutionalization stage of consumerism.[11] Venezuela lags considerably behind Turkey and is placed at the organizational stage. In the 1970s, the Venezuelan government through its regulatory activities was able to

FIGURE 5.1. Consumerism Stages in World Markets

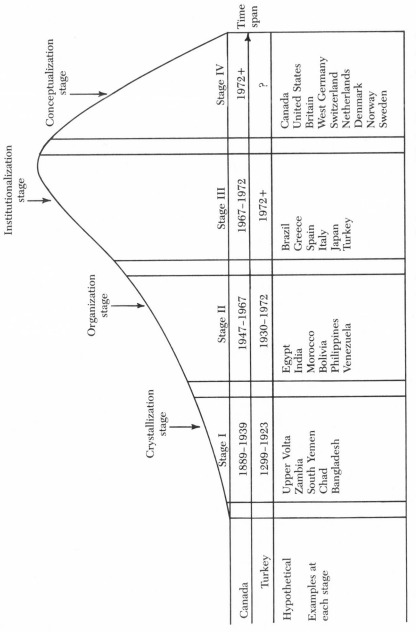

	Stage I	Stage II	Stage III	Stage IV	Time span
Canada	1889–1939	1947–1967	1967–1972	1972+	
Turkey	1299–1923	1930–1972	1972+	?	
Hypothetical					
Examples at each stage	Upper Volta Zambia South Yemen Chad Bangladesh	Egypt India Morocco Bolivia Philippines Venezuela	Brazil Greece Spain Italy Japan Turkey	Canada United States Britain West Germany Switzerland Netherlands Denmark Norway Sweden	

Crystallization stage · Organization stage · Institutionalization stage · Conceptualization stage

Source: Adapted from E. Patrick McGuire, *Consumer Protection: Implications for International Trade.* (Ottawa: The Conference Board of Canada, 1980).

133

dampen the effects of inflation through the use of price controls.[12] Whether at stage I or stage IV, countries have to deal with micro- as well as macro-level consumerism issues, in the short and long runs. These issues will be dealt with later on in the chapter.

Figure 5.1, which examines how far consumerism has evolved in different economic environments, is a useful managerial and public policy planning tool. Knowledge of the different stages of consumerism development is crucial in planning future corporate strategies.[13]

What happens to consumerism activity after stage IV? Does it stop? When the cycle completes its turn, it goes back to stage I and a new cycle may begin. This is the case now in Sweden, for instance, where there is a high degree of government involvement in regulating the market for the well-being of citizens.

The concept of the consumer protection life cycle is an analytical tool that emphasises the movement from micro to macro issues, as will be shown later. However, consumerism as a social issue apparently goes through alternating periods of high and low activity. It is generally believed that three such sequences have already occurred in North America during the twentieth century. The relevant role of these cycles and the impact that the existence of consumer protection agencies might have in altering this pattern would appear to be a point deserving empirical analysis.

CONSUMER ISSUES

One definition of consumerism for any country is "the organized efforts of consumers seeking redress, restitution and remedy for dissatisfaction they have accumulated in the acquisition of their standard of living."[14] The problem, at least partially, stems from the fact that all consumers cannot be informed about all aspects of their complex markets and the marketing practices of companies. Thus, there is a need for outside agencies to undertake certain consumer protection activities. This protection may take place against clear-cut abuses such as fraud, deceit, or unsafe practices or products. Or it may take place in cases where consumers cannot make informed decisions due to lack of information. Finally, protection may be offered to those who cannot protect themselves—less-privileged citizens. Thus, one of the first things that marketing is likely to do in the way of helping consumerism activity and consumerists is to provide more information and more protection for the consumer at large.

The second area of consideration is protection of ecology. The concept of ecology implies the science of survival. The ecological problems in marketing stem perhaps from an over-emphasis on the short-run micro concepts of need satisfaction and profit generation. When the marketing practitioner brings about the production of goods and services to satisfy the immediate needs of consumers and stimulates unnecessary consumption, he is primarily short-run oriented. He is, therefore, not trying to satisfy consumer needs in the long run and hence improve the long-range survival and growth objective of his company. In such a situation there are no checks and balances against pollution or careless and unbalanced use of scarce resources. If today's marketing practitioner does not do something about air, soil, and water pollution and the better utilization of scarce resources, then indeed in the long run our scarce resources will be depleted.

Thus, a major task confronting consumerists is to cope with ecological problems in order to ensure survival in the long run. Marketing, therefore, is given not only the task of making the right product available at the right time, place, and price, but it is also commissioned to care for the ecological balance, without which societies cannot survive and prosper. This will, in turn, help the economic development of a country.

For those countries at the initial stages of consumerism development the major concern has always been poverty. Since poverty is inversely related to effective demand or ability to buy, and since the vitality of the marketing sector is determined by demand, poverty has a significant and direct bearing on marketing. According to some broadly defined criteria some 20 percent of all U.S. residents are relatively poor and acquire less than adequate food and other necessary goods and services.[15] "They (the poor) represent not only a loss of human resources but also a loss of markets and profits."[16] There are, furthermore, other inequalities that exist in the markets of developed countries. For instance, the poor pay more for the same goods and services than their well-to-do counterparts who reside in wealthier neighborhoods.[17] This is a net loss in the incomes of those who can least afford such a loss. The role of consumerism in income distribution is undeniable. In the future this role will somehow have to be reversed. As a more equitable distribution of income will be acheived by this reversal process, consumerism in developed countries will benefit consumers by granting them increased purchasing power. Consumerists in developed countries will also see to it that more and more people can buy more of everything, aiding the reversal of the price discrimination process. In the poorer regions of developed societies goods and services will have to be priced within the ranges that the poor can afford.

In the United States, consumerism cuts across traditional social and political boundaries. Consumerism in the 1980s will provide a format for U.S. public affairs agendas in the years to come. A comparative study conducted in the United States shows that consumers in the 1980s are more concerned about certain consumer problems than they were in 1976, and believe there has been a decline in several aspects of the marketplace. As well, consumers believe that certain marketplace improvements have taken place for the benefit of consumers at large.[18] American consumer worries in 1976 versus 1982 are shown in Figure 5.2.

RECENT DEVELOPMENTS

Less-developed countries are reaching the point where various private and public corporations play major roles in the economy but, in

FIGURE 5.2. American Consumer Worries, 1982 versus 1976

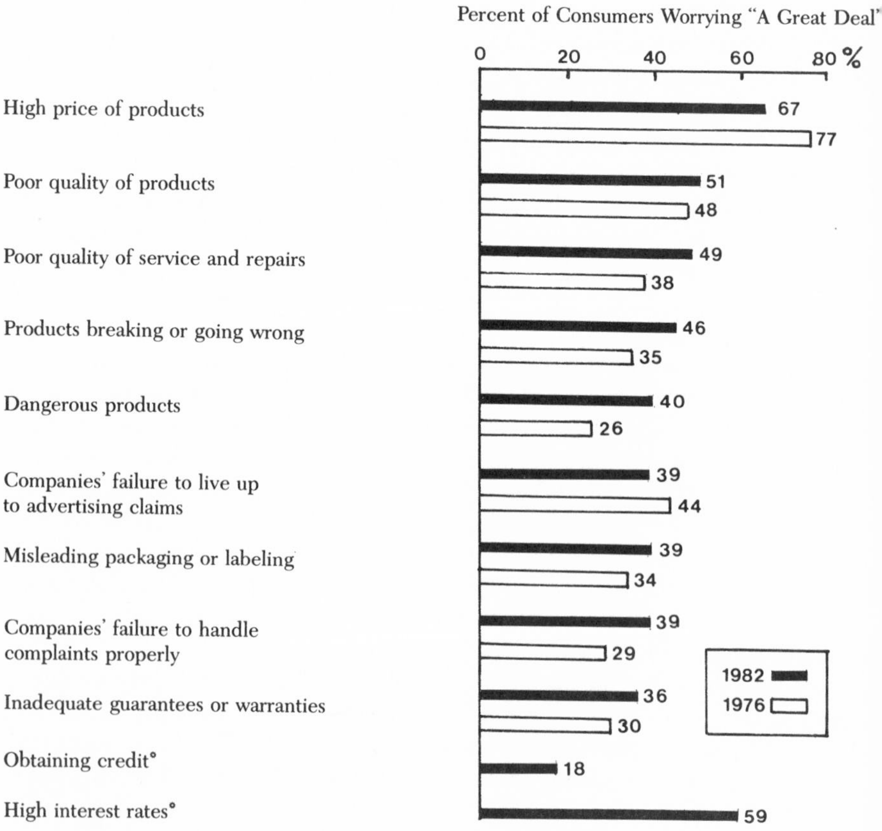

Percent of Consumers Worrying "A Great Deal"

| | 0 | 20 | 40 | 60 | 80 % |

High price of products — 67 / 77

Poor quality of products — 51 / 48

Poor quality of service and repairs — 49 / 38

Products breaking or going wrong — 46 / 35

Dangerous products — 40 / 26

Companies' failure to live up to advertising claims — 39 / 44

Misleading packaging or labeling — 39 / 34

Companies' failure to handle complaints properly — 39 / 29

Inadequate guarantees or warranties — 36 / 30

1982 ■ 1976 □

Obtaining credit° — 18

High interest rates° — 59

°Obtaining Credit (18 percent) and High Interest Rates (59 percent). Asked in 1982 but not in 1976.

Source: Consumerism in the 1980s poll of 1,252 adults, October 15–26, 1982, conducted by Louis Harris and Associates, sponsored by ARCO. Reprinted in M. Evers, "Consumerism in the Eighties," *Public Relations Journal* 39, no. 8 (August 1983): 26. Reprinted with permission.

essence, no consideration has been given to the protection of consumers. The proliferation of goods and services produced for these markets has brought about an urgent need for the protection of consumers. In this respect, there have been limited and uncoordinated efforts. In recent years there has been some enthusiasm for the study of consumer complaints but only on a piecemeal basis. It is thought that certain preventative measures need to be taken by both government and private organizations in LDCs. For this purpose, some less-developed countries have considered voluntary consumer protection associations. Factors leading to the rise of consumerism in LDCs are shown in Figure 5.3.

The development of consumerism in any country can be traced to changes in the macroeconomic environment. Paradoxically, modern consumerism is found only in the affluent countries. It finds its roots mostly with middle- or upper-income consumers.[19]

Differences in consumption patterns of consumers are caused by a variety of factors. Macro-level variations in culture, income levels, and government programs as well as micro-level variations in price levels, credit availability, expected incomes, and degree of exposure to consumption habits of other countries create consumption differences across cultures. As the movement from poverty to wealth takes place, there is a general evolution of consumer spending patterns. Consumers with a certain level of income and education demonstrate similar spending patterns and behavioral traits around the world.

Weber and Shipchandler hypothesize that wealthier consumers the world over are very much alike in their spending and shopping behavior, as are poorer people.[20] We can purposefully state that consumerism activity will show corresponding similarity among nations of equal economic development. There may also be a relationship between the level of consumer income (worldwide) and the intensity of demand for particular goods and services. This is to say that the worldwide demand preferences of households at different income levels for different goods and services should show dissimilarities. For instance, a household living on a bare subsistence income would spend its first incremental income on items of basic necessity. As the household income rises so does the type, quantity, and variety of purchases (see Table 5.2). We can conclude by saying that consumers at certain income levels would have the same demand preferences for goods and services regardless of the country of residence.

LDCs at the development (or takeoff) stage have structural characteristics that permit or create the potential for consumerism activity: advances in income and education, growth of technology, exploitation of the environment, and disparities between the quality of local and exported products.[21] The existence of these elements, in most cases, leads to social contradictions, resulting in conflicting and deteriorating relations between consumers, business, and government.

FIGURE 5.3. Factors Leading to the Rise of Consumerism

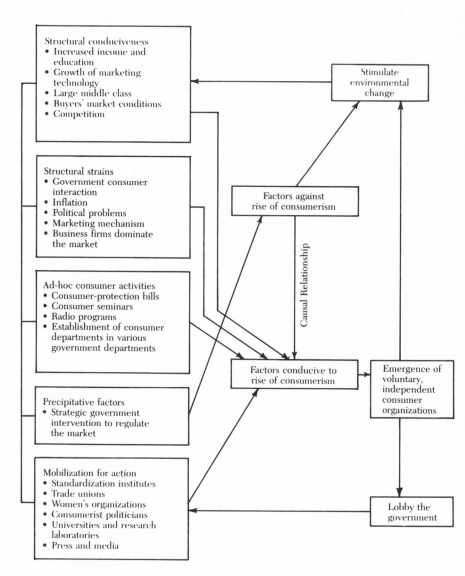

Source: Adapted from Philip Kotler, "What Consumerism Means to Marketers," *Harvard Business Review* (May–June 1972): 48–57. Vol. 50 No. 3.

TABLE 5.2. Order of Consumer Goods and Services Expenditures as Income Rises

Income level		Goods	Services
Subsistence-level consumers (Annual Income Under $200/Capita)			
	Sustenance	• Food, primarily staples • Clothing	
Low-income consumers (annual income $200–$1000/capita)			
	Sustenance	• More non-staples (food) • Housing • Hand implements	• Public transportation • Fuel, light, electricity • Basic medical care
	Labor saving	• Sewing machines • Kerosene stoves	• Movies • Basic education
	Leisure & mobility	• Bicycles	
Lower middle-income consumers (Annual income $1000–$2000/capita)			
	Labor saving & convenient	• Iron • Range • Refrigerator • Clothes washers (wringer type) • Radio • Phonograph • Television (black & white)	• Expanded use of: • Public utilities (transp., electricity, etc.) • Medical care • Education • Basic dental care

(continued)

TABLE 5.2. (Continued)

Income level	Goods	Services
Leisure & mobility	• Motor scooters/cycles • Still camera • Inexpensive sporting goods • Some styled clothing • Some personal care items	• Some travel
Upper middle-income consumers (Annual income $2000–$5000/capita)		
Labor saving & convenient	• Vacuum cleaner • Clothes drier • Electric mixer • Power tools • Hair drier • Styled clothing • Personal care items	
Leisure & mobility	• Wide range of sporting goods • Automobile	• More travel • Restaurants • Spectator sports • Participant sports • Some domestic help • Some donations • More educational expenditures

High-income consumers
(Annual income over
$5000/capita)

Labor saving & convenient	• Air conditioners • Water softeners • Electric toothbrush • Electric blender • Electric garage door opener • Trash compactors • Microwave ovens • Multiple autos, TVs, radios, etc. • Replacing goods purchased earlier—with new refinements (e.g., color t.v., self-cleaning range)
Leisure & mobility	• Expensive leisure products Boats, travel trailers, camping equipment Vacation houses More sporting goods

	• Domestic and foreign travel
	• Country club, tennis club, etc.
	• Frequent dining out
	• More domestic help
	• More donations
	• More medical and dental care
	• Professional services:
	   Attorney
	   Financial advisor
	   Psychiatrist

Source: J. A. Weber and Z. Shipchandler, "The Worldwide Evolution of Consumer Spending Patterns", in *1978 Proceedings of the Academy of International Business*, Chicago, Illinois, August 1978, edited by Sion Raveed and Y. R. Puri, p. 144. Reprinted with permission.

The improved education and higher incomes of consumers makes them more vociferous and more secure in their claims. Consumers expect higher product quality while at the same time product performance, in most cases, is decreasing. Many consumers feel that business should assume greater social responsibility in the face of the greater public concern over social problems. More unsafe and defective products are emerging, marketing claims are excessive, and advertising is often misleading. Products are also becoming more and more complex, making product and brand choice difficult.[22]

It can be seen from Figure 5.4 that there are goal conflicts in the marketing systems of countries. Producers and distributors want to maximize their economic surplus at the same time as consumers want to maximize their utility surplus. Increasing benefits to consumers will probably imply lower revenues or higher costs to other groups. Governments come in as mediators to decide on suitable distributions of surpluses in the system. Competition is influencing both producers and distributors and may improve the efficiency of the system, but at the same time strong competition can lead to higher advertising costs and meaningless product differentiation.[23]

These conflicting attitudes and relations produce structural strains on parts of the socioeconomic systems of LDCs. If these were the only conditions needed for consumerism, one would expect that all LDCs would have a very active and strong consumer movement. Yet this has not been the case.

The existence of stress leads to the proliferation of certain consumer predispositions and beliefs. As a social movement consumerism cannot develop unless there is a general belief about problems in the marketplace. This general belief is *not* well developed in most LDCs. The existence of a common belief is a necessary condition for the evolution of a social movement such as consumerism. In LDCs consumerism may also be stimulated by the growth of leaders, such as Anwar Faisal, the current president of the International Organization of Consumer Unions. Catalysts or precipitating factors are usually specific events or major problems that spark the growth of the consumerism movement. The success of any consumerism movement, however, depends on how effectively it is organized and managed. The progression of consumerism in LDCs will ultimately depend on the reaction of business and government leaders. Countervailing forces must be considered in assessing the progress and course of consumerism activity.[24]

CONSUMERISM LEGISLATION AND BYLAWS

Despite the continuous interest of both international agencies and indigenous LDC governments, there are certain problems with extending

FIGURE 5.4. The Consumerism Setting

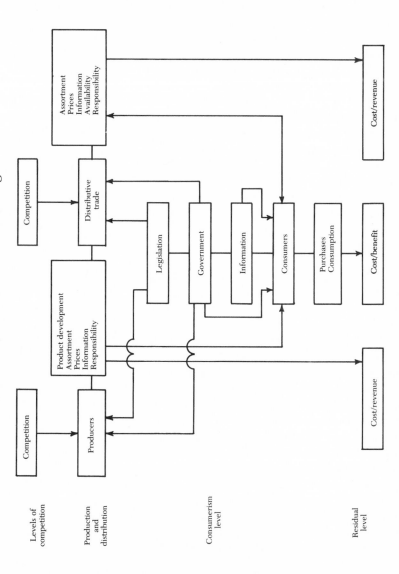

Source: Adapted from Bo Wickstrom, "Consumerism and the Control of Marketing," in *Increasing Marketing Efficiency in East Africa*, edited by B. Wickstrom and E. Gustafsson (Göteborg, Sweden: SIMS, 1975), p. 202. Reprinted with permission.

143

consumer protection into developing countries. The reason for this apparent dilemma can be attributed to the following factors:

a. Lack of information on consumer protection legislation and protective institutions in LDCs.

b. Consumer protection measures which have been developed and used in advanced countries in the last two decades seem less relevant for the prevailing conditions of LDCs.

c. When consumer protection is evident in LDCs, it seems to be mainly the middle and upper classes that get protection rather than the large number of people most in need of it. This is also true in most of the developed countries, where poorer consumers do not get the same level of protection as their counterparts who live in wealthier regions.[25]

Consumerism activity is gaining more momentum in international markets. When we look at the recent developments following repeated judicial remedies and appeals, proven programs have moved toward governmental enforcement, and new practices eventually have become institutionalized.[26] Some of the legislation and bylaws enacted in recent years are as follows.[27]

In 1973 the International Labor Office published a *Study Guide on Consumer Protection*. This was followed in June 1977 by a report of the UN Administrative Committee on activities of the United Nations' systems related to consumer protection. In June of 1978 a report was prepared by the Secretary General of the UN on consumer protection. This was a comprehensive survey of institutions and legislation in developed countries and LDCs. In 1980 the UN Secretary General produced a report on options for action in promoting consumer protection in developing countries. Recently the UN Commission on Transnational Corporations was asked by the Secretary General to take the lead in preparing a report on how to protect the consumers of LDCs.[28]

CONCEPTUAL FRAMEWORK

There are a number of differences between developed and less-developed countries in terms of how consumers are protected and how consumer issues are handled. Consumerism in most LDCs is more a matter of legislation and its efficient implementation than a matter of an engaged public effort. So far there has been very little consumerism activity in most of these countries. Whatever is evident in the way of consumerism is started by political parties, trade unions, professional associations, and the mass media, which initiate and sustain many efforts to protect consumers and improve their standing in the marketplace.

In free-market economies of the West, firms are free to make decisions on what to manufacture and how to market it. Consumers also are free to choose the products/services they wish to purchase. Consumers have free and informed choice in the selection of products and services offered by a variety of competing suppliers. This means that there is sovereignty on the demand side of the buyer–seller equation (see Figure 5.5). Whenever there is a conflict between company interest and customer interest, the available consumer protection agencies are on the side of the customer. Marketing is a challenge to competition. In a free-enterprise system with strong but fair competition, marketing theoretically would help the best product to achieve the greatest success. As such, in these economies,

FIGURE 5.5. Functioning of Consumerism in Dissimilar Environments

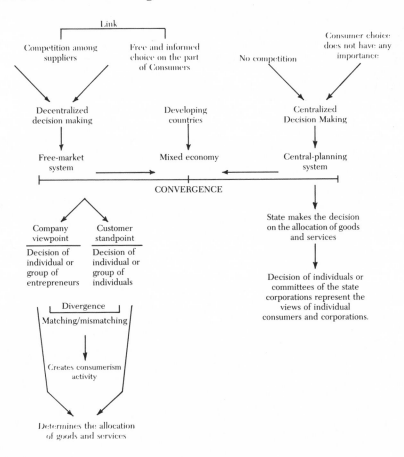

Source: Compiled by the author.

marketing contributes to technological as well as to general economic development.[29]

On the other hand, the decision-making process in centrally planned economies does not leave much room for company or customer point of view in the distribution of goods and services. In most of these economies state corporations are seen to represent the consumer. Consequently, individual consumer choice does not have much importance in broader decision making.

In most of the LDCs, there is a departure from either a pure free-market or centrally planned economic system toward a mixed economic system—a convergence. As a result, the consumers' role and the interface between the consumer and the manufacturer has also shifted. The functioning of free market and centrally planned economies is shown in Figures 5.6 and 5.7.

In free-market economies consumerism is a social movement, the goal of which is to strengthen the rights of buyers, to make consumer sovereignty a meaningful term, and to bring about greater equality in the buyer–seller equation. In developing countries, on the other hand, there are two ways to protect the consumer. One is through government agencies, the other is through private associations. In these countries, this causes a dilemma. On one hand there is public mistrust of government agencies; on the other, it is difficult to provide financial assistance for independent consumer protection associations. This fundamental problem is the main source of consumerism in LDCs. Thus, a model should be designed for each country according to its needs. Since LDCs with market economies tend to present similar characteristics, a common model can be developed. The type of organization best suited to protect consumer rights appears to be an independent consumer association with support from universities, trade unions, professional organizations, women's leagues, and consumer cooperatives (see Figure 5.8).[30]

CONSUMERISM AS A MEANS OF SOCIAL ADAPTATION TO INNOVATION

Consumerism is considered to be part of the theory of social adaptation to innovation. According to this theory, an innovation interacts with relevant environmental variables in three successive phases of development.[31]

Phase I. The innovation occurs in the form of a product, a group of products, the development of a new territory, a new social idea, or a major technological change. In most cases, the introduction of the innovation has

FIGURE 5.6. Free-Market Economy Injection of Independent Voluntary Consumer Association
(Countervailing Power)

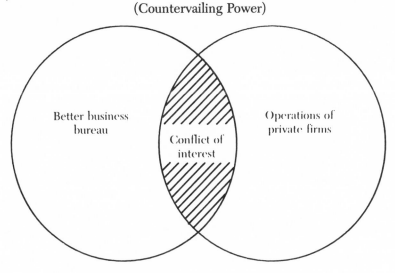

FIGURE 5.7. Centrally Planned Economy Injection of State-Operated Standards and Quality Control Institute
(Countervailing Power)

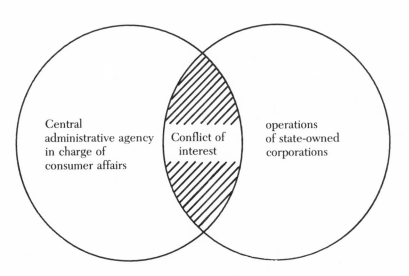

Source: Both compiled by the author.

FIGURE 5.8. Government–Business Firm–Consumer Interfaces in Mixed Economies
(Countervailing Power)

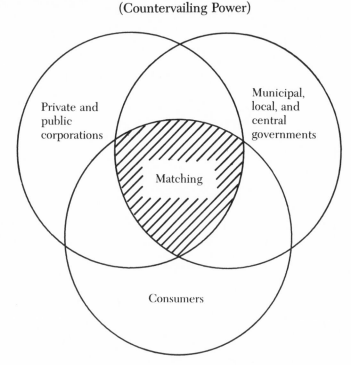

Private and public corporations

Municipal, local, and central governments

Matching

Consumers

Independent voluntary consumer associations act as a countervailing power among the three parties, providing a matching device.
Source: Compiled by the author.

a small impact on its relevant environmental determinants. At this first stage, the innovators are busy innovating, and the consequences of the novelty are neither far-reaching nor very significant. This is the seller's market phase.

Phase II. At the second stage, there is a tendency toward consolidation of the relationship between the innovators and the rest of the environment. There are no longer new markets for sellers. Instead there is a switch to repeat business, which is a direct result of the growing stability of the innovator–environment relationship. The environment has an increasing effect on the innovators. As a result, consumerism begins to make itself heard at the later stage of the repeat-business phase.

Phase III. At this stage, environmental factors take control. This leads to eventual regulation and control of the innovators as government

FIGURE 5.9. The Pattern of Social Adaptation to An Innovation

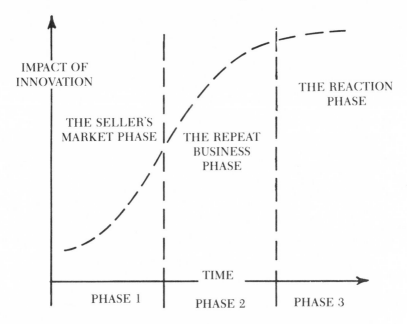

Source: D. W. Hendon, "Toward a Theory of Consumerism", *Business Horizons*, 18, no. 4 (August 1975): 20. Reprinted with permission.

authorities heed consumer protests, and to possible nationalization in the public interest (see Figure 5.9).

Having constructed this general framework, Hendon developed eight specific hypotheses for a study of consumerism. These are summarized below:

Hypothesis 1: Wheel of Consumerism. Consumerism activities and movements occur in periodic cycles. As shown in Figure 5.7, the seller's market, repeat-business, and reaction phases take place over and over.°

Hypothesis 2: Early Stages of Inflation. Generally, a high rate of inflation is one predictor of more intense consumerism activity, up to a

---

°For fuller treatment of the life-cycle phenomenon of consumerism across nations see E. Kaynak and S. Wickström, "Methodological Framework for a Cross-National Comparison of Consumerism Issues in Multiple Environments," *European Journal of Marketing* 19, no. 1 (1985): 31–46.

point. When inflation becomes endemic, consumers become less concerned with consumerism. Instead, they convert their money to hard goods. This has been the case in countries such as Argentina, Israel, and Brazil in recent years.

Hypothesis 3: Proximity of Actors. In both developed and less-developed economies, consumerism movements can occur only when a sufficient number of individuals who live close to each other move and act collectively. The low-income consumers of Egypt, Morocco, and Algeria who revolted collectively against the rising prices of major staple food items are good contemporary examples.

Hypothesis 4: Environmental Factors. Certain environmental factors such as restrictive political and legal systems and a long-standing tradition of class distinction can also trigger intense consumerism activity.

Hypothesis 5: Sophisticated Issues–Economic Development. It can be stated that consumer issues tend to grow in sophistication with the passage of time. A certain degree of economic development is needed for consumerism to evolve. For different stages see Figure 5.1.

Hypothesis 6: Sophisticated Issues–Violence Level. Generally, actions over consumer issues are more violent if the issues at hand are less sophisticated, and vice versa.

Hypothesis 7: Class Distinctions–Affluence Level. Class distinctions somehow diminish as less-wealthier consumers gain more affluence in a society.

Hypothesis 8: Over-Sophistication Reaction. In an economy where the problems of consumption outweigh the problems of production (most Western societies), the over-sophisticated economy returns to basic consumer issues for certain groups in the economy. In Figure 5.1, return from Stage 4 to Stage 1.[32]

DEVELOPED VERSUS LDC PRACTICES

Consumerism is a social movement dependent on the national economic conditions of countries, be they developed or less-developed. However, the economic and technological maturity of a country dictates the sophistication of the current state of consumerism in a given country. Of course, cross-national differences/conditions also vary greatly, and these affect the development of consumerism.

Conditions vary greatly in less-developed countries. Inflation is often endemic and products and product performance often fall short of consumer expectations. Some blame the "system" and others attribute responsibility to the operations of transnational corporations. It is, of course, relevant to ask whether the growth of consumerism in less-developed countries should be regarded as part of the development process itself, and whether priority should be given to consumerism measures. The crisis of third-world countries as a result of the influence of the European and American multinationals is accelerating. Less-developed countries are now beginning to experience exactly the same pattern of rising expectations to which Western customers are accustomed. Whereas in many LDCs consumer expectations go little beyond an adequate supply of the physical necessities of life, in Europe and North America consumers are so far past that stage they can afford to let social goals and the satisfaction of self-actualization needs come to the fore.[33]

Consumerism requires a healthy macroeconomic and social environment, a condition which is badly lacking in most LDCs. There are acute disparities between developed and less-developed countries in the growth of the macroeconomic and social environment. For comparative purposes, the different characteristics of the macroenvironment of developed and less-developed countries are shown in Table 5.3.

One of the problems with extending consumerism in less-developed countries is that conditions, which vary widely, are so different from those in developed countries. Information on the progress of consumerism legislation and institutions in less-developed countries is required in order to set sound priorities for action. Gathering this information presents problems of some complexity. The consumerism measures that have made such progress in developed countries in the last quarter of the century at times seem less relevant for conditions in less-developed countries.[34]

Consumerism activity is more likely to be transferred between similar

TABLE 5.3. The Macroeconomic and Social Environment

Less-developed country	Developed country
Low standards of living	High standards of living
Low level of aspiration	High level of aspiration
Seller's market conditions exist	Buyer's market conditions exist
Consumer information outreach is very low	Consumers engage in constant problem-solving activities
Lower level of expectations for products	Higher level of expectations for products
Consumers are not organized	Consumers are well organized
Consumerism is a matter of legislation and its efficient implementation	Consumerism is a matter of engaged public support

Source: Erdener Kaynak and Solveig Wickstrom, "Methodological Framework for a Cross-National Comparison of Consumerism Issues in Multiple Environments," *European Journal of Marketing* 19, no. 1 (1985): 34. Reprinted with permission.

and culturally alike environments. Before any transfer takes place, it is first necessary to control the other cross-national/cultural differences of the two countries. Better operational definitions of the various types of precursors and transfer are needed. At the same time we need to know much more about the determinants of the relative degrees of transferability of consumer policy between nations and cultures. In addition to transfer, there is the international cooperative development of consumer policy measures. As yet there is no solid research of direct relevance to this area. It would be inappropriate for individual LDCs to become heavily engaged in policy formulation without an adequate research base. There is every reason to believe that blind transfer of consumer policy measures from the industrialized countries is not what the LDCs need and want.[35]

Researchers should also examine the potential and actual frictional issues of consumerism, and prescribe the appropriate "lubricants" to overcome the difficulties encountered in the interface. There are, of course, certain preconditions for the smooth functioning of a market economy where consumerism can be an instrument to facilitate the process. These preconditions are: heightened regulation of business activity, implementation of a national industrial strategy, and public utility regulation replacing the free-market mechanism (prediction of the demise of the market-run economy).

The healthy macroeconomic and social environment necessary for consumerism is sadly lacking in most LDCs. As a result, consumerism in LDCs has reached only one of the first three stages, depending on the country's level of socioeconomic and technological development. In recent years consumerists in LDCs have been preoccupied with micro issues (traditional concerns) such as package sizes, unit pricing, credit disclosure, product safety, misleading advertising information, labeling, and product quality. By contrast, in developed countries consumerists are mainly trying to deal with macro issues (socioeconomic, cultural, and technological concerns). Major policy issues such as pollution, poverty, the welfare system, health care, tariffs, the tax system, collective bargaining, foreign ownership, and the anti-nuclear drive all come under the realm of the consumerism movement of developed countries (see Figure 5.10). The effective functioning of any socioeconomic system depends on adequate feedback about the system's performance. In marketing systems of both developed and less-developed countries, measures of performance on the producers' side are relatively well developed. Measures on the consumers' side are now relying, for the most part, on either sales or market share (producers' measures), or global measures of consumer discontent over or support of consumerism.[36] However, in recent years more studies have been done on consumer satisfaction and complaint behavior in LDCs.[37, 38]

FIGURE 5.10. Consumerism Issues in Diverse Cultures

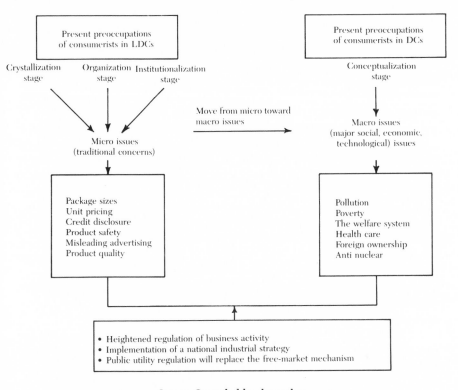

Source: Compiled by the author.

WHAT NEEDS TO BE DONE TO INCREASE CONSUMER PROTECTION ACTIVITIES?

Under the prevailing circumstances, the priorities of consumers in less-developed countries differ in at least two ways from those of their counterparts in developed countries. First, there is an urgent need to increase the quantity of products and services produced and to redirect industrialization toward the long-run benefits of the LDC consumers. This effort, in turn, will accelerate the process of economic development. At present, this dimension of consumerism is almost negligible in developed countries, since they have all solved the problem of production a long time ago. Second, there is the need to provide an equal distribution of income and to improve the educational level of most LDC consumers. There are apparent differences in the patterns of private-consumption expenditures among different social strata of most less-developed countries, mainly due to changing socioeconomic conditions and the prevailing unequal distribution of income.

It is apparent that these two conditions are dependent on a country's level of socioeconomic development. Of course, this does not mean that consumerism cannot help with the solution of these problems. On the contrary, a voluntary consumer movement, through various means and methods, can do a great deal to provide solutions to previously stated problems. Organized consumer movements can show consumers of these countries not only the sources of their problems, but also the ways and means to overcome them.

In LDCs the development of consumer cooperatives can also play an important part in the protection of consumers. Perhaps the urgent need is to collect more information directly from LDC consumers about their personal priorities, which may be quite different from those of more sophisticated consumers in industrialized countries. It is not going to be enough simply to transplant the laws or institutions that have served consumers well in industrialized countries into the different conditions of less-developed countries. A catalyst is needed to precipitate consumerism activities in LDCs. If the environmental conditions conducive to consumerism are not prevalent, its development will be slower.

In recent years a new agenda of consumer concerns has developed.

> This new agenda recognizes that the contemporary consumer is both rich and poor at the same time, and is confronted with new and complex problems involving both scarcity and abundance. The mutual interest of business and government—as well as consumer groups—in identifying and responding to consumer concerns should provide a basis for increasing use of participative and conciliatory rather than adversary policy processes.[39]

Consumers in the 1980s and beyond will face a new environment. They will encounter new kinds of problems which will necessitate different kinds of policy needs in different consumption situations.

> The distinction between the problems arising from scarcity and those arising from abundance offers a basis for re-formulating the consumer policy agenda. Process issues take on a new importance in the new high-communication, anti-regulation environment. Concerns involving the quality, availability and cost of public services become more and more pressing as consumers come to rely increasingly on the public sector for essential daily needs.[40]

The consumer policy agenda for the 1980s and beyond is shown in Table 5.4.

TABLE 5.4. Consumer Policy Agenda

Scarcity issues

Meeting the basic needs of the poor.

Responding to emerging needs of the "new" poor.

Identifying economy values and "best buys."

Protecting vulnerable consumers against scams and deceptions.

Using self-service and limited selection to hold down costs.

Allocating short supplies among uses and users.

Developing reserve stocks and potential substitution possibilities in advance.

Bringing the consumer impact of supply-limiting policies into explicit consideration in the policy process.

Abundance issues

Developing appropriate product/service descriptions and corresponding information in areas of important innovation and change—particularly: communications and electronics, financial services, and health care.

Helping consumers to cut through the volume and variety of available information (and misinformation) to isolate relevant alternatives.

Highlighting the long-term cost implications of new product/service offerings and lifestyles.

Process issues

Monitoring the cost and effectiveness of regulation; minimizing its restrictive impact on both business and consumers.

Seeking optimal combinations of state/federal authority and responsibility.

Assessing the need and impact of subsidies for both production and consumption.

Reducing the unnecessary use, length and cost of private litigation of consumer problems.

Seeking non-adversarial methods of identifying and resolving consumer issues.

Encouraging more business initiative in developing innovative responses to consumer concerns.

Making more effective use of consumer education and information programs.

Increasing two-way communication and participation in consumer policy decisions in both business and government.

Public services issues

Mitigating effects of government monopoly on service provision and pricing.

Maintaining and/or improving service quality, controlling cost, and adapting activity to community needs.

Experimenting with innovative approaches and consumer-oriented operating modes.

Source: © 1983 by the Regents of the University of California. Reprinted from CALIFORNIA MANAGEMENT REVIEW, volume XXVI, no. 1, p. 117, by permission of the regents.

CONSUMERISM AND ECONOMIC DEVELOPMENT: PUBLIC POLICY IMPLICATIONS

Irrespective of a country's stage of socioeconomic development, what is needed is a conceptualization of the policies concerning consumers in that country. If we return to the basic notion that marketing is about matching what is offered with what customers need and want, then we can see consumerism as a simple frictional issue.[41] How can we examine the potential and current frictional issues and find ways and means to overcome them?

In his research, Thorelli points to a steadily increasing level of consumer dissatisfaction in both developed and less-developed countries which instigates consumerism activity.[42] How is this possible when the quality of supply in many aspects is increasing at the same time? There are a number of possible explanations for this: (a) As the number of products purchased increases, there is a larger potential for unsuccessful transactions. (b) The increasing complexity of goods and services makes it more difficult for consumers to assess the quality and suitability of what they purchase. They are becoming more insecure and more worried. (c) The growing variety of products and brands creates difficulties of choice. (d) Consumers, in a country like Sweden, trust the public consumer policy and are therefore less careful in evaluating company product offerings. (e) Consumers have less time for search activity and buying and therefore are more irritated if the products they select do not perform properly, which means going through the buying process once more. (f) The increase in educational level of consumers causes higher expectations. Occasionally consumers in highly developed countries may even have expectations that go beyond the capabilities of the economic system at that time.[43]

Looking at the developments over the last three decades, one can conclude that consumerism is here to stay. The breadth, depth, and speed of consumer change will continue. There is much unfinished business. Public forecasts of consumer issues can provide management with information with which to: identify new marketing opportunities and problems; gain lead time required to develop, redesign, reformulate or reposition products; avoid or minimize costly impacts of government mandates (product bans, product pruning, restrictions, recalls); or pursue lobbying, public relations, and image-building potentials. The initiative is there for the taking. Public forecasting provides an important informational tool to planners who are concerned with these alternative courses of action.[44]

Consumerism in LDCs, when it matures as a movement, will lead to demands for more product information and more protection against malfunctioning products, including the establishment of government as well as independent testing agencies. Consumerism in LDCs will mobilize "consumer opinion" to influence product design development and marketing practices in directions that will improve the quality of life. Increasingly, product packaging and marketing practices will be required to pass the test of "social usefulness" as judged from the consumer viewpoint.[45] This, in turn, will have tremendous implications for the economic development efforts of countries.

Pricing will have to be simplified and restrictions placed on the use of price as a promotional tool. Obscure pricing methods and false price comparisons need to be eliminated. The real cost of credit will have to be revealed to the consumer at large. Consumers need to be provided with accurate and relevant information about the product, thus ensuring that consumer expectations about the performance of the product are realistic. Advertising should not create expectations that the product cannot meet, and copy that relies heavily on exaggeration needs to come under the closest scrutiny. Advertising must also contribute to consumers' education with respect to correct product use and maintenance. In some countries distributors' margins need to come under close scrutiny and increasingly will have to be justified in cost terms. Pricing and inventory handling methods will have to be managed in light of new legislative restrictions.[46] The role of consumerism in matching what is offered by manufacturers with what is demanded by consumers in any economy is depicted in Figure 5.11. This shows that consumerism facilitates the free movement of need-satisfying goods and services by offering profit to the company and satisfaction to the consumer, which is conducive to higher levels of economic development.[47]

Will consumerism issues cease after a time? Or is it a never-ending cycle?

In general, as a nation experiences economic growth, consumerism issues grow more sophisticated and violent. Differences due to environmental factors are to be expected. . . . If there is a limit to growth, an economy of scarcity will defuse consumerism movements up to a point.

If worker rebellions are the result of broadly defined consumerism issues, Marx was wrong when he hypothesized that worker revolts would begin in the more highly developed nations; instead, they began in the relatively underdeveloped nation of Russia. He was wrong because consumerism issues—prerequisites to and leading indicators of general workers' rebellions—grow more sophisticated and less violent as a nation experiences economic growth. Violent workers' rebellions arising from broadly defined consumerism issues occur in less-developed nations because of less-sophisticated issues and class distinctions, and are fanned by inflation and proximity.

. . . . The United States experienced only a relatively few violent

FIGURE 5.11. Manufacturer–Consumer Matching Process

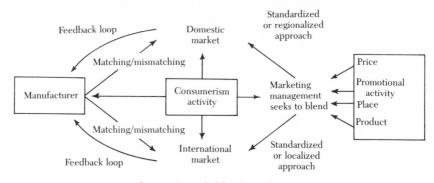

Source: Compiled by the author.

consumer protests in its history, but not so few as Britain or France at comparative stages in those nations' economic development, primarily because of the lack of class distinctions in the United States and the prevalance of these disinctions in Britain and France.[48]

Modern consumerism is a widespread social movement that is growing rapidly in both developed and less-developed economies of the world.

FIGURE 5.12. Input–Processor–Output Model of Consumerism

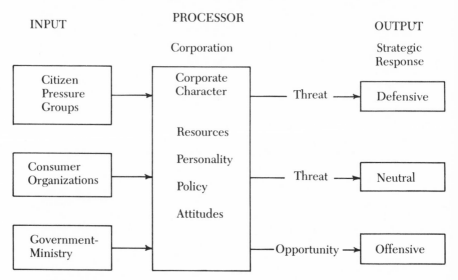

Source: Reprinted by permission of the publisher from "International Consumerism: A Threat or Opportunity," *Industrial Marketing Management* 3, p. 7. Copyright 1973 by Elsevier Science Publishing Co., Inc.

Although the level of development of consumerism is different at varying stages of economic and social development of countries, it is an enduring force whose effect should be taken into consideration by private-sector operators as well as public-policy workers. Kaufman and Channon pointed out certain factors that cause private firms to respond to consumerism in three different ways:

Defensive strategy. The defensive strategy to consumerism is counterattack. This results in a confrontation, either overt or covert, between consumerists and private firms.

Neutral strategy. The neutral strategy is to ignore the challenges of government or the public or both.

Offensive strategy. The use of an offensive strategy is an attempt to meet the challenge of consumerism with a positive attitude (see Figure 5.12).[49]

NOTES

1. S. Wickström, "Another Look At Consumer Dissatisfaction as a Measure of Market Performance," *Journal of Consumer Policy* 6, no. 1 (1983): 19–35; S. A. Greyser, *Consumerism at the Crossroads* (Boston, MA: Sentry Insurance, 1977); A. Sapiro and J. Lendrevie, "On the Consumer Front in France, Japan, Sweden, U.K. and the U.S.A.," *European Business* (Summer 1973): 43–52; J. K. Johansson, "The Theory and Practice of Swedish Consumer Policy," *Journal of Consumer Affairs* (1976): 19–32; H. B. Thorelli and S. V. Thorelli, *Consumer Information Handbook: Europe and North America* (New York: Praeger, 1974); H. B. Thorelli, H. Becker, and J. Engeldow, *The Information Seekers* (Cambridge, MA: Ballinger, 1975).

2. D. W. Hendon, "Toward a Theory of Consumerism," *Business Horizons* 18, no. 4 (August 1975): 16.

3. J. Stanton, R. Chandran, and J. Lowenhar, "Consumerism in Developing Countries— The Brazilian Experience," in *Advances in Consumer Research*, edited by Kent B. Monroe (Arlington, VA, October 8, 1980), pp. 718–22; E. Kaynak, *Marketing in the Third World* (New York: Praeger, 1982); H. B. Thorelli and G. D. Sentell, *Consumer Emancipation and Economic Development: The Case of Thailand* (Greenwich, CT: JAI Press, 1982); R. A. Layton and G. Holmes, "Consumerism as an Element of Ongoing Social Change," *Management Decision* 12, no. 5 (1974): 313–28.

4. A. R. Andreason, "Consumerism Dissatisfaction as a Measure of Market Performance," *Journal of Consumer Policy* 1, no. 4 (1977): 311–22.

5. E. Kaynak and S. Wickström, "Methodological Framework For a Cross-National Comparison of Consumerism Issues in Multiple Environments," *European Journal of Marketing* 18, no. 8 (1984); R. M. Gaedeke and U. Udo-Aka, "Toward the Internationalization of Consumerism," *California Management Review* 27, no. 1 (Fall 1974): 86–92; I. Kaufman and D. Channon, "International Consumerism: A Threat or Opportunity," *Industrial Marketing Management* 3 (1973): 1–14.

6. R. S. Alexander, F. M. Surface, and W. Alderson, *Marketing* (Boston, MA: Ginn and Company, 1949).

7. H. C. Barksdale and W. A. French, "The Response of U.S. Business to Consumerism," *European Journal of Marketing* 10, no. 1 (1976): 13–27; A. R. Andreason and A. Best,

"Consumers Complain—Does Business Respond," *Harvard Business Review* 55, no. 4 (July–August 1977): 93–101; J. Arndt, E. Crane, and K. Tallhaug, "Opinions about Consumerism Issues among Present and Future Norwegian Business Executives," *European Journal of Marketing* 11, no. 1 (1977): 13–20; J. Arndt, H. C. Barksdale, and W. D. Perreault, "Comparative Study of Attitudes toward Marketing, Consumerism and Government Regulation: The United States versus Norway and Venezuela," in *New Findings on Consumer Satisfaction and Complaining*, edited by R. L. Day and H. K. Hunt (St. Louis, MO: November 6–8, 1980), pp. 66–72; R. Nader, "The Great American Gyp," in *The New York Review of Books* (New York: NYREV, 1968); R. O. Herrman, "The Consumer Movement in Historical Perspective," Department of Agricultural Economics and Rural Sociology, University Park, PA: Pennsylvania State University, February, 1970.

8. R. J. Kroll and R. W. Stampfl, "The New Consumerism," in *Proceedings of 27th Annual Conference of the American Council on Consumer Interests, April 8–11, 1981, Minneapolis, Minnesota,* edited by C. B. Meeks, pp. 97–100.

9. E. P. McGuire, *Consumer Protection: Implications For International Trade* (New York: The Conference Board, 1980); D. A. Aaker and G. S. Day, *Consumerism: Search For the Consumer Interest,* 3d ed. (New York: Free Press, 1978).

10. W. Straver, "The International Consumerist Movement: Theory and Practical Implications For Marketing Strategy," *European Journal of Marketing* 11 (1977): 93–117.

11. Kaynak and Wickström, "Methodological Framework." See note 5.

12. Arndt, Bardsdale, and Perreault, "Comparative Study," p. 67. See note 7.

13. Kaufman and Channon, "International Consumerism," pp. 4–5. See note 5.

14. David A. Aaker and George S. Day, "A Guide to Consumerism," *Journal of Marketing* vol. 34, no. 3 (July 1970): 12–19; Richard H. Buskirk and James T. Rothe, "Consumerism—An Interpretation," *Journal of Marketing* (October 1970): 62; G. Day and D. A. Aaker, *Consumerism* (New York: Free Press, 1981).

15. Eli P. Cox, "Poverty and Demand," *MSU Business Topics* (Autumn 1971): 25–32.

16. A. C. Samli, "Role of Marketing in Economic Development: What Should International Marketers Know," in *International Marketing Management* edited by E. Kaynak (New York: Praeger, 1984), pp. 34–50.

17. David Caplowitz, *The Poor Pay More* (New York: Free Press, 1963); A. Coskun Samli, "Differential Price Structures for the Rich and the Poor," *University of Washington Business Review* (Summer 1969):35–43; A. Coskun Samli and Larry French, "De Facto Price Discrimination in the Food Purchases of the Rural Poor," *Journal of Retailing* (Summer 1971): 48–60.

18. M. Evers, "Consumerism in the Eighties," *Public Relations Journal* 39, no. 8 (August 1983): 24–26.

19. Arndt, Barksdale, and Perreault, "Comparative Study," p. 66. See note 7.

20. J. A. Weber and Z. Shipchandler, "The Worldwide Evolution of Consumer Spending Patterns," in *1978 Proceedings of the AIB, Chicago, Illinois, August, 1978,* edited by S. Raveed and Y. R. Puri, pp. 142–43.

21. Stanton, Chandran, and Lowenhar, "Consumerism in Developing Countries." See note 3.

22. Bo Wickström, "Consumerism and the Control of Marketing," in *Increasing Marketing Efficiency in East Africa,* edited by B. Wickström and E. Gustafsson (Göteborg, Sweden: SIMS, 1975), pp. 200–10.

23. Ibid., p. 201.

24. J. O. Onah, "Consumerism in Nigeria," in *Marketing in Nigeria,* edited by J. O. Onah (London: Cassell, 1979), pp. 126–34.

25. E. Kaynak, "Consumerism: A Neglected Aspect of Marketing Planning in Developing Economies," *Development in Marketing Science* Proceedings of the Academy of Marketing Science Annual Conference (Las Vegas, Nevada), 5 (May 1981): 607–10.

26. McGuire, *Consumer Protection,* p. 36. See note 9.

27. United Nations, *International Co-operation and Coordination Within the United Nations System,* Consumer Protection Report of the Secretary-General, Economic and Social Council, May 27, 1983, report no. E/1983/71.

28. McGuire, "Consumer Protection." See note 9.

29. *Marketing Management and Strategy for the Developing World,* United Nations Industrial Development Organization (New York, 1975), p. 30.

30. E. Kaynak and R. Culpan, *Consumer Protection Movement in a Developing Economy: The Case of Turkey,* Mediterranean Consumer Conference, March 1977, Athens, Greece, pp. 11–12.

31. Hendon, "Toward a Theory," pp. 19–20. See note 2.

32. Ibid., pp. 20–21.

33. G. S. C. Wills, "Marketing's Social Dilemma," *European Journal of Marketing* 8, no. 1 (1974): 4–14; H. B. Thorelli, "Consumer Policy For the Third World," *Journal of Consumer Policy* 3 (Summer 1981): 197–211.

34. S. Dandapani, "Consumer Protection in Developing Countries," *Consumer Affairs Bulletin* 4 (1975): 1–2.

35. H. B. Thorelli, "Consumer Policy at the Enterprise Level," *Marknads Vetande* 3, no. 4 (1980): 41–47.

36. T. P. Hustad and E. A. Pessemier, "Will the Real Consumer Activist Please Stand Up: An Examination of Consumers' Opinions About Marketing Practices," *Journal of Marketing Research* 10 (1973): 319–24; R. L. Day, "Consumer Satisfaction/Dissatisfaction with Services and Intangible Products," paper presented at Marketing Research Seminar, Institut d'Administration des Entreprises, Université d'Aix Marseilles, France, 1975.

37. R. L. Day and H. K. Hunt, *New Findings on Consumer Satisfaction and Complaining* (St. Louis, MO: Indiana University Press, November 6–8, 1980).

38. H. B. Thorelli and G. Sentell, *Consumer Emancipation,* see note 3; H. B. Thorelli, "China: Consumer Voice and Exit," in *Consumer Satisfaction/Dissatisfaction,* proceedings from CS/D Conference at Knoxville TN 1982, edited by H. K. Hunt.

39. L. E. Preston and P. N. Bloom, "The Concerns of the Rich/Poor Consumer," *California Management Review* 26, no. 1 (Fall 1983): 100.

40. Ibid., p. 116.

41. G. S. C. Wills, "Customer Policies," editorial, *European Journal of Marketing* 14, no. 1 (1980).

42. Thorelli, "Consumer Policy." See note 35.

43. S. Wickström, "Consumer Dissatisfaction Scope and Policy Implications," University of Lund, Lund, Sweden, 1981.

44. McGuire, "Consumer Protection." See note 9.

45. P. T. Drucker, *Managing for Results* (New York: Harper & Row, 1964), pp. 91–110.

46. M. J. Thomas, "Marketing Management: A View of the Future," *Quarterly Review of Marketing* (Autumn 1975): 9–10.

47. Erdener Kaynak, "Some Thoughts of Consumerism in Developed and Less-Developed Countries," *Marketing International Review* 2, no. 2 (Summer 1985): 15–30.

48. Hendon, "Toward a Theory," p. 24. See note 2.

49. Kaufman and Channon, "International Consumerism," pp. 6–9. See note 5.

6
The Role and Relevance of Marketing Research to the Economic Development of Less-Developed Countries

INTRODUCTION

Marketing research methods and techniques prove to be the best means for determining the controlling factors of changes in the marketing environment. As the economic structure of less-developed countries gradually changes from a production phase to a consumption phase, the consumption-oriented economy intensifies the importance of marketing and marketing research, which are competitive tools used by companies in a competitive economy. Marketing bridges the gap between producers and consumers of goods and services. Without this exchange mechanism, the transformation of a subsistence economy into a market-oriented economy cannot be realized. Surprisingly enough, these are not "self-evident truths" for many decision makers in less-developed countries. Their appreciation of marketing as an effective catalyst of socioeconomic progress is hindered both by lack of relevant data and by a series of more or less conscious biases against marketing activities.[1] The modern consumer-oriented marketing concept is based on integrated marketing and has the goal of profits through customer satisfaction. Such a system can be preserved only through close contact with the end customers themselves. This is where marketing research helps the private firm and public policymakers in forming policies and designing marketing strategies.[2]

If markets have failed to expand or in fact have declined in less-developed countries, marketing research would seek the causes of market stagnation and suggest remedies. Products themselves may face diminishing demand because of changes in demand, the opening up of new and better resources through discovery or development, or because of restrictions imposed by importing countries. Marketing research would be directed toward the discovery of substitute products or the development of industries in which the less-developed countries or regions can exercise some degree of differential advantage.[3]

MICRO- VERSUS MACRO-MARKETING

The problems arising from the nonadaptability to a given economic system of individual firms' marketing policies call for training in micro-marketing. This is the process of planning and carrying out transactions for the distribution of goods and services within a given economic system and cultural pattern. It comprises price policy, product development, and communications policy. Micro-marketing is concerned with the adaptation of production and supply to demand (see Figure 6.1).

The infrastructural problems faced by LDCs call for another type of marketing activity, often referred to as *macro-marketing*. This is the activity of creating and adapting an economic infrastructure to the needs of ultimate consumers, be they individual or institutional. The parameters of action are changed, but it is difficult to tell where macro-marketing lies between micro-marketing and the economic policy of a country. The trading orientation of a country, whether a free-market or centrally planned economy, also plays a major role here.

One major reason for inadequate marketing development in LDCs is sheer lack of knowledge of the marketing processes themselves. The necessary information for determining government policies and especially intervention is still lacking or incomplete. In only a few countries has applied marketing research received any priority in national research

FIGURE 6.1. Impact of Marketing on Economic Policy

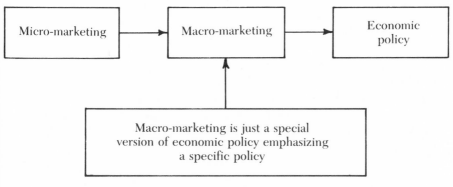

Source: Compiled by the author.

FIGURE 6.2. Philosophy Guiding the Marketing Efforts of Firms and Public Policymakers

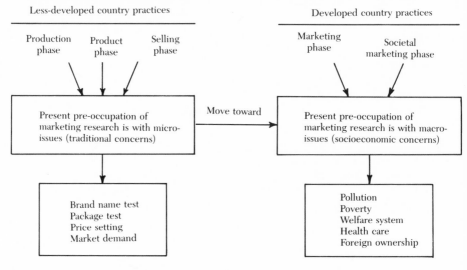

Source: Compiled by the author.

programs. Indeed this explains why so little is known about how to accurately identify and assess deficiencies in marketing, how to determine their causes, and how to design appropriate policies for incentives, institutions, and investments.[4]

In less-developed countries, little of what we refer to as marketing research has usually been undertaken. Public officials and economic development planners of these countries are of the opinion that the growth and development that occurred in the developed countries is due to the application of superior marketing techniques. Marketing research orientation of firms in developed versus less-developed countries is shown in Figure 6.2.

In less-developed countries the entire market structure needs to be analyzed to determine the extent to which inefficiencies place the industry at a less favorable competitive advantage than other producing areas. In these countries, inefficiencies in marketing that cause cost increases are only one type. Price efficiency, which reflects consumer market premiums for quality back through the marketing system to the producer, are equally important.[5] Finally, analyses need to be made of the profile of demand of firms as well as individual consumers in the main markets of less-developed countries to determine whether or not product policy, quality of products, and marketing methods are changing in such a manner as to necessitate changes in market structure or in production.[6]

Although marketing research proves to be the best tool of the marketing manager, its reliability depends on certain factors. A well-organized, highly talented team of interviewers well-acquainted with the respondents, a correctly chosen representative sample, a carefully designed survey questionnaire that will reveal the sincere thoughts of the respondents, and financial facilities appear to be the boundary conditions for achieving successful research. Such research will be fruitful for the marketing manager in facilitating his decision-making process.[7] Even in developed nations it is quite difficult to filter unbiased information from the respondents due to various reasons that have their base in human nature. This being the case, it is difficult to predict the chances of getting fruitful results from marketing research in less-developed countries where problems of illiteracy, communication obstacles, social structure, lack of competent staff, traditional behavior, and financial limitations are encountered in undertaking marketing research.[8] The different limiting factors affecting marketing research practices in developed versus less-developed countries are shown in Table 6.1.

Marketing research is expected to contribute to market expansion and through market expansion to the economic development of less-developed countries. Marketing research in market expansion is needed to determine the areas in which comparative advantage exists; to study consumer preference, whether of final consumers or of consumers of intermediate products; to set up standards of pricing and marketing efficiency; and to seek out complementarities and externalities that can expand industries based on changing factor endowments.[9] As a result, Tinbergen noted the link between economic development planning for LDCs and the use of marketing research.[10] On the other hand, social forecasters are helping companies to align their marketing strategies and policies to a more realistic view of the future.[11]

IS MARKETING RESEARCH NECESSARY FOR LDCs?

Since the publication of the classic article of Boyd et al.[12] in 1964, "On the Use of Marketing Research in the Emerging Economies," the study of marketing research in LDCs and its impact on economic development has received considerable attention.[13] Most of these studies advocated that it would be very difficult, if not impossible, to conduct surveys in these countries. They pointed out micro (firm-specific) and macro (country-specific) research difficulties. Very few studies, so far, have offered

TABLE 6.1. Marketing Research Infrastructure in Developed versus Less-Developed Countries

Developed country practices	Less-developed country practices
Single language and nationality	Multilingual/multinational/multicultural factors
Availability of relatively homogeneous population	Fragmented and diverse markets
Data available, usually accurate, and collection easy	Data collection a formidable task, requiring significantly higher budgets and personnel allocation
Political factors relatively unimportant and the system is stable	Political factors frequently vital and the system is in most cases unstable
Relative freedom from government interference	Government involvement and influence in business decisions
Relatively stable business environment	Multiple environments, many of which are very unstable
Legal and regulatory constraints	Same
Availability of research infrastructure and technological advancement	Lack of research infrastructure and technological advancement
Marketing research stresses operational issues	Marketing research stresses strategic issues
Availability of cultural homogenity	Cultural taboos and trends
Media availabilities and mix satisfactory	Unsatisfactory media
Telephone and postal systems adequate	Inadequate telephone and postal systems

Source: E. Kaynak, "Marketing Research Needs of Less-Developed Countries: Standardization versus Localization," in *Developments in Marketing Science VI*, edited by J. D. Lindquist (Kalamazoo, MI: Academy of Marketing Science, 1984), p. 61. Reprinted with permission.

managerially oriented prescriptions for ways of undertaking optimum-level marketing research studies.[14] Different types of research difficulties encountered by managers of companies are shown in Table 6.2.

CURRENT PROBLEMS OF MARKETING RESEARCH

Marketing research for balanced economic development in less-developed countries needs to focus on answering the following fundamental question: which type of marketing system and distribution techniques and methods do less-developed countries need to adequately support an efficient and equitable socioeconomic development process? A marketing

TABLE 6.2. Uses and Problems of Marketing Research in LDCs

Micro use	*Macro use*
Increase market share and profitability of individual firms (facilitatory tool to meet individual company objectives)	Facilitate socioeconomic development process (facilitatory tool to meet developmental objectives)

Collection of primary and secondary
data

Firm-specific problems encountered (technical)	*Country-specific problems encountered (nontechnical)*
Probability sampling very difficult (kept at rudimentary level)	Lack of good research facilities
Inaccessibility to respondents	Lack of trained researchers, research organizations, interviewers, and supervisors
Interviewing difficult	Cultural and societal factors hinder data collection
Widespread sampling errors	Technical staff dominate the marketing research process
Telephone and mail surveys are very difficult to conduct	Poor transportation network
Many dwelling units are unidentified	No common language in most cases
High response errors and nonexistent sampling frames	Low literacy rates
Use of outdated, incomplete or nonexistent sampling frames	Family structures are extended and complexly interwoven
Measurement errors common	
Lack of sufficient or accurate basic background data	

Source: E. Kaynak, "Marketing Research Techniques and Approaches for LDCs," in *Marketing in Developing Countries*, edited by G. S. Kindra (London: Croom Helm, 1984): p. 241. Reprinted with permission.

system is a socioeconomic process dealing with an exchange of information, property titles, goods, and value units and the transformation of goods in space, time, quality, and quantity.[15]

To relate marketing to economic development objectives and structural conditions in less-developed countries requires consideration of the following four factors:

a. Interaction between various sectors relevant to the economic development process
b. Workable diagnosis of marketing problems/opportunities
c. Definition of relevant performance criteria related to economic development
d. Evaluation and preparation of a marketing research blueprint as a basis for devising more effective and workable institutions for economic development[16]

Despite a considerable degree of multi-country marketing research,[17] the question of universal or unique approaches to undertaking marketing research in LDCs still remains an unresolved international marketing policy issue.[18] In the vast majority of LDCs, development of marketing research is in an "embryonic stage," whereas the current status of marketing research in the newly emerging economies of Asia, such as Singapore, Thailand, Malaysia, and the Philippines has moved from an embryonic to a growth stage in the last decade.[19]

One can easily hypothesize that the transferability of North American marketing research techniques to LDCs depends, to a greater extent, on the stage of socioeconomic and technological development and the cultural characteristics of the population in the recipient LDC. Generally, however, it does not depend on the intrinsic worth and usefulness of marketing research techniques or on their ultimate benefit.[20]

Undertaking marketing research in LDCs hence necessitates the use of innovative and adaptive marketing research techniques, as well as approaches to elicit information from respondents who portray entirely different socioeconomic and cultural characteristics.[21] Factors affecting cross-national marketing research in different LDC market environments is shown in Figure 6.3. The way marketing research is conducted in an LDC is affected by the culture-bound as well as respondent-related impediments. In addition, limited availability of research technology and prevailing legal and business environments serve as delimiting factors.[22]

However, some European researchers who have conducted marketing research in the Arab countries of the Middle East talk about their success stories.[23] It is apparently quite possible to conduct sophisticated and modern marketing research programs in the Persian Gulf. Because the area is a wealthy and rapidly developing market, it offers the best research infrastructure to would-be researchers.

A satisfactory solution to the above-mentioned marketing research problems needs to be found. For this reason, original empirical work is required, including fact-finding field surveys. The need for an empirical

FIGURE 6.3. Factors Affecting Cross-National Marketing Research Respondent-Related Impediments

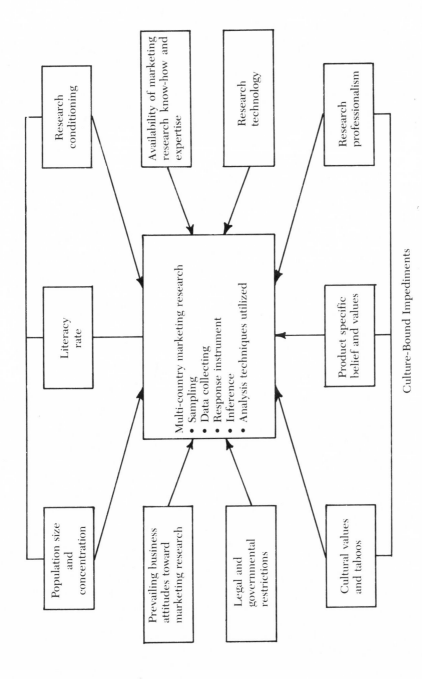

Source: E. Kaynak, "The Use of Marketing Research to Facilitate International Marketing within Developing Countries," in *International Marketing Management,* edited by E. Kaynak (New York: Praeger Special Studies, 1984), p. 159. Reprinted with permission.

type of marketing research is justified in less-developed countries on at least five counts:

a. Statistical documentation is often unsatisfactory in less-developed countries because of insufficient facilities for collection and retrieval of relevant data and limited financial funds available to universities and other research institutions.

b. The importance of empirically obtained information and its relevance to economic development policies is acknowledged by both research institutions and policymakers alike in many less-developed countries. Yet domestic research capacity is frequently underutilized, and qualified research workers are assigned to other tasks. There is an unreasonable and unfounded distrust of the knowledge of native marketing researchers and their studies.

c. Analyses are frequently limited to macro and global aspects, while micro-level problems on the grass-roots level are overlooked.

d. Studies often concentrate on planning and target-setting, while neglecting implementation and control stages.

e. Socioeconomic and technological contexts of the problems tend to be neglected.[24]

In order to achieve fruitful and objective results in marketing research a competent organization is required. A general look at the less-developed countries reveals the fact that most such organizations are government sponsored, and in fact very few are in the line of marketing research. This shows that the importance and the critical role of marketing in the economic development of these countries has been underestimated by the people in the area of management. The answer to "Why has it been like this?" lies in the fact that the major obstacle to the use of marketing research in less-developed nations is the attitude toward marketing of business and government administrators. These people are inclined to view marketing as a mechanistic process and think that they have no marketing problems because of the production-oriented character of the prevailing economy. Since the demand typically exceeds the supply there is little concern about profits through customer satisfaction.[25]

Besides limited effective demand the government usually follows the policy of not encouraging competition. Most firms are also bound by the constraint of limited availability of managerial competency. Most of the firms in such countries are family owned, and very few of these have an academic background along the lines of management. Their objective being merely to preserve the status quo, they have no interest in spending money on development or for marketing research. As far as product development is concerned there is little if any attempt being made, since most products are copies of Western products.[26] Although these company owners lack the managerial talent to utilize the tools of marketing and marketing research effectively, they very seldom think of obtaining qualified help. The people who are qualified to conduct marketing research in less-developed countries are associated with either government research organizations or universities. The gap, on the other hand, between the academic and business sectors is considerably greater in these nations than in industrialized countries. Unfortunately, firms do not refer to the academic environment as a source of expert advice.[27]

The "bureaucratic attitude" observed in the social and economic environment of the less-developed nations proves to be a major obstacle to obtaining meaningful and reliable information from civil servants. There is insecurity and a fear of "losing one's status" which hinders free and sincere response in that area. Questions are rarely welcome and the respondents suspect that their answers may reveal certain deficiencies.[28] As a consequence it seems that cultural and social progress are prerequisites for economic development. Only then can efficient tools such as marketing research be fully utilized within the economic environment of LDCs. Nevertheless, the existence of methodological and technical obstacles will not prevent marketing researchers from establishing the basis for effective planning and control of the economic development process.[29]

In line with the rapidly expanding economy, officials of less-developed countries try to adopt advanced marketing research techniques for the benefit of private industry and commerce. Through marketing research techniques, analyses are made of the profile of demand of firms as well as consumers, in the main markets, to determine whether or not the marketing methods are changing in such a manner as to necessitate changes in market structure or in marketing systems.[30]

In a planned economy, on the other hand, research is not only a means of obtaining market information, it is an indispensable factor in the formulation of plans for the national economy and for supervision of the fulfillment of economic development plans.[31] In these economies the need for large-scale macro economic market research is emphasized, while market research by manufacturing units is principally concerned with the sales possibilities of individual products, with competition analysis taking second place. Macroeconomic market research has to extend to considerable depth with regard to production, consumption, and public opinion.[32]

USE OF MARKETING RESEARCH IN LDCs

It has been stated that marketing research information can help managers of firms and public policymakers in LDCs at both the individual

TABLE 6.3. Micro and Macro Roles of Marketing Research in Economic Development

Use of marketing research	
Individual firm level (Micro-role)	Societal level (Macro-role)
The planning and execution of transactions of distribution of goods and services within a given economic system and cultural pattern ↓	The system construction of the infrastructure as well as the whole production–marketing system interaction ↓
Identification of profitable sales opportunities, prediction of changes in the competitive environment, efficient allocation of advertising expenditures, isolation and pinpointing of trouble spots as well as lucrative market opportunities when formulating marketing strategies. ↓	Fostering and stimulating economic development of LDCs. Development of models of performance in marketing by use of marketing research techniques. ↓
Application • Product policy • Pricing policy • Promotion policy • Distribution channel policy • Policies of industry and government	Application • Information network • Warehousing • Transportation • Banking and insurance • Communication • Product development and testing • Quality control • Credit information

Source: Compiled by the author.

firm (micro) level as well as economic development planners at the societal (macro) level.[33] In most cases, conducting surveys in LDCs is difficult because of their socioeconomic, technological, and cultural structures, which hinder the utilization of certain marketing research techniques and methods.

There are certain important characteristics of the LDC environment that impinge on the role of marketing research. This role of marketing research cannot be fully assessed unless one elaborates on the micro (firm-specific) and macro (societal-level) roles of marketing research in the economic development endeavors of LDCs (see Table 6.3). Although the

TABLE 6.4. Utilization of Different Marketing Research Techniques

	Application to different environments	
Uses	Third-world countries	Developed countries
Frequency of research	Ad-hoc	Continuous
Type of research	Market research	Marketing research
Type of inputs	Generate data	Generate information
Research focus	Micro-issues	Macro-issues
Marketing research institutions	Government-sponsored	Privately-sponsored
Type of research techniques utilized	Adaptive	Innovative
Sampling methods	Convenience	Systematic random
Interviewing techniques	Personal interviews	Mail and telephone interviews
Use of rating scales	Visual (graphic)	Verbal (numerical)
Sampling frame	Outdated or nonexistent	Updated and available
Most common scales used	Three-point	Five- to seven-point

Source: E. Kaynak, "Marketing Research Needs of Less-Developed Countries: Standardization versus Localization," in *Developments in Marketing Science VII*, edited by J. D. Lindquist (Kalamazoo, MI: Academy of Marketing Science, 1984), p. 162. Reprinted with permission.

difficulties in undertaking marketing research in LDCs are great, with the will and appreciation of local needs and business practices they can be overcome. As a result, marketing research techniques developed in the economically advanced countries of the West need to be tailored or localized before they can be used with a similar degree of effectiveness and usefulness in LDCs. Utilization of marketing research techniques in developed versus less-developed environments is shown in Table 6.4.

MARKETING RESEARCH AND ECONOMIC DEVELOPMENT IN LDCs

During the economic development process of LDCs, marketing research activity at micro (firm) level identifies profitable sales opportunities, predicts changes in the competitive business environment, deals with efficient allocation of advertising expenditures, and isolates and pinpoints trouble spots as well as lucrative market opportunities when formulating marketing strategies.[34] Besides these micro-level uses, marketing research can also play an indispensable role at the macro- (country) level by fostering and stimulating the economic development of LDCs.[35]

If research is to become an effective tool for analysis leading to market expansion in LDCs, specialists will have to devote more time in devising effective research tools. For this purpose, some of the methods used will have to be less sophisticated than those used in developed countries. If these countries are to be assisted in their economic development, public policymakers, by use of marketing research techniques, will have to devise attainable models of performance in marketing if LDCs are to be competitive in world markets. These kinds of performance models have already been developed and tested in a number of East European countries.[36]

Because of inadequate organizational arrangements, the limited availability of reliable statistics, quantifying factors and staff support, the speed at which information is obtained, the instability of government regulations and the economic instability of the country, the use of quantitative marketing research techniques has been limited.[37] As formal and reliable basic data is frequently difficult to obtain in LDCs, unconventional sources of data collection may prove to be the most useful. Qualitative research has a special value in LDC research. For instance, the practice of qualitative research in Turkey was pioneered by the focus group interview, which has made significant inroads in this LDC in recent years.[38]

Educational factors and social psychology as well as the sociological structure of the population of LDCs have to be taken into consideration before conducting marketing research in these countries. The questionnaire, for instance, has to be adapted to the educational level of the group and questions have to be arranged in such a way that they will achieve the results desired. In most LDCs, respondents with low educational attainment tend to have a shorter span of attention, to react more to real products than to ideas, and to prefer discussing the present rather than speculate about future possibilities.[39] As a result, the time span considered in the questions asked needs to be shorter.[40]

In developed countries, verbal rating scales with numerical values attached are used very successfully. Low literacy rates in most LDCs preclude this method of eliciting information from respondents. Instead, visual scales with graphics are commonly used in LDCs because they are easily understood by most respondents.[41] Also, the low literacy rate would render the Likert or Gutman-type scaling techniques inapplicable in LDCs. In these countries, respondents with low levels of education are usually unable to make the fine distinction between "strongly agree" and "moderately agree." Some languages do not even have words describing these alternatives. A solution to this dilemma may lie in the use of judgment-type scaling techniques like Thurstone's equal appearing interval scale, but with fewer intervals.[42] Instead of the usual attitude scale items to which the respondent is asked to indicate agreement or disagreement, behavioral items might be used.[43]

National differences among LDCs can have a considerable effect on the formulation of the initial design of a multi-country survey. Unless these differences are understood and taken into consideration at the planning stage, and allowed for in the design of the survey, the marketing research may completely fail to achieve its set objectives.[44] Differences in behavior and attitude patterns among LDC consumers necessitate considerable differences and adaptation in survey design. For instance, most LDC respondents do not understand the fine distinctions among adjectives in five- or seven-point scales. In some languages there are not that many alternative adjectives to describe a particular life-style phenomenon. The solution to this problem has been the use of three-point scales, which apparently make greater sense to respondents, especially at lower income and educational levels. There is also a tendency among LDC respondents to favor midpoints when five- to ten-point scales are used. When the shorter and simpler scales are utilized, the problem of favoring midpoints is eliminated.[45]

In developed countries of the West, quantitative marketing research techniques and experimentation are utilized much more. Because of differences in market research facilities, capabilities, and marketing conditions, the research design and techniques utilized in LDCs must be adapted to local conditions. As a result, marketing researchers use more observation and juries of experts.[46]

CONCLUSIONS

In LDCs marketing research has certain major roles to play both in the domestic market and in the evaluation of external demand for the country's output. Because of the socioeconomic, cultural, technological, and government-related difficulties involved in the marketing research process, certain steps should be taken. First of all, marketing research techniques that have been used and applied in the developed countries cannot be transferred without considering the prevailing conditions of the marketplace in LDCs. Second, there is an urgent need to upgrade the research capabilities of local managers as well as to improve their appreciation of marketing research as a "legitimate" decision-making tool. Third, LDC governments should improve their research infrastructure, which is badly

Perspective," in *Agricultural Market Analysis: Development, Performance, Process,* edited by V. L. Sorensen (East Lansing, MI: Michigan State University, 1964), p. 16.

21. S. Gordon Reeding, "Cultural Factors in the Marketing Process in Southeast Asia," *Journal of the Market Research Society* 24, no. 2 (1982): 98-114.

22. P. T. Bauer, "State Control of Marketing," p. 30. See note 1.

23. Glen Carter, "Modern Marketing Research in an Arab Environment," in *Taking Stock: What Have We Learned and Where Are We Going?* Paper presented at the 33d ESOMAR Congress, Monte Carlo, September 14-18, 1980.

24. E. Kaynak, "The Use of Marketing Research to Facilitate International Marketing Within Developing Countries," in *International Marketing Management,* edited by E. Kaynak (New York: Praeger Special Studies, 1984), pp. 160-61.

25. Kaynak, "Marketing Research Techniques," p. 243. See note 18.

26. Erdener Kaynak, *Marketing in the Third World* (New York: Praeger, 1982).

27. Ugur Yavas and Erdener Kaynak, "Current Status of Marketing Research in Developing Countries: Problems and Opportunities," *Journal of International Marketing and Marketing Research* 5, no. 2 (June 1980): 82-83.

28. Kaynak, "Marketing Research Techniques," pp. 245-46. See note 18.

29. E. D. Smith, "Agricultural Marketing Research," p. 666. See note 16.

30. G. Rice and E. Mahmoud, "Forecasting and Data Bases in International Business," *Management International Review* 24, no. 4 (1984): 59-71.

31. Laszlo Szabo, "Market Research in the European Socialist Countries," in *Marketing East/West: A Comparative View,* ESOMAR/WAPOR Congress, Budapest, 1973, pp. 191-203.

32. L. Szabo, "Market Research in Hungary," *European Research* 7, no. 2 (March 1979): 71.

33. Paul Howard Berent, "International Research is Different," in *AMA Combined Proceedings,* series no. 37, edited by Edward M. Mazze, pp. 293-97.

34. Ugur Yavas, "Marketing Research Usage by Domestic and Foreign Manufacturing Firms in Turkey," *Management International Review* 23, no. 2 (1983): 59.

35. John Z. Kracmar, *Marketing Research in the Developing Countries: A Handbook* (New York: Praeger, 1973); Folz, "The Relevance of Marketing." See note 3.

36. A. C. Samli, "An Approach for Estimating Market Potential in East Europe," *Journal of International Business Studies* 8, no. 2 (Fall/Winter 1977): 49-53.

37. Guvenc G. Alpander, "Use of Quantitative Methods," pp. 71-77. See note 14.

38. Yavas, "Marketing Research Usage," p. 59. See note 34.

39. Mary Goodyear, "Qualitative Research in Developing Countries," *Journal of the Market Research Society* 24, no. 2 (1982): 86-96.

40. George M. Gaither, "Researching Latin America," in *New Directions in Marketing,* proceedings of the American Marketing Association, New York, June 14-16, 1965, edited by Frederick E. Webster, pp. 538-47.

41. N. Morris and A. P. van der Reis, "An Investigation of the Transferability of Rating Scale Techniques to Transport Research in a Developing Country" (National Institute for Transport and Road Research, CSIR, South Africa, September 1980), pp. 110-14.

42. R. Angelmar and B. Pras, "Verbal Rating Scales for Multinational Research," *European Research* 6, no. 2 (March 1978): 62-67.

43. Godwin C. Chu, "Problems of Cross-Cultural Communication Research," *Journalism Quarterly* (Autumn 1964): 557-68.

44. A. O. Ogunmodede, "The Role of Research Marketing," in *Marketing in Nigeria,* edited by Julius O. Onah (London: Cassell, 1979), pp. 95-96.

45. A. Graeme Cranch, "Modern Marketing Techniques Applied to Developing Coun-

Dawson, L. M. "Facing the New Realities of International Development." *Business* 31, no. 1 (January–February 1981): 29–35.

_____. "Setting Multinational Industrial Marketing Strategies." *Industrial Marketing Management* 9, no. 3 (July 1980): 179–86.

DeJoya, A. R. "Government's Role in Marketing." *Marketing Horizons* 17, nos. 6–7 (June–July 1978): 11–14.

Dholakia, N. and R. R. Dholakia. "Marketing in the Emerging World Order." *Journal of Macromarketing* 2 (Spring 1982): 47–56.

_____. "Missing Links: Marketing and the Newer Theories of Development." In *Marketing in Developing Countries,* edited by G. S. Kindra (London: Croom Helm Limited, 1984), pp. 57–75.

Dholakia, N. and F. A. Firat. "The Role of Marketing in the Development of Non-Market Sectors and Conditions Necessary for Success." In *Marketing Systems for Developing Countries,* edited by D. Izraeli, D. N. Izraeli, and F. Meissner, (New York: John Wiley & Sons, 1976), pp. 50–60.

Dholakia, R. R. "Intergeneration Differences in Consumer Behavior: Some Evidence from a Developing Country." *Journal of Business Research* 12, no. 1 (March 1984): 19–34.

DiPaolo, G. A. *Marketing Strategy for Economic Development.* (New York: Dunellen, 1976).

Dixon, D. F. "Role of Marketing in Early Theories of Economic Development." *Journal of Macromarketing* 1 (Fall 1981): 19–27.

Dominguez, L. V. and Christina Vanmarcke. "Studying the Role of Marketing in the Development of Industrial Enterprise in Resource-Rich, Market-Poor Countries." University of Miami School of Business Administration, Working Paper no. 83–5, November 1983.

Douglas, E. *Economics of Marketing.* (New York: Harper & Row, 1975).

Douglas, S. P. "Patterns and Parallels of Marketing Structures in Several Countries." *M.S.U. Business Topics* 19 (Spring 1971): 38–48.

Douglas, S. P. and Y. Wind. "Environmental Factors and Marketing Practices." *European Journal of Marketing* 7, no. 3 (Winter 1973–1974): 155–65.

Drucker, P. F. "Marketing and Economic Development." *Journal of Marketing* 23 (January 1958): 29–33.

El-Namaki, M. S. S. *Problems of Management in a Developing Environment.* (Amsterdam: North-Holland, 1979).

El-Sherbini, A. A. "Behavioral Analysis of the Role of Marketing in Economic Development." *Journal of Macromarketing* 3, no. 1 (Spring 1983): 76–79.

_____. "Marketing in the Industrialization of Undeveloped Countries." *Journal of Marketing* (January 1965): 28–32.

Elton, W. W. "The Developing World." In *Changing Marketing Systems: Consumer, Corporate and Government Interfaces,* edited by R. Moyer (Washington, D.C.: American Marketing Association, 1967), pp. 242–43.

Emlen, W. J. "Let's Export Marketing Know-How." *Harvard Business Review* 35, no. 6 (November–December 1958): 70–76.

Etemad, H. "Is Marketing the Catalyst in the Economic Development Process?" In *Marketing in Developing Countries*, edited by G. S. Kindra (London: Croom Helm, 1984), pp. 29–56.

Etgar, M. "A Failure in Marketing Technology Transfer: The Case of Rice Distribution in the Ivory Coast." *Journal of Macromarketing* 3 (Spring 1983): 59–68.

Fisher, A. G. B. "Marketing Structure and Economic Development: Comment." *Quarterly Journal of Economics* 68 (February 1954): 151–54.

Forman, S. and J. F. Riegelhaupt. "Market Place and Marketing System: Toward a Theory of Peasant Economic Integration." *Comparative Studies in Society and History* 12 (1970): 188–212.

Foster, T. "Latin America—Land of Opportunity." *Distribution Worldwide* 76, no. 10 (October 1977): 45–48.

Frank, A. G. "The Development of Underdevelopment." *Monthly Review* 18, no. 4 (September 1966): 17–31.

Freedman, D. S. "The Role of the Consumption of Modern Durables in Economic Development." *Economic Development and Cultural Change* 19, no. 1 (October 1970): 25–48.

Friedman, I. S. "The New World of the Rich-Poor and the Poor-Rich." *Fortune* (May 1975): 244–52.

Garlick, P. C. *African Traders and Economic Development in Ghana.* (Oxford: Clarendon Press, 1971).

Gilbreath, K. "From Fruited Plain to Industrial State: Market Trends in American Economic History." *Baylor Business Studies* 11, no. 2 (May–July 1980): 81–96.

Geertz, C. "The Bazaar Economy: Information and Search in Peasant Marketing." *American Economic Review* 68, no. 2 (May 1978): 28–32.

Gillis, M. "The Role of State Enterprises in Economic Development." *Social Research* 47 (Summer 1980): 248–89.

Glade, W. P., W. A. Strong, J. G. Udell, and R. Littlefield. *Marketing in a Developing Nation* (Lexington, MA: D.C. Heath, 1970).

Glade, W. P. and J. G. Udell. "The Marketing Concept and Economic Development: Peru." *Journal of Inter-American Studies* 10, no. 4 (October 1968): 533–46.

Goertz, J. "KETA: A Force Behind Exports." *International Trade Forum* 15, no. 3 (July–September 1979): 16–20, 27–35.

Goldman, A. "Outreach of Consumers and the Modernization of Urban Food Retailing in Developed Countries." *Journal of Marketing* 38 (October 1974): 8–16.

Goldsmith, R. W. "The Comparative Approach to the Problems of Economic Growth and Structure." In *Comparative Management and Marketing*, edited by J. J. Boddewyn (Glenview, IL: Scott, Foresman and Company, 1969), pp. 14–19.

Gorle, P. "Why Change Means Money." *Marketing* (Britain) 19, 1 (October 4, 1984): 58–62.

Green, B. L. and G. R. Hawkes. "Development as a Multistage Process, Growth and Change." *Journal of Regional Development* 5, no. 4 (October 1974): 21.

Griggs, J. E. "Marketing in Economic Development." In *Evaluating Marketing Change: An Application of Systems Theory* (East Lansing, MI: M.S.U. International Business and Economic Studies, Michigan State University, 1970), pp. 1-14.

Guthrie, C. B. "Economics of Voluntary Chains in Latin America." In *Marketing Systems for Developing Countries*, edited by D. Izraeli, D. N. Izraeli, and F. Meissner (New York: John Wiley & Sons, 1976), pp. 160-71.

Hanna, N., A. H. Kizilbash, and A. Smart. "Marketing Strategy Under Conditions of Economic Scarcity." *Journal of Marketing* 39 (January 1975): 63-80.

Hansz, J. E. and J. D. Goodnow. "A Multivariate Classification of Country Market Environments." In *Marketing Education and the Real World and Dynamic Marketing in a Changing World*, edited by B. W. Becker and H. Becker (Chicago, IL: American Marketing Association, 1973), pp. 191-98.

Harrison, K. "Development, Unemployment, and Marketing in Latin America." Occasional paper no. 2, Latin American Studies Center, Michigan State University, April 1972.

Heenan, D. A. and W. J. Keegan. "The Rise of Third World Multinationals." *Harvard Business Review* 57 (January–February 1979): 101-109.

Heldmann, H. "The Role of Transport and Traffic in National Economy." *Inter Economics*, no. 11 (1973): 340-43.

Helleiner, G. K. "World Market Imperfections and the Developing Countries." *Overseas Development Council NIED Series*, Occasional paper no. 11, May 1978.

Henry, P. M. "Economic Development, Progress and Culture." *Development: Seeds of Change* 3, no. 4 (1981): 17-25.

Hilger, M. T. "Consumer Perceptions of a Public Marketer in Mexico." *Columbia Journal of World Business* 15, no. 3 (Fall 1980): 75-82.

———. "Theories of the Relationship between Marketing and Economic Development: Public Policy Implications." In *Macro-Marketing: Distributive Processes from a Societal Perspective, An Elaboration of Issues*, edited by P. D. White and C. C. Slater, pp. 333-378, Boulder, CO: University of Colorado, August 14-17, 1977.

Hill, J. S. and R. R. Still. "Effects of Urbanization on Multinational Product Planning: Markets in Lesser-Developed Countries." *Columbia Journal of World Business* 19, no. 2 (Summer 1984): 62-67.

Hirsch, L. V. "The Contribution of Marketing to Economic Development—A Generally Neglected Area." In *The Social Responsibility of Marketing*, edited by W D. Stevens (Chicago, IL: American Marketing Association, 1961), pp. 413-18.

Holton, R. H. "How Advertising Achieved Responsibility Among Economists." *Advertising Age* 51 (April 30, 1980): 56-64.

———. "Marketing Structure and Economic Development." *Quarterly Journal of Economics* 67 (August 1953): 344-61.

Hong, A. "1980s Promise Top Market Opportunities." *Advertising Age* 49, no. 50 (December 11, 1978): 29, 47.

Hoselitz, B. F. "Problem of Adapting and Communicating Modern Techniques to Less Developed Areas." *Economic Development and Cultural Change* 2, no. 1 (January 1968): 249–68.

Howard, C. A. "Continuing Challenges of Economic Integration: How Far the Distance Between Asean and CER?" In *Proceedings of the Academy of International Business Asia—Pacific Dimensions of International Business*, edited by S. M. Dawson and J. R. Wills (College of Business Administration, University of Hawaii, December 18–20, 1982), pp. 617–27.

Hughes, H. "Industrialization and Development: A Stocktaking." *Industry and Development*, no. 2 (1980): 1–27.

Hung, C. L. "Economic and Market Environment: The Case of Hong Kong." In *Marketing in Developing Countries*, edited by G. S. Kindra (London: Croom Helm, 1984), pp. 95–114.

Hunt, L. J. "Marketing Education in Developing Environments." In *New Marketing for Social and Economic Progress*, 1975 AMA Combined Proceedings, series no. 36, edited by R. C. Curhan (Chicago, IL: American Marketing Association, 1975), pp. 642–46.

Jacobs, L., R. Worthley, and C. Keown. "Perceived Buyer Satisfaction and Selling Pressure versus Pricing Policy: A Comparative Study of Retailers in Ten Developing Countries." *Journal of Business Research* 12, no. 1 (March 1984): 63–74.

Jansson, H. "Interfirm Linkages in a Developing Economy." Department of Business Administration, University of Uppsala, Uppsala 1981.

Jessop, G. "Greece: A Nation at the Crossroads." *Marketing* (Britain) (December 1979): 73–77.

Kaitati, J. G. "Marketing Without Exchange of Money." *Harvard Business Review*, vol. 60, no. 6 (November–December 1982): 72–74.

Katona, G. "Selling Government Programs." *Journal of Macromarketing* 2 (Fall 1982): 38–42.

Kay, W. G. "Marketers Must Feel the Winds of Exchange, Point U.S. Business in Direction of Success." *Marketing News* (July 10, 1981): 7.

Kaynak, E. "A Proposed National Food Distribution Plan for a Burgeoning Developing Economy." *Agricultural Administration* 17 (1984): 33–50.

_____. "Comparative Analyses of the Socio-Economic, Cultural and Regulatory Environments of Distributors in L.D.C.s." *Singapore Management Review* 7, no. 1 (January 1985): 65–76.

_____. "Food Distribution Systems: Evolution in Latin America and the Middle East." *Food Policy* 6, no. 2 (May 1981): 78–90.

_____. *Global Perspectives in Marketing.* (New York: Praeger, 1985).

_____. "Government and Food Distribution in LDCs: The Turkish Experience." *Food Policy* 5, no. 2 (May 1980): 132–42.

_____. *International Marketing Management.* (New York: Praeger, 1984).

_____. *Marketing in the Third World.* (New York: Praeger, 1982).

_____. "The Adaptation of Marketing Institutions of the West into a Less-Developed Economy: The Turkish Experience." *Nigerian Journal of Business Management* 2, no. 2 (July–August 1978): 304–308.

_____. "The Role and Relevance of Marketing Research to Economic Development of Less-Developed Countries." *Hong Kong Journal of Business Management* 2 (1984): 63–73.

Kaynak, E. and S. T. Cavusgil. "The Evolution of Food Retailing Systems: Contrasting the Experience of Developed and Developing Countries." *Journal of the Academy of Marketing Science* 10, no. 3 (1982): 249–67.

Kaynak, E. and R. Savitt. *Comparative Marketing Systems.* (New York: Praeger, 1984).

Kindra, G. S. *Marketing in Developing Countries.* (London: Croom Helm, 1984).

Kinsey, J. "The Role of Marketing in Economic Development." *European Journal of Marketing* 16, no. 6 (1982): 64–77.

Kirpalani, V. H. "Opportunities/Problems in the International Transfer of Marketing/Technology to the Third World." In *AMA Combined Proceedings,* edited by E. M. Mazze (Chicago, IL: American Marketing Association, 1975), pp. 285–88.

Kotler, P. "Neglected Areas Demand Attention of Scholars if Marketing Discipline is to Reach Maturation." *Marketing News* 41 (September 3, 1982).

Kotler, P. and L. Fahey. "The World's Champion Marketers: The Japanese." *Journal of Business Strategy* 3, no. 1 (Summer 1982): 3–13.

Kunkle, J. H. "Values and Behavior in Economic Development." *Economic Development and Cultural Change* 13, no. 3 (April 1963): 257–77.

Lace, G. "Cashing in on a Black Economy." *Marketing* (Britain) 12, no. 3 (January 20, 1983): 18–20.

Lamont, D. "A Theory of Marketing Development: Mexico." In *Marketing and Economic Development,* edited by P. D. Bennett (Chicago, IL: American Marketing Association, 1965), pp. 44–45.

Lamont, D. L. "Opportunities for Marketing Growth in the Mexican Market." *Southern Journal of Business* 4, no. 2 (April 1969): 272–78.

Langley, J. and J. Foggin. "Selected Aspects of Economic Development as Related to Distribution." *Survey of Business* 15 (Spring 1980): 30–35.

Layton, R. A. "Trade Flows in Macromarketing Systems." *Journal of Macromarketing* 1 (Spring 1981): 35–48.

Linde, V. *Marketing in Developing Countries.* (Götheborg: Marknowlsvetenskap, Vasastadens Bokbinderi, 1980).

Littlefield, J. E. "The Relationship of Marketing in Economic Development in Peru." *Southern Journal of Business* 3, no. 3 (July 1968): 1–14.

Loeb, M. "For a Bigger Economic Pie, Stir in Five Ingredients." *Marketing News* (July 9, 1982): 9.

Lomax, D. F. "International Trade and Industrial Policy." *National Westminster Bank Quarterly Review* (May 1976): 45–56.

Luqmani, M., Z. A. Qurueshi, and L Delene. "Marketing in Islamic Countries: A Viewpoint." *M.S.U. Business Topics* 28, no. 3 (Summer 1980): 17–25.

McCarthy, E. J. "Effective Marketing Institutions for Economic Development." In *Toward Scientific Marketing,* edited by S. A. Greyser (Chicago, IL: American Marketing Association, 1964), pp. 393–404.

McClenahen, J. S. "Japan—Trade Troubles Disturb Her Economic Maturity." *Industry Week* 196, no. 1 (January 9, 1978): 34–38.

McCullough, J. "The Role of Traditional Markets in the Economic Development of an Agrarian Region." In *1978 Proceedings of the Academy of International Business* (Chicago, IL, August 1978), pp. 130–33.

Mallen, B. "Marketing Channels and Economic Development: A Literative Overview." *International Journal of Physical Distribution* 5, no. 5 (1975): 230–37.

Meissner, F. "Rise of Third World Demands Marketing Be Stood on Its Head." *Marketing News* 12 (October 6, 1978): 1, 16.

Michell, P. "Infrastructures and International Marketing Effectiveness." *Columbia Journal of World Business* 14, no. 1 (Spring 1979): 91–101.

Miller, C. J. (ed.). *Marketing and Economic Development.* (Lincoln: University of Nebraska Press, 1967).

Mitchell, I. S. "Marketers' Attitudes Toward the Marketing Concept in Nigerian Business and Non-Business Operations." *Columbia Journal of World Business* 19, no. 3 (Fall 1984): 62–71.

Mittendorf, H. F. "The Challenge of Organizing City Food Marketing Systems in Developing Countries." *Zeilschrift für auslandische Landwirtschaft* 17, no. 4 (October–December 1978): 323–41.

Moore, T. E. "Analysis of the Chinese Market for Light Industry Manufacturing Equipment." *Business America* 5, no. 9 (May 3, 1982): 16–19.

Moyer, R. "Marketing in Economic Development." International Business Occasional Paper no. 1 (East Lansing, MI: Michigan State University, 1965).

Moyer, R. S. "The Structure of Markets in Developing Economies." *Business Topics* 12 (Autumn 1964): 43–60.

Moyer, R. S. and S. C. Hollander (eds.) *Markets and Marketing in Developing Economies.* (Homewood, IL: Richard D. Irwin, 1968).

Muller-Heumann, G. and R. Bohringer. "Stimulating Consumption—An Alternative." *Intereconomics,* no. 11 (1973): 344–47.

Myers, K. H. "Marketing's Role in the Economy." In *Towards Scientific Marketing* edited by S. A. Greyser (Chicago, IL: American Marketing Association, 1963), pp. 355–65.

Myers, K. H. and O. A. Smalley. "Marketing History and Economic Development." *Business History Review* 33 (Autumn 1959): 387–401.

Nielsen, R. P. "Marketing and Development in LDCs." *Columbia Journal of World Business* 9 (Winter 1974): 46–49.

Nnolim, D. A. "Marketing as a Tool of Economic Development." In *Marketing in Nigeria,* edited by J. O. Onah (London: Cassell, 1979), pp. 7–21.

Norman H. R. and P. Blair. "The Coming Growth in 'Appropriate' Technology." *Harvard Business Review* 60, no. 6 (November–December 1982): 62–64, 68.

Odia, S. G. "Marketing: The Neglected Managerial Function of a Booming Economy." In *Marketing in Nigeria,* edited by J. O. Onah, (London: Cassell, 1979), pp. 3–6.

O'Gorman, F. *Role of Change Agents in Development.* (East Lansing, MI: Non-Formal Education Information Centre, Michigan State University, 1978).

Onah, J. O. *Marketing in Nigeria.* (London: Cassell, 1979).

Organization for Economic Co-operation and Development. *Food Marketing and Economic Growth.* Paris, 1970.

Oritt, P. L., and A. J. Hagan. "Channels of Distribution and Economic Development." *Atlanta Economic Review* 27, no. 4 (July–August 1977): 40–44.

Padolecchia, S. *Marketing in the Developing World.* (New Delhi: Vikas Publishing House, 1979).

Petrof, J. V. "Economic Development and Marketing." In *Selling to the Global Shopping Center,* edited by H. W. Berkman and J. K. Fenyo (New York, 1977), pp. 87–90.

_____. "Small Business and Economic Development: The Case for Government Intervention." *Journal of Small Business Management* 18, no. 1 (January 1980): 51–56.

_____. "The Role of Marketing in a Developing Society." *Optimum* 7, no. 4 (1976): 27–36.

Pfaff, M. "The Marketing Function and Economic Development: An Approach to a Systematic Decision Model." In *Proceedings of 1965 Fall Conference AMA* (Chicago, IL: American Marketing Association, 1965), pp. 46–47.

Prasad, S. B. "Comparative Managerialism as an Approach to International Economic Growth." In *Comparative Management and Marketing,* edited by J. J. Boddewyn (Glenview, IL: Scott, Foresman and Company, 1969), pp. 75–84.

Preston, L. E. "Consumer Goods Marketing in a Developing Economy." Center of Planning and Economic Research, Research Monograph Series no. 19, Athens, Greece, 1968.

_____. "Market Control in Developing Economies." *American Marketing Association Proceedings* 26 (Winter 1967): 223–27.

_____. "Market Development and Market Control." In *Changing Marketing Systems: Consumer, Corporate and Government Interfaces,* edited by R. Moyer (Washington, D.C: American Marketing Association, 1967), pp. 223–27.

_____. "Marketing Organization and Economic Development: Structure, Products, and Management." In *Vertical Marketing Systems,* edited by L. P. Bucklin (Glenview, IL: Scott, Foresman and Company, 1970), pp. 116–34.

_____. "The Commercial Sector and Economic Development." In *Markets and Marketing in Developing Economies,* edited by R. Moyer and S. Hollander (Homewood, IL: Richard D. Irwin, 1968), pp. 9–23.

Rae, I. "Solving the Chinese Puzzle." *Marketing* (Britain) 2, no. 20 (August 27, 1980): 24–25.

Rao, C. P. "Industrial Marketing in the International Setting." *Arizona Business* 21, no. 3 (March 1974): 12–18.

Rao, T. R. "Marketing and Economic Development." *Marketing and Management Digest* (January 1976): 15–18.

Reddy, A. C. and C. P. Rao. "Beware These Pitfalls When Marketing U.S. Technologies in Developing Countries." *Marketing News* 19 (March 1, 1985): 3, 6.

_____."Japanese Marketing: Underlying Reasons for its Success." *Mid-South Business Journal* 2, no. 1 (January 1982): 3–6.

Reddy, A. C., J. E. Oliver, C. P. Rao, and A. L. Addington. "A Macro Behavioral Model of the Japanese Economic Miracle." *Akron Business and Economic Review* 15, no. 1 (Spring 1984): 40–45.

Riddle, D. I. "Differing Models of Economic Development: Implications for Corporate Strategy." Paper presented at the Annual Meeting of the Academy of International Business, Cleveland, Ohio, 1984.

Riley, H. M. "Improving Internal Marketing Systems as Part of National Development Systems." Occasional paper no. 3, May 1972, Latin American Studies Center, Michigan State University.

Rist, G. "Alternative Strategies to Development." *International Development Review* 22, nos. 2–3 (1980): 102–15.

Robbins, G. W. "Notions About the Origins of Trading." *Journal of Marketing* (January 1947): 228–36.

Rostow, W. W. "The Concept of a National Market and Its Economic Growth Implications." In *Marketing and Economic Development,* edited by P. D. Bennet (Chicago, IL: American Marketing Association, 1965), pp. 11–20.

Ruttan, V. "Agricultural Product and Factor Markets in Southeast Asia." *Economic Development and Cultural Change* 7 (July 1969).

Samli, A. C. "Exportability of American Marketing Knowledge." *Business Topics* 13, no. 4 (Autumn 1965): 34–42.

_____. *Marketing and Distribution Systems in Eastern Europe.* (New York: Praeger, 1978).

_____. "The Necessary Micromarketing Functions in LDCs for Macro Benefits." In *Developments in Marketing Science,* edited by J. D. Lindquist (Kalamazoo, MI: Academy of Marketing Science, 1984), pp. 153–55.

Samli, A. C. and W. Jermakovicz. "The Stage of Marketing Evolution in East European Countries." *European Journal of Marketing* 17, no. 3 (July 1983): 26–33.

Samli, A. C. and E. Kaynak. "Marketing Practices in Less-Developed Countries." *Journal of Business Research* 12, no. 1 (March 1984): 1–14.

Samli, A. C. and J. T. Mentzer. "A Model for Marketing in Economic Development." *Columbia Journal of World Business* 16, no. 3 (Fall 1981): 91–101.

Savitt, R. "Some Conceptual Issues Between Marketing Change and Economic Development." In *Developments in Marketing Science,* edited by J. D. Lindquist (Kalamazoo, MI: Academy of Marketing Science 1984), pp. 156–59.

Scherb, O. H. "Brazil Pursues Industrial Eminence." *Advertising Age* 51, no. 21 (May 12, 1980): 5–8.

Schooler, R. D. and C. Ferguson. "A Model to Determine the Activated Potential of Foreign Markets." *Marquette Business Review* (Fall 1974): 129–36.

Seers, D. "The Meaning of Development." *International Development Review* 11, no. 4 (December 1969): 2–6.

Sethi, S. P. "Comparative Cluster Analysis for World Markets." *Journal of Marketing Research* 8 (August 1971): 348–54.

Shama, A. *Marketing in a Slow-Growth Economy.* (New York: Praeger, 1980).

Shapiro, S. J. "Comparative Marketing and Economic Development." In *Science in Marketing,* edited by G. Schwartz (New York: John Wiley & Sons, 1965), pp. 398–429.

Sherbini, A. A. "Import-oriented Marketing Mechanisms." *M.S.U. Business Topics* (Spring 1968): 70–73.

_____. "Marketing in the Industrialization of Underdeveloped Countries." *Journal of Marketing* 28 (January 1965): 28–32.

Silver, S. R. and J. J. Schwartz. "The U.S. Industrial Marketer's Position in International Trade." *Industrial Marketing Management* 6 (1977): 337–52.

Simmons, A. "Economic Planning in Africa." *M.S.U. Business Topics* 23, no. 3 (Summer 1975): 19–28.

Sinclair, S. *Third World Economic Handbook.* (London: Euromonitor Publications 1982).

Singh, S. P., R. Chaganti, and P. Kelley. "Corporate Strategy and Public Policy in the Context of Social and Economic Development." In *Proceedings of the Academy of International Business Asia—Pacific Dimensions of International Business,* edited by S. M. Dawson and J. R. Wills (College of Business Administration, University of Hawaii, December 18–20, 1982), pp. 52–61.

Slater, C. C. "A Theory of Market Process." In *Macromarketing: Distribution Processes from a Societal Perspective,* edited by C. C. Slater (Boulder, CO: University of Colorado, 1976), pp. 117–40.

_____. "Market Channel Coordination and Economic Development." In *Vertical Marketing Systems,* edited by L. P. Bucklin (Glenview, IL: Scott, Foresman and Company, 1970), pp. 135–57.

_____. "Marketing—A Catalyst for Development." In *Marketing Systems for Developing Countries,* edited by D. Izraeli, D. N. Izraeli, and F. Meissner (New York: John Wiley & Sons, 1976), pp. 3–17.

_____. "Marketing Processes in Developing Latin American Societies." *Journal of Marketing* 32 (July 1968): 50–55.

_____. "Towards an Operational Theory of Market Processes." In *Macromarketing: Distribution Processes from a Societal Perspective, An Elaboration of Issues,* edited by P. D. White and C. C. Slater (Boulder, CO: University of Colorado, 1977), pp. 115–29.

Smith, C. A. "Economics of Marketing Systems: Models from Economic Geography." *Annual Review of Anthropology* 3 (1974): 167–201.

Smith, G. W. "Marketing and Economic Development: A Brazilian Case Study, 1930–70." *Food Research Institute Studies* 12, no. 3 (1973): 179–98.

Soffer, B. "Patent Activity and International Competitiveness." *Research Management* 21, no. 6 (November 1978): 34–37.

Spinks, G. R. "Attitudes Toward Agricultural Marketing in Asia and the Far East." *Monthly Bulletin of Agricultural Economics and Statistics* 19, no. 1 (January 1970): 1–8.

Stefflre, V. "Market Structure Studies: New Products for Old Markets and New Markets (Foreign) for Old Products." In *Applications of the Sciences in Marketing Management,* edited by F. M. Bass, C. W. King, and E. A. Pessemier (New York: John Wiley and Sons, 1968), pp. 251–68.

Still, R. R. and J. S. Hill. "Adapting Consumer Products to Lesser-Developed Markets." *Journal of Business Research* 12, no. 1 (March 1984): 51–61.

Symanski, R. and R. J. Bromley. "Market Development and the Ecological Complex." *The Professional Geographer* 26, no. 4 (November 1974): 382–88.

Taimni, K. K. "Employment Generation Through Handicraft Cooperatives: The Indian Experience." *International Labor Review* 120, no. 4 (July–August 1981): 505–17.

Tan, A. "Implications of Cooperatives for Economic Development." *Hacettepe Bulletin of Social Sciences and Humanities* 7, no. 1–2 (June–December 1975): 59–69.

Tanniru, R. R. "Developing Countries: Roles of Marketing." *Marketing and Management Digest* (January 1976): 23–30.

Tavis, L. A. "Multinationals as Foreign Agents of Change in the Third World." *Business Horizon* 26, no. 5 (September–October 1983): 2–6.

Thomson, J. R. "Foreign Marketers Rush Into Sadat's 'Open' Arms." *Advertising Age* (August 18, 1980): p. V–2.

Thorelli, H. B. "The Multinational Corporation as a Change Agent." *Southern Journal of Business* 1, no. 3 (July 1977): 1–9.

Thorelli, H. B. and G. D. Sentell. *Consumer Emancipation and Economic Development: The Case of Thailand* (Greenwich, CT: JAI Press 1982).

Ting, W. "Marketing Development of Asian-Pacific NICs Multinationals—A Transitional Perspective." In *Proceedings of the Academy of International Business Asia—Pacific Dimensions of International Business,* edited by S. M. Dawson and J. R. Wills (College of Business Administration, University of Hawaii, December 18–20, 1982), pp. 430–37.

Ugoh, S. U. "The Economic Consequences of Sole Agency Distribution." In *Marketing in Nigeria,* edited by J. O. Onah, (London: Cassell, 1979), pp. 29–33.

Unger, L. "Consumer Marketing Trends in the 1980s When Growth Slows." *European Research* 9, no. 2 (April 1981): 69–73.

United Nations Industrial Development Organization. "Marketing Management and Strategy for the Developing World." Report of an Expert Group Meeting Vienna, December 2–7, 1984.

VanDam, A. "Marketing in the New International Economic Order." *Journal of Marketing* 41, no. 1 (January 1977): 19–23.

Wadinambiaratchi, G. "Channels of Distribution in Developing Economies." *Business Quarterly* (Winter 1965): 74–82.

Wadinambiaratchi, G. H. "Theories of Retail Development." *Social and Economic Studies,* no. 4 (December 1972): 391–403.

Warrack, A. A. "A Conceptual Framework for Analysis of Market Efficiency." *Journal of Agricultural Economics* 20, no. 3 (1968): 9–22.

Wheatly J. J. and O. Sadaomi. "Marketing in Japan: Problems and Possibilities for American Business." *Journal of Contemporary Business* 8, no. 2 (1979): 63–79.

Williams, S. "Negotiating Investment in Emerging Countries." *H.B.R.* 43, no. 1 (January–February 1965): 89–99.

Worth, D. "The Wherein of the Green." *New Englander* 25 (September 1978): 51–52, 54.

Wynn, S. "The Taiwanese Economic Miracle." *Monthly Review* 33 (April 1982): 30–40.

Yavas, U. "Transferability of Marketing Know-How to a Developing Country." *Der Markt* 21, nos. 2–3 (1982–1983): 69–74.

Yoshino, M. Y. "The Japanese Marketing System." (Cambridge, MA: MIT Press, 1971).

Index

About the Author

Erdener Kaynak is a Professor of Marketing, Division of Business Administration, the Pennsylvania State University at Harrisburg, U.S.A. He holds a B. Econ. degree from the University of Istanbul, an M.A. in Marketing from the University of Lancaster, and a Ph.D. in Marketing Management from the Cranfield Institute of Technology. He has taught at Hacettepe University in Ankara, Turkey, Acadia University in Wolfville, Nova Scotia, Canada, and Mount Saint Vincent University in Halifax. He has conducted post-doctoral research studies at Michigan State University, the Universities of Lund and Uppsala, Sweden, the University of Stirling, Scotland, and the Chinese University of Hong Kong where he also lectured at both graduate and undergraduate levels. Dr. Kaynak has lectured widely in diverse areas of management and held executive training programs in Europe, North America, the Middle East, the Far East, and Latin America. He is the founder and president of a Halifax-based company, Cross-Cultural Marketing Services Incorporated.

Dr. Kaynak has served as a business consultant to a number of Canadian and international organizations. He has been the recipient of a number of research scholarships and distinctions, most notably: Fulbright Post-Doctoral Research Scholarship, Turkish Government Scholarship, Fellowship of the Salzburg Seminar in American Studies, British Council Fellowship, Swedish Institute Research Scholarship, and German Academic Exchange Service Scholarship. He has published over fifty articles in refereed scholarly journals, including the *Journal of Macromarketing, Journal of Business Research, Journal of Advertising Research, Journal of the Academy of Marketing Science, European Journal of Marketing, International Journal of Physical Distribution and Materials Administration, European Management Journal, Management International Review, European*

199

Research, International Journal of Marketing and Marketing Research, Journal of International Advertising, and many others. He is the author of six books, four of them published by Praeger Publishers of New York, entitled *Marketing in the Third World* (1982), *Comparative Marketing Systems* (1984; co-authored), *International Marketing Management* (1985), *Global Perspectives in Marketing* (1985), *International Business in the Middle East* (1986; published by Walter De Gruyter of Berlin and New York), and *World Food Marketing Systems* (1986; published by Butterworth Scientific Publishers of London).

In addition to this, he has read papers and chaired sessions in more than fifteen countries at over thirty conferences. He is on the Editorial Review Board of the *Journal of the Academy of Marketing Science,* editorial board member of *Management Decision,* the *Service Industries Journal* and *International Studies of Management and Organization,* a regional editor for the Middle East of the *Journal of Enterprise Management;* and North American editor for *Management Research News,* and editorial board member of the *Journal of International Marketing and Marketing Research* and *International Journal of Advertising.* As guest editor, he has prepared special issues of a number of leading North American and European journals. He was the organizer and chairperson of four international congresses: one on tourism; one on housing development; the First World Marketing Congress, devoted to managing the international marketing function ("Creative Challenges of the Eighties"); and the Second World Marketing Congress, devoted to marketing in the 1990s and beyond. At present, he is the only Canadian member of the Board of Governors and Director of International Programs of the Academy of Marketing Science.

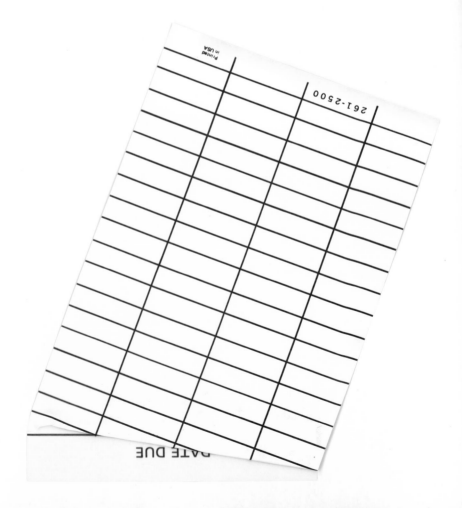

DATE DUE

261-2500

Printed
in USA